The Truth-Seeker's Handbook:

A Science-Based Guide

The Truth-Seeker's Handbook:

A Science-Based Guide

Dr. Gleb Tsipursky

Published November 2017 by Intentional Insights Press.

For more information on this book, including for bulk discounts, email info@intentionalinsights.org or write to 450 Wetmore road, Columbus, OH, 43214.

Publisher's Cataloging-in-Publication. Tsipursky, Gleb. The Truth-Seeker's Handbook: A Science-Based Guide. Gleb Tsipursky. 1st ed. Includes bibliographical references. Contents: critical thinking, rational thinking, rationality, emotions and reason, psychology, behavioral economics, politics, self-help, philosophy, health, wellbeing, spirituality, education, therapy.

ISBN-13: 978-0-9964692-2-7
ISBN-10: 0-9964692-2-2

1. Critical Thinking. 2. Rational Thinking. 3. Rationality. 4. Emotions and Reason. 5. Psychology. 6. Behavioral Economics. 7. Politics. 8. Self-help. 9. Philosophy. 10. Health. 11. Wellbeing. 12. Spirituality. 13. Education. 14. Therapy.

The book was mainly written and edited by Gleb Tsipursky, with additional contributions of chapters by Jeff Dubin, Joel Lehman, Hunter Glenn, Diogo Gonçalves, Max Harms, Peter Livingstone, Agnes Vishnevkin, Amy K. Watson, and Alex Weissenfels. The main illustrator and designer for the book was Lexie Holliday.

Dedication and Acknowledgment

This book is dedicated to all the supporters of Intentional Insights who helped make it possible. Thank you for your contributions of time, money, and other resources to promoting truth, rational thinking, and wise decision-making. I want to acknowledge in particular all the Intentional Insights supporters who helped create this book, including by doing editing, contributing chapters, providing graphic design skills, and other ways: you all know who you are!

The majority of the profits from this book are pledged to the nonprofit work done by Intentional Insights.

Table of Contents

Introduction

"You can't handle the truth!"
--- A Few Good Men (1992)

There's a reason that this movie quote became a cultural touchstone. These words speak to a deep tension within us as individuals. We may think we want the truth, but sometimes the facts can be very difficult to handle, since they cause us very unpleasant emotions and make us really uncomfortable. Our minds tend to flinch away from these facts, preferring instead to seek out the comfort of our pre-existing beliefs. Being a truth-seeker involves undertaking the sometimes-difficult work of expanding one's comfort zone and challenging one's pre-existing notions for the sake of seeing the truth of reality. If you are not prepared to put some labor into this endeavor, I recommend you put this book down and turn to something better suited to your preferences. If you are, read onward!

For those who read onward, I want you to know that the effort you put into truth-seeking will be very much worth it. Even from a purely emotional perspective, a more clear view of reality will pay great dividends down the road. Sticking to pre-existing beliefs that do not align with reality causes us to develop unrealistic expectations, and we inevitably grow stressed, anxious, and depressed when our bubble is popped by the sharp needle of reality. So while it might not be pleasant to face the facts in the moment, in the long run you will be much better off in getting to the unpleasant realizations quickly, updating your beliefs to match the facts, and aligning your emotions to a more accurate understanding of reality.

Caption: Meme saying "It would be very convenient if the things that are most comfortable to believe are also the ones that happen to be the most true" (Created for Intentional Insights by Isabelle Giuong)

Of course, the emotional payoff is just one part of the benefit you gain in orienting toward inconvenient truths instead of comfortable falsehoods. Perhaps an even bigger benefit comes from avoiding bad decisions.

Everything in our lives results from our decisions: who we spend time with, what we buy or don't buy, who we support politically. Making good decisions depends on us having the right information. Did you ever hear the acronym GIGO? That stands for "garbage in, garbage out" and stems from the field of information technology in reference to computers producing the wrong output if they get fed bad information. Our brains are in essence organic computers that make decisions based on the information they get. If we feed them bad information based on us holding false beliefs, we will make bad decisions, in our private, professional, and civic lives.

These bad decisions are costly. In our everyday life, bad decisions cause us to lose money, time, relationships, health, and happiness. Making bad decisions in the workplace results in our organizations losing money, time, and reputation, as well as undermining teamwork and employee morale. Making bad decisions in the political sphere, often due to deceptive information from politicians, leads to fundamental challenges and dangerous risks, including catastrophic and existential ones, for our society.

Now, you may not want to hold false beliefs and suffer the consequent unrealistic expectations or bad decisions. However, avoiding false beliefs is not easy. Research shows that false beliefs and their consequences come from faulty wiring in our brains that causes flawed thinking, feeling, and behavior patterns: what the scientific literature calls cognitive biases.

When I began to learn about this field while pursuing my doctoral degree, what surprised me most was that much of our bad decision-making comes from failing to understand the role of emotions in making decisions. I thought of myself as a relatively unemotional person, one who lets his cold analysis determine his behavior. Boy, was I wrong! Fortunately, recent scholarship shows we can address these problems by using debiasing strategies discovered by scholars in behavioral science fields to address these cognitive biases. Unfortunately, much of this research is trapped in dry academic papers in journals read only by other academics.

To me, this situation is intolerable. It is appalling to see these resources that can address some of the worst problems we face confined to so few. My knowledge of this situation comes from my professional experience as a scholar specializing in truth-seeking, rational thinking, and wise decision-making in politics and business. I researched these topics as a professor at The Ohio State University, specializing in the history of behavioral science. Deciding to reorient my efforts from research toward the popularization of science, I co-founded, together with my wife, Agnes Vishnevkin, the nonprofit organization Intentional Insights, dedicated to promoting scholarly research to a broad audience. Currently, I volunteer my time as President of the Board of Directors, and donate 10 percent of my income, and 50 percent of the profits from this book, to that nonprofit to support its mission. My science popularizing activities also includes writing books; publishing pieces in prominent venues such as *Time, Scientific American, Psychology Today, The Conversation*, and elsewhere; appearing as a guest on network TV, including affiliates of Fox and ABC, and radio stations such as NPR, WBAI (New York City), KGO (San Francisco), 700WLW (Cincinnati), KRLD (Dallas), AM980 (Canada), and elsewhere.

If you wish to join me as a fellow truth-seeker, you can take advantage of the research-based strategies described in this book to address the cognitive biases present in all of us. We need to avoid trusting our gut reactions and recognize when our intuitions steer us awry. While we all are impacted by such problematic mental patterns to some degree, studies show that each of us has our own peculiar mix, and it is up to you to learn your own vulnerabilities and how to address them.

For instance, I suffer from optimism bias, the belief that everything will go well. As a result, if I just go with my intuitions, I will take excessive risks, not prepare for potential problems, and run into many bad situations when interacting with others due to assuming the best of people, which is unfortunately not a safe assumption. This failure mode resulted in a systematic pattern both of unmet expectations and bad decisions that has seriously harmed my quality of life in the past. Only by using the debiasing strategies discussed in this book have I been able to address this debilitating problem.

My wife, on the other hand, suffers from pessimism bias, the belief that everything will go poorly. If I think the grass is always green on the other side, she thinks the grass is always yellow on the other side; if I see light at the end of the tunnel, she worries that it is an oncoming train. Her problem can be as bad in its own way as my problem. As you can imagine, due to this difference, our conversations can sometimes grow heated. However, knowing the debiasing strategies has helped us turn this source of conflict into an opportunity to help correct for each other's biased perspectives. Indeed, together we are better than the sum of our parts, as we can maximize taking advantage of opportunities with my optimism and addressing potential problems with her pessimism.

The external perspective we provide to each other is one of the many strategies that can be used to deal with the false beliefs caused by cognitive biases. While research on a variety of mental states such as happiness suggests that about half of our mental patterns are determined by our genes, the other half is determined by our environment and experience. The large majority of the population let their thought, feeling, and behavior patterns drift on the waves of life experience, buffeted by the storms of dramatic events and floating calmly in more quiet times. Yet as a truth-seeker, you can choose to take control of your environment and life experience to develop the kind of thought, feeling, and behavior patterns that would most align with an accurate view of reality. By doing so, you can improve your decision-making in private, professional, and civic life, and avoid the kind of emotional turmoil that comes with suddenly realizing you've been leading a life with blinders on for the last decade.

In fact, research shows that just a single training intervention can substantially improve one's ability to see reality clearly and avoid bad decisions. According to research on this topic, this ability – called rationality – is just as important as intelligence. However, while it is very difficult to improve one's intelligence level, it is quite simple to improve one's rationality. This book has the pragmatic tools to help you improve your rationality by discarding false beliefs and developing a more clear vision of reality. It was written by myself with contributions from some others with relevant expertise, and you can read their bios in the back of the book. Originating from a series of blog posts on the Intentional Insights website, and revised and edited with some additional content, the book was "born digital," and it has citations in the form both of references to research and of links to various articles of relevance to the topic. For those reading a paper version from Amazon.com and want to see the citations, you can get a digital copy for a much reduced price via the Amazon Kindle Matchbook program.

So read onward, fellow truth-seeker, and I look forward to hearing any feedback you may have. You can email me at gleb@intentionalinsights.org.

Book Outline

In the first section, the book lays out truth-seeking from an individual perspective.

The first chapter delves into the three key components of being rational: 1) Thinking rationally, meaning having accurate beliefs and expectations; 2) Making rational decisions, meaning ones that are most likely to lead you to having the kind of life you want; 3) Reaching your goals rationally, by using research-based strategies for goal achievement.

The second chapter deals more concretely with the distinction between logic and emotions. It describes the two systems of thinking uncovered by researchers. The Autopilot System (System 1) is our quick, intuitive, emotional thinking pattern. It predominates our everyday decision-making, and makes most decisions well. However, going with our gut is not always the best option, and leads to a series of systematic mental errors – cognitive biases. Thus, we sometimes need to use our Intentional System (System 2), our slow, deliberate, reason-oriented, logical system. It's effortful to use, but is needed in many cases where the Autopilot System steers us wrong.

Chapter three gets at the concept of map and territory. This is a very helpful framework for recognizing the difference between the mental map of the world that we have in our heads and the reality of the actual world as it exists – the territory. Our brains tend to forget that what we think about reality is often different from the truth of reality. When we have a constant awareness of the difference between the map in our heads and the territory of reality, we minimize our unrealistic expectations and false beliefs.

The fourth chapter connects more accurate beliefs and realistic expectations to the results you want to achieve. Looking for the truth about your environment – both external and internal – is not always easy. However, doing so is the most important thing you can do to put your life under your own control and be happy and successful through managing your thoughts, feelings, and behaviors.

In the fifth, sixth, and seventh chapters, the book goes into more depth on when we should go with our guts versus our heads. The fifth chapter addresses going with our gut in everyday life. It describes a number of scenarios when going with our gut is wise, such as in dangerous situations, or in one-time minor tasks. In contrast, for systematic activities or ones that have a significant impact on us, it's best to go with our heads and take the time and effort to turn on our Intentional System.

The sixth chapter covers going with your gut in workplace relationships. You might have heard that first impressions of people are generally accurate. Well, the research shows that this is a false belief. Our Autopilot System is optimized for the ancestral environment, and our first impressions simply indicate whether we perceive that person to belong to our tribe and be friendly to us. The chapter discusses when and how we should apply our Intentional System to address the problems with our Autopilot System, and when we should let our gut determine our behavior.

Chapter seven discusses another important area of life: altruism. Our gut tends to respond to stories about problems in the world that tug at our heartstrings, and we do good in response to these stories. Unfortunately, this makes us vulnerable to what scholars call the narrative fallacy, when we are more moved by stories than facts. As a result, we have a false model of how much good we are doing when we try to address suffering and advance flourishing. Stepping back from the story and letting the Intentional System shape our decision-making helps ensure that we achieve our goals in doing good. The narrative fallacy impacts many other areas of life besides doing good, of course, and should be kept in mind for all storytelling contexts.

The eighth, ninth, and tenth chapters cover a topic of great importance to being intentionally aware: probabilistic thinking. When we think about what we believe about the world, we usually consider ourselves to either believe in something or not believe in something. For instance, you may believe that your date will be on time or not, or that your boss will give you a raise or not, or that gun control is a good policy or not.

Thinking probabilistically involves cultivating a much more accurate approach to our beliefs. Instead of a binary "true" or "false" approach to our beliefs, probabilistic thinking assigns a percentage estimate to what we believe. As an example, you may have a belief that there is a 70% likelihood that your date will be on time. You are thus making a specific prediction about the actual state of the world. Then, based on new information, for example about your date being on time or late, you can develop more accurate beliefs and expectations. The eighth chapter introduces probabilistic thinking and describes how you can use this strategy to predict the future much better than just going with your gut.

When was the last time you thought you remembered something, but it turned out you were mistaken? Feels weird to know that we can't trust our memory, doesn't it? The ninth chapter delves into how our memory is quite a bit less reliable than we assume it to be. It uses the technique of probabilistic thinking to help address this problem and bring our perception of our past under our control.

There are many people who think that unusual coincidences have some sort of deep significance. They believe that karma or fate or a deity causes these events to occur. Probabilistic thinking provides an alternative explanation, as the tenth chapter describes. It shows how it's very unlikely for some crazy coincidences not to happen in your life, and attributing them to something other than random chance sets up unrealistic expectations and false beliefs.

The next set of chapters address dealing with problematic beliefs and feelings around truth-seeking. Chapter eleven helps you protect yourself from holding on to false beliefs. It walks you through gaining awareness of potentially false beliefs, evaluating them, and updating these beliefs to more accurate ones if needed.

In chapter twelve, I describe one example of the process of updating beliefs. It discusses how the process of updating takes place through a case study on a somewhat controversial sociopolitical issue, basic income. Through using this case study, I show how I updated my perspective as more and more evidence swayed me to reconsider my previous position.

Lucky chapter thirteen discusses a key concept: identity management. By managing your sense of self-identity – the story you tell yourself about who you are and how you label yourself – you can choose to place a higher value on seeking the truth, and remove inhibitions to doing so. This chapter's tactics are rooted in reframing and distancing, two research-based methods for changing our thought frameworks.

The fourteenth chapter addresses healthy ways to address finding out you made a mistake. Dealing with mistakes represents a particularly challenging area for truth-seekers, as our minds tend to flinch away from the negative emotions involved in learning about our errors. This chapter provides ways around this emotional roadblock.

The next chapter deals with the related topic of addressing negative feedback from others. While finding out you made a mistake on your own feels bad, learning about it from others can feel even worse. Moreover, you have to react in a way that protects your relationship with the other person. This chapter describes how to do so in a strategic manner.

We are prone to self-delusion when our attention is drawn to one aspect of a broader whole, and we don't consider the whole package. This cognitive bias, called attentional bias, impacts us in many areas of our life. The sixteenth chapter uses the example of house shopping to illustrate the harmful impact of this mental error and gives some suggestions for how to prevent it from undermining our decision-making.

On a related financial note, the seventeenth chapter deals with money management. Unless we are lucky, we do not get an education in financial literacy. Lacking this education, it is very easy to develop the wrong beliefs about money, and get ripped off. For example, did you know it's almost always a bad idea to keep your savings in a savings account? Did you know that, barring unusual circumstances, mutual funds are a rip-off? Using probabilistic thinking, this chapter shows you how to maximize the likelihood of beneficial financial outcomes.

Another common money management error has to do with the sunk costs fallacy, the topic of chapter eighteen. We tend to develop the false belief that if we invested money or other resources into a project, we should keep going, otherwise we would just have thrown the original investment away for nothing. However, too often that results in throwing good money after bad, based on our inability to detach from the emotional attachment to the original investment. This chapter helps clarify how to prevent such problematic behaviors.

A third financially-themed chapter deals more squarely with the relationship between financial decision-making and emotions. Chapter nineteen addresses three kinds of mistakes we tend to make that result in us failing to evaluate reality accurately. Loss aversion refers to the greater priority we put on avoiding the loss of a sum of money as compared with gaining that same sum of money. Diminishing sensitivity describes how we place less value on a resource as we get more of that resource. Reference point causes us to anchor ourselves to an arbitrary set point, without any objective reason. All of these mental errors cause us to develop unfounded beliefs.

In chapter twenty, the book gets more squarely at challenging feelings. The chapter goes through how to think about one's feelings, and how much responsibility we should take for them. It elaborates on distancing one's feelings from one's actions. Finally, it talks about strategies to change one's feelings to be more aligned with the truth of reality.

Chapter twenty-one addresses how to deal with challenging feelings in a situation of extreme emotional distress. It relates how the author figured out she was experiencing a nervous breakdown. Admitting this unpleasant situation was not easy, as we are often reluctant to acknowledge that our brain is not under our control. The chapter describes how the author overcame this discomfort to take charge of her mental well-being.

The next section of the book focuses on truth-seeking as it relates to other people. Sometimes, the false beliefs that we hold spring up primarily from our own internal preconceptions; at other times, they originate primarily externally, coming from other people. Societal pressures and expectations can feed us bad information and cause us to make bad choices, and it's important to recognize when that occurs and how to stop it. This chapter uses the example of family and friends pressuring us in deciding what career to pursue as a means of demonstrating how to recognize and prevent social norms from leading us astray.

While in some cases the external pressure is obvious, in others it is less so. Research on network effects shows that our social connections can influence our beliefs in subtle ways to cause us to develop counterproductive beliefs and make bad decisions. Chapter twenty-three describes ways of recognizing when such problems might be occurring and how to deal with these challenges.

Following that, chapter twenty-four introduces the concept of failing at other minds. This crucially important concept gets at the most basic mistake our brains tend to commit when trying to model other people, namely imagining them as ourselves. Other people differ from us! They have different values, motivations, backgrounds, expectations, beliefs, and as well as different thought, feeling, and behavior patterns. Only by recognizing that other people are different from us will we start to make more accurate predictions about their behavior and thus let go of false beliefs and unrealistic expectations.

One of the basic ways we fail at other minds is in giving and getting advice. We tend to give advice that works for us, forgetting that other people differ from us; in turn, we get advice from other people that works for them. If we believe the advice as fully correct for us, we will develop false beliefs and make bad decisions. Chapter twenty-five addresses how to study and understand ourselves so that we can adapt the kind of advice given by others to our own needs.

The next chapter builds on the focus of the previous two chapters on understanding people around you and goes into how to communicate with other people well. It describes how to notice and address different communication preferences to get the outcome that you desire. The chapter also introduces the concept of cached patterns, habits of thought and feeling in our mind that we absorbed uncritically from the social environment around us, as opposed to conclusions we arrived at by our own intentional reasoning. Re-evaluating our cached patterns is key not only to communicating well with other people, but for more broadly developing an accurate understanding of the world around us.

Truth-seeking often requires engaging with others who hold a different perspective on the truth than you do. These engagements typically take place in the form of debates, where we argue with those people to try to convince them that our point of view is correct and theirs is not. However, research suggests that debates are not well suited to how most people change their minds. Chapter twenty-seven describes the problems with debates as a means of addressing false beliefs, whether your own or those of others.

Chapter twenty-eight offers a solution: collaborative truth-seeking. This more productive, research-based approach to addressing differences of opinion may not be as intuitive and natural as debates, but it is much more likely to succeed in helping yourself and those with whom you engage orient toward the truth.

Chapter twenty-nine builds up on collaborative truth-seeking and offers further tactics to improve your ability to resolve disagreements in a successful manner that results in one or more people updating their beliefs toward the truth. It focuses on how to speak to people's emotions and help them feel heard, so as to prevent negative feelings from impeding effective collaborative truth-seeking.

It's always hard to talk to professional colleagues – whether those in your own workplace or external stakeholders – who hold false beliefs. Chapter thirty provides some suggestions on how to do so, summarized under the acronym EGRIP (Emotions, Goals, Rapport, Information, Positive Reinforcement), which provides clear guidelines on how to deal with colleagues who deny the facts.

The next chapter shows you how to use EGRIP in a different situation: when talking to people in civic contexts who deny the facts. Chapter thirty-one uses the example of science denialism and shows how to help encourage climate change deniers to accept the facts on global climate change. With these two examples of EGRIP, you should be able to use it yourself in a wide variety of contexts.

The last section of the book delves into perhaps the most troublesome area of truth-seeking: the political arena. Chapters in this section combine a mix of timeless analytical pieces, similar to the previous sections, as well as ones written in reaction to immediate politically-salient events. The latter pieces, I hope, will provide insights on how to respond in a truth-oriented manner to emotionally challenging and politically provocative topics.

Voters are inherently irrational. Their cognitive biases cause them to make bad political decisions. We need to shape our political process around their irrationality, and manipulate them to get them to make more rational choices. So claim many analysts and commentators, but chapter thirty-two argues they do not take into account the research showing the effectiveness of debiasing tactics to help voters grow more rational.

As the previous chapter argues, voters are not simply irrational. However, the large majority of voters lack training in growing more rational. Given that lack, voters tend to fall into a host of cognitive biases described in chapter twenty-eight. Breaking with the analysts who suggest we need to focus on manipulating voters who are inherently irrational, this chapter suggests we need to emphasize providing them with training in growing more rational.

Chapter thirty-four uses the case study of the 2016 US presidential debates to show how candidates appealed to voter irrationality. The two candidates, Donald Trump and Hillary Clinton, both played to people's cognitive biases. The chapter illuminates how they did so, and suggests that what we need to do is not simply fact-check the debates, but also do fallacy-checking to catch times when candidates try to appeal to our problematic mental patterns.

Next, the book goes into a specific set of thinking errors related to overconfidence. All of us tend to be overconfident in our beliefs, to one degree or another. Since our beliefs are often false, this overconfidence leads to failures on the truth-seeking front. When applied to politics, the systematic overconfidence results not simply in false beliefs but also bad decisions. Chapter thirty-five discusses what can be done to address such overconfidence.

The following chapter addresses the related problem of political precommitment. Due to our overconfidence, we tend to commit ourselves to false beliefs. Often, our precommitment stems from our pre-existing political affiliation, meaning the political party or group to which we belong. Having made the initial commitment, it feels very uncomfortable to back away from those beliefs, especially because that would imply a break with our political party. Such political precommitment greatly hinders truth-seeking.

Chapter thirty-seven addresses the challenging topic of how to respond to terrorist attacks. Our emotions of fear and anger drive us to lash out and take revenge against the terrorists. However, this emotional reaction usually stems from the false belief that this revenge will result in us being safer. Using probabilistic thinking, this chapter demonstrates how such revenge-driven emotional responses actually result in us being less safe, and instead offers more effective solutions.

The next chapter builds further on the same topic of responding to terrorist attacks. It describes how political leaders responded to a terrorist attack by calling for revenge and violence in response. The chapter points out how doing so plays into the hands of terrorists, who benefit from such reactions. Such responses let the terrorists win and are counterproductive from the perspective of promoting safety and security.

Another application of probabilistic thinking to a challenging issue is discussed in chapter thirty-nine. It deals with the controversial shooting of Tyre King, a 13-year-old black teenager by a white police officer in a dark alley. With little evidence to go on besides the words of the police officer about what happened, we need to make an evaluation of whether the shooting was justified, and probabilistic thinking provides a key path forward.

Next, the book turns to addressing why and how people develop false beliefs, using the lens of the 2016 US presidential campaign. Despite credible fact-checkers pointing out that Trump lied much more often and extensively than Clinton, polls show that more people falsely believed Trump to be more truthful than Clinton. Chapter forty unpacks some of the reasons behind this phenomenon.

Written shortly after the election, chapter forty-one discusses how to develop a healthy perspective on the new administration. It is tempting to look forward with hope to a new day after the turmoil of the US presidential campaign. However, the comfort of optimism may prevent a more truth-oriented perspective, one which suggests preparing for a situation where Trump's rule may not match optimistic predictions.

Another chapter written shortly after the election describes how Trump changed the author's perspective on marriage. The election pushed the author of this chapter to recognize that his view of marriage was mistaken, and stemmed from a cognitive bias where he simply desired to go against social norms. Impelled by the election, the author then went ahead and proposed to his long-time girlfriend. A perfect example of how a change in beliefs was followed by a change in behavior!

The phrase "alternative facts," coming from the Trump administration, has been mocked by many people who care about the truth. However, this mockery reveals an underlying false belief that there is a strong concern among the broad populace for the truth. This incorrect belief stems from a cognitive bias termed the false consensus effect, which refers to us tending to overestimate the extent to which other people value what we value. Chapter forty-three explains how this false belief steers us wrong and suggests some effective strategies to appeal to encourage people who do not intuitively care about the truth to recognize the dangers of alternative facts in politics.

Chapter forty-four provides a more thorough analysis of our post-truth present and suggests some strategies to get to a post-lies, pro-truth future. The venerable Oxford Dictionary chose "post-truth" as its 2016 word of the year, in large part due to Trump's success in the presidential election. It defined post-truth as "relating to or denoting circumstances in which objective facts are less influential in shaping public opinion than appeals to emotion and personal belief." However, research on behavioral science suggests a number of strategies that we can use to get beyond our post-truth present into a pro-truth future, and this chapter outlines such strategies.

The following chapter gets at how the media inadvertently helps politicians who spread alternative facts, and what can be done about this problem. The style of media reporting on unsupported or downright false claims by politicians usually leads with the claim in the title of the article, and then refutes it in the body of the piece. However, the majority of people read the headlines only, skipping the article. As a result, media reporting spreads misconceptions, and we need to push the media to change their reporting style to address this problem.

The following chapter goes in-depth into how those who care about promoting truth should engage with the Pro-Truth Pledge. The pledge is designed to roll back the tide of lies in our public discourse through combining behavioral science with crowdsourcing. The pledge asks signees to commit to 12 behaviors that research in behavioral science shows correlate with an orientation toward truthfulness, such as clarifying one's opinions and the facts, citing one's sources, and celebrating people who update their beliefs toward the truth. It's a perfect set of behaviors for truth-seekers to follow, and I encourage you to check out and take the pledge at ProTruthPledge.org.

The next pair of chapters deal with the firing of FBI director James Comey by Trump. The latter claimed he fired Comey to ensure competent leadership of the FBI, but many Democrats stated the firing occurred due to Trump's desire to prevent Comey from digging deeper into Trump's potential connections with Russia. Chapter forty-seven, written shortly after the firing without more evidence on hand, discusses how we can evaluate the situation using probabilistic thinking. In this sense, it echoes the earlier chapter on Tyre King: while more information would be valuable to make a more accurate assessment, we often have to make an initial judgment with limited data.

Written somewhat later, chapter forty-eight follows up on the Comey incident. In the period between two chapters, clear evidence emerged that Trump fired Comey to ease the pressure from Comey's inquiry into the Trump campaign's potential collusion with Russia to fix the 2016 US presidential election. The general population, based on this evidence, changed their beliefs about Trump's motivation for Comey's firing, according to polls. However, the same polls also showed that Republicans did not change their minds. The chapter discusses how to encourage people to change their minds based on evidence through using behavioral science-based tactics.

While Trump's attacks of the media are highly problematic from the perspective of truth-seeking, in some cases criticism of these attacks go too far. Chapter forty-nine focuses on one such instance, when a Republican candidate for congress body-slammed a journalist. Many mainstream media outlets linked the Republican candidate's behavior to Trump's example, yet the connection was frequently overstated. Such exaggerations undercut the credibility of the critics, and go against the truth.

Chapter fifty showcases another example of such excessive criticism. After a far-right rally that resulted in extensive violence between far-right and far-left groups, included domestic terrorism from someone belonging to the far right, Trump blamed both sides for the violence. He faced extensive backlash, including many who claimed 100 percent of the blame for the violence lay on the far-right groups. In reality, evidence showed that some far-left groups engaged in aggressive violence as well. Denying this fact subverts the aim of truth-seeking.

Of course, pointing out that Trump is sometimes unfairly criticized does not mean he does not deserve criticism at other times. The crucial thing to focus on is the behavior, not the person. For instance, chapter fifty-one discusses the Trump administration's spin around his transgender directive, which bans new transgender recruits to the US military and orders the re-evaluation of the status of transgender soldiers already in the military. The decree clearly discriminates against transgender people, yet the Trump administration denied this plain fact. Such spin is an example of gaslighting, a psychological manipulation that aims to create doubt about the nature of reality, which goes squarely against truth-seeking.

Next, chapter fifty-two gives another example of deceptive behavior by Trump. It examines Trump's extensive and blatant falsehoods at a prominent rally, and shows how Trump benefits from these falsehoods. His behavior deeply undercuts trust in the government, thus undermining the fabric of American democracy, but win him short-term political gains. Other politicians, seeing Trump's success, are adopting his tactics. This chapter discusses how to address this problem using successful tactics from the environmental movement.

The last chapter discusses the Pro-Truth movement, which is centered around the Pro-Truth Pledge. It uses the example of the environmental movement to show how movements can take off quickly with sufficient coordination and sense of shared values. Similarly, if enough people who care about fighting fake news and post-truth politics coordinate together around the Pro-Truth Pledge as a central coordinating mechanism, a successful Pro-Truth movement can take off and fight back the tide of misinformation.

Next follows the Conclusion, which summarizes the essence of the book and suggests next step to follow. After that comes the "Appendix," which includes the full text of the Pro-Truth Pledge, along with the Frequently Asked Questions about it. Following that is a "Select Annotated Bibliography" section, with behavioral science-based books related to truth-seeking that helped inform the chapters of this book. If you enjoyed the strategies described in the book and want to learn the science behind the strategies, check out that section. The final part of the book is the biography of authors who contributed to this book.

Thanks again for reading, and enjoy the journey!

Section 1: Individual Truth-Seeking

Chapter 1: 3 Steps to Living Intentionally

By Gleb Tsipursky

Caption: Meme saying "Keep calm and be intentional" (created for Intentional Insights by Agnes Vishnevkin)

Are you getting all you want? Are you achieving all of your goals? Are you living a fully intentional life?

If you are, I salute you. I can't make the same claim. I do aspire to live more intentionally, though – I am an aspiring intentionalist.

To live a more intentional life, I constantly strive to gain greater agency, the quality of living intentionally. In doing that, it helps to take the following 3 steps:

1. Evaluating reality clearly, to
2. Make effective decisions, that
3. Achieve our short and long-term goals.

Now, these steps may sound simple in theory, but they are not so simple in practice at all. Our mental patterns of thinking and feeling make it quite challenging to enact these 3 steps in the most effective manner. Let's unpack these steps to see exactly what each of them means.

What does it mean to evaluate your reality clearly? That means gaining a deep understanding of your external environment – your immediate surroundings, your social circle, your career, and anything else of relevance. That also means your own internal environment – your patterns of feeling, thinking, and behaving. Four factors obstruct our ability on this front, including:

• Social prescriptions about appropriate ways of perceiving reality;
• Internalized preconceptions based on our previous experiences;
• Thinking errors that our brain makes due to faulty wiring;
• Finally, an emotional reluctance to face the truth of reality when that requires changing our minds and updating our beliefs based on new information.

Learning about and watching out for these challenges in a systematic manner improves our decision-making. Gaining agency in this area involves studying and practicing research-based strategies for evaluating and making decisions, and for enacting these decisions into life in an intentional manner.

In the moment, doing the latter involves having an intentional response to situations, as opposed to relying on autopilot reflexes, in order to accomplish our immediate goals. In the long term, agency involves intentionally planning one's time and activities so that one can accomplish one's aims in the future. You can gain agency in both the short and the long term by learning about and implementing intentional approaches to refining and achieving your goals.

Next, you want to make effective decisions about how to reach your goals. Consider your options, based on your knowledge of your outer and inner environment. Be aware that you can change both your external surroundings, and your own thoughts, feelings, and behaviors, to help you to get what you want in life. Evaluate the various paths available to you, assess the probability that each path will get you to your goals. Then make a plan for how to proceed, and take the path that seems best suited to go where you want.

Finally, implement the decisions you made and travel along the path. Remember, you will usually encounter some unknown obstacles on your road to what you want. Be excited about getting feedback from your environment and learning about better paths forward. Take the opportunity to change your path if a new one opens up that seems better suited to help you meet your goals. Be open to changing your very goals themselves based on what you learn.

As you can imagine, these things are easy to say, but hard to do. It's very helpful to get support along the way, through learning about strategies oriented toward this purpose. However, above all, it takes your own commitment to the goal of gaining greater agency over your life and living intentionally.

• What personal experiences did you have that illustrate the benefits of gaining agency and living intentionally?

What strategies have you found to be most helpful in these areas?

• What specific steps can you take to implement the strategies described here into your life?

References

Dennett, D. C. (1989). *The intentional stance.*

Lilienfeld, S. O., Ammirati, R., & Landfield, K. (2009). Giving debiasing away: Can psychological research

on correcting cognitive errors promote human welfare? *Perspectives on psychological science, 4*(4), 390-398.

Chapter 2: Autopilot vs. Intentional System: The Rider and the Elephant

By Gleb Tsipursky

Caption: Meme saying "Who we think we are; who we really are" (Created for Intentional Insights by Cerina Gillilan)

Let's start with why it matters. If we know about how our minds work, we can be intentional about influencing our own thinking and feeling patterns. We can evaluate reality more clearly, make better decisions, and improve our ability to achieve goals, thus gaining greater agency, the quality of living intentionally.

Ok, then how do our minds work? Intuitively, our mind feels like a cohesive whole. We perceive ourselves as intentional and rational thinkers. Yet cognitive science research shows that in reality, the intentional part of our mind is like a little rider on top of a huge elephant of emotions and intuitions.

Roughly speaking, we have two thinking systems. Daniel Kahneman, who won the Nobel Prize for his research on behavioral economics, calls them System 1 and 2, but I think "autopilot system" and "intentional system" describe these systems more clearly. The term "intentional system" in particular is useful as a way of thinking about living intentionally and thereby gaining greater agency.

The autopilot system corresponds to our emotions and intuitions. Its cognitive processes take place mainly in the amygdala and other parts of the brain that developed early in our evolution. This system guides our daily habits, helps us make snap decisions, and reacts instantly to dangerous life-and-death situations, like saber-toothed tigers, through the freeze, fight, or flight stress response. While helping our survival in the past, the fight-or-flight response is not a great fit for modern life. We have many small stresses that are not life-threatening, but the autopilot system treats them as tigers, producing an unnecessarily stressful everyday life experience that undermines our mental and physical well-being. Moreover, while the snap judgments resulting from intuitions and emotions usually feel "true" because they are fast and powerful, they sometimes lead us wrong, in systematic and predictable ways.

The intentional system reflects our rational thinking, and centers around the prefrontal cortex, the part of the brain that evolved more recently. According to recent research, it developed as humans started to live within larger social groups. This thinking system helps us handle more complex mental activities, such as managing individual and group relationships, logical reasoning, probabilistic thinking, and learning new information and patterns of thinking and behavior. While the automatic system requires no conscious effort to function, the intentional system takes deliberate effort to turn on and is mentally tiring. Fortunately, with enough motivation and appropriate training, the intentional system can turn on in situations where the autopilot system is prone to make errors, especially costly ones.

Here's a quick visual comparison of the two systems:

Autopilot System	Intentional System
<ul><li>Fast, intuitive, emotional self</li><li>Requires no effort</li><li>Automatic thinking, feeling, and behavior habits</li><li>Mostly makes good decisions, 80% of time</li><li>However, prone to some predictable and systematic errors</li></ul>	<ul><li>Conscious, reasoning, mindful self</li><li>Takes intentional effort to turn on + drains mental energy</li><li>Used mainly when we learn new information, and use reason and logic</li><li>Can be trained to turn on when it detects Autopilot System may be making error</li></ul>

The autopilot system is like an **elephant**. It's by far the more powerful and predominant of the two systems. Our emotions can often overwhelm our rational thinking. Moreover, our intuitions and habits determine the large majority of our life, which we spend in autopilot mode. And that's not a bad thing at all – it would be mentally exhausting to think intentionally about our every action and decision.

The intentional system is like the elephant **rider**. It can guide the elephant deliberately to go in a direction that matches our actual goals. Certainly, the elephant part of the brain is huge and unwieldy, slow to turn and change, and stampedes at threats. But we can train the elephant. Your rider can be an elephant whisperer. Over time, you can use the intentional system to change your automatic thinking, feeling, and behavior patterns, and become a better agent in achieving your goals.

I hope this information fills you with optimism. It does me. This is what Intentional Insights is all about – learning how to be intentional about using your rider to guide your elephant.
- What steps do you think you can take to evaluate where your emotions and intuitions may lead you to make mistakes?
- What can you do to be prepared to deal with these situations in the moment?
- What can you do to be an elephant whisperer and retrain your elephant to have thinking, feeling, and behavior patterns that match your long-term goals?

References
Baumeister, R. F., & Tierney, J. (2012). *Willpower: Rediscovering the greatest human strength.*
Dennett, D. (2009). Intentional systems theory. *The Oxford handbook of philosophy of mind*, 339-350.

Heath, C., & Heath, D. (2010). *Switch: How to change when change is hard.*
Kahneman, D. (2011). *Thinking, fast and slow.*
Stanovich, K. (2011). *Rationality and the reflective mind.*

Chapter 3: Where Do Our Mental Maps Lead Us Astray?

By Gleb Tsipursky

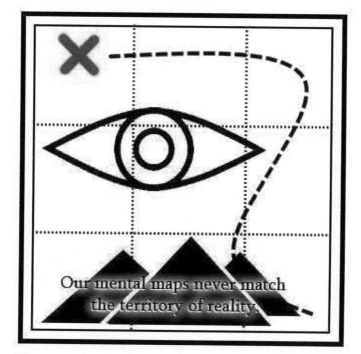

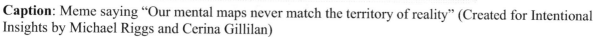

Caption: Meme saying "Our mental maps never match the territory of reality" (Created for Intentional Insights by Michael Riggs and Cerina Gillilan)

So imagine you are driving on autopilot, as we all do much of the time. Suddenly the car in front of you cuts you off quite unexpectedly. You slam your brakes and feel scared and indignant. Maybe you flash your lights or honk your horn at the other car. What's your gut feeling about the other driver? I know my first reaction is that the driver is rude and obnoxious.

Now imagine a different situation. You're driving on autopilot, minding your own business, and you suddenly realize you need to turn right at the next intersection. You quickly switch lanes and suddenly hear someone behind you honking their horn. You now realize that there was someone in your blind spot and you forgot to check it in the rush to switch lanes. So you cut them off pretty badly. Do you feel that you are a rude driver? The vast majority of us do not. After all, we did not deliberately cut that car off, we just failed to see the driver. Or let's imagine another situation: say your friend hurt herself and you are rushing her to the emergency room. You are driving aggressively, cutting in front of others. Are you a rude driver? Not generally. You're merely doing the right thing for the situation.

So why do we give ourselves a pass, while attributing an obnoxious status to others? Why does our gut always make us out to be the good guys, and other people bad guys? Clearly, there is a disconnect between our gut reaction and reality here. It turns out that this pattern is not a coincidence. Basically, our immediate gut reaction attributes the behavior of others to their personality and not to the situation in which the behavior occurs. The scientific name for this type of error in thinking and feeling is called the fundamental attribution error, also called the correspondence bias. So if we see someone behaving rudely, we immediately and intuitively feel that this person IS rude. We don't automatically stop to consider whether an unusual situation may cause someone to act this way. With the driver example, maybe the person who cut you off did not see you. Or maybe they were driving their friend to the emergency room. But that's not what our automatic reaction tells us. On the other hand, we attribute our own behavior to the situation, and not our personality. Much of the time, we feel like we have valid explanations for our actions.

Learning about the fundamental attribution error helped me quite a bit. I became less judgmental about others. I realized that the people around me were not nearly as bad as my gut feelings immediately and intuitively assumed. This decreased my stress levels, and I gained more peace and calm. Moreover, I realized that my intuitive self-evaluation is excessively positive and that in reality I am not quite the good guy as my gut reaction tells me. Additionally, I realized that those around me who are unaware of this thinking and feeling error, are more judgmental of me than my intuition suggested. So I am striving to be more mindful and thoughtful about the impression I make on others.

The fundamental attribution error is one of many feeling patterns. It is certainly very helpful to learn about all of these errors, but it's hard to focus on avoiding all of them in our daily life. A more effective strategy for evaluating reality more intentionally to have more clarity and thus gain greater agency is known as "map and territory." This strategy involves recognizing the difference between the mental map of the world that we have in our heads and the reality of the actual world as it exists – the territory.

For myself, internalizing this concept has not been easy. It's been painful to realize that my understanding of the world is by definition never perfect, as my map will never match the territory. At the same time, this realization was strangely freeing. It made me recognize that no one is perfect, and that I do not have to strive for perfection in my view of the world. Instead, what would most benefit me is to try to refine my map to make it more accurate. This more intentional approach made me more willing to admit to myself that though I intuitively and emotionally feel something is right, I may be mistaken. At the same time, the concept of map and territory makes me really optimistic, because it provides a constant opportunity to learn and improve my assessment of the situation. Others to whom I taught this concept in videotaped workshops for Intentional Insights also benefited from learning about both the fundamental attribution error and the idea of map and territory. One workshop participant wrote in an anonymous feedback form: "with relation to the fundamental attribution error, it can give me a chance to keep a more open mind. Which will help me to relate to others more, and view a different view of the "map" in my head."

Now, what are the strategies for most effectively learning this information, and internalizing the behaviors and mental patterns that can help you succeed? Well, educational psychology research illustrates that engaging with this information actively, personalizing it to your life, linking it to your goals, and deciding on a plan and specific next steps you will take are the best practices for this purpose.

So take the time to answer the questions below to gain long-lasting benefit from reading this:
- What do you think of the concept of map and territory?

- How can it be used to address the fundamental attribution error?
- Where can the notion of map and territory help you in your life?
- What challenges might arise in applying this concept, and how can these challenges be addressed?
- What plan can you make and what specific steps can you take to internalize these strategies?

References

Ayres, I. (2010). *Carrots and sticks: Unlock the power of incentives to get things done.*

Schunk, D. H. (1989). Social cognitive theory and self-regulated learning. *Self-regulated learning and academic achievement: Theory, research, and practice*, 83-110.

Gilbert, D. T., & Malone, P. S. (1995). The correspondence bias. *Psychological bulletin, 117*(1), 21.

Shuell, T. J. (1986). Cognitive conceptions of learning. *Review of educational research, 56*(4), 411-436.

Shuell, T. J. (1990). Phases of meaningful learning. *Review of educational research, 60*(4), 531-547.

Chapter 4: How to Be Perfect!

By Hunter Glenn

Caption: Woman looking up (Tachina Lee/Unsplash)

Once, alchemists sought the secret formula for turning lead into gold. Nowadays, we seek things that are rather more unattainable. The perfect job. The perfect relationship. The perfect family life. Perfect health. Perfect everything!

Our Automatic Approach

Sam, for instance, tries to get the perfect body. His diet is whatever TV says is the latest "right way." He exercises however his Facebook feed says is "the best way it's done" (*which is it again: cardio or strength?*).

However, it's hard to keep good habits; mostly Sam just tries until he fails (which is often).

When Sam was a student, he studied the one way he knew how. He picked his major, his profession, his job based on advice from his parents, with just a few moments reflecting on his own desires or how to do the most good with his career. Medical treatment? He gets whatever he hears is best according to hearsay and best friends.

You probably don't need me to tell you how that's working for Sam. Sometimes things go well, sometimes they don't, more or less at random. Things just…*happen* to Sam; he rarely feels in control.

Sam lives his life on autopilot. And he sometimes wonders if this is really the best he can do.

For that, I admire Sam. He has a sense that there's a better way, that he himself can do better. He's self-aware, seeing that his "any ole' way" strategy isn't working for him. Realizing that if you're lacking results, you must be lacking…*something* important… is the first great key.

A golden life needs a silver bullet. Without it, for all his admirable drive to improve his life, all his energy, I fear Sam will just move from one not-very-impressive strategy to another. Life often fails to reward our effort, if that effort is not properly directed.

What approach can make us powerful, succeeding in every area of life? You might have heard it before:
Seek the truth all the days of your life
And "the truth will set you free."

The Rational Approach

Unlike Sam, Sally seeks the truth. She looks on a mess of a thousand lies and plucks the one nugget of truth out of it. She grows more powerful as the years pass; the diamonds in the rough inevitably end up in her hands; others may be satisfied by fool's gold, but her kind want the genuine article, and they get it.

Results. Sally's work is rewarded with results. She sifts through diet advice and finds what really works. Changing habits isn't easy for anybody, but Sally figured out how to make that work for her, too. Her exercise plan works. She has a feeling of control in her life. She knows exactly why she chose what to study and the work she wants to do. The truth has served her well.

The star's natural state is to shine surrounded by darkness on every side. Truth's natural state is to shine amid frustrated, useless lies on every side. The truth-seeker's natural state is to succeed on every side, while others ask "What's your secret?" Sally's secret is not assuming that she holds the truth, but to keep checking whether what she believes is true, and how well her beliefs enable her to accomplish her goals.

It's so tempting to believe that we have the truth, isn't it? Who would admit otherwise? Indeed, anyone you ask will be willing to tell you the way to success.

Fake Answers

If we want to get to New York, which is worse, having no map, or following a map to Congo? The answer is even more obvious when maps to New York are *right there* for the taking, but we're not taking them because we "already have our map."

Caption: Picture of people looking at a map *(Sanja Gjenero/FreeImages)*

This is why seeking the truth is only a first step. What if we just fall for the most convincing fake "truth" on the market?

Nate Silver, enjoying incredible success in his work of *predicting the future*, wrote a book called *The Signal and the Noise*, all about how to find the true "signal" (the truth) when it's cut up in a thousand pieces and hidden, scattered in "The Noise" (fake answers). This is our second great key, finding *the* answer. Not just finding *an* answer, finding *the* answer, the truth.

These are the two great trials in life, the two gates on the road to success. First, asking the question, and second, finding the (right) answer. Finding our ignorance, then finding its cure. Starting a quest for truth, then resisting the siren call of fake answers.

Rationality is Results

What will happen when Sam learns to find the *signal*, the lighthouse in the distance, the guiding star, instead of going from one noise to the next?

He will succeed. He will move from one area of his life to the next, finding the useful tricks out of the useless, each adding to his chest of knowledge like precious gemstones. One area of his life after another will shine like the sun, as Sam himself begins to, one challenge after another defeated and triumphed, a victory to be rightly proud of.

This is called rationality, of the real kind. Rationality is about *results*. And results come from finding the one path that leads upwards out of a thousand confused paths going nowhere.

Why rationality? Why not just be satisfied with what we've got, never looking for a better way to study, to work, to make decisions, to parent, or date, or get in shape, or get our *life* in shape? Why not be satisfied with whatever answer we picked up along the way, and be satisfied with the results our efforts give us?

…

Then again, why shouldn't you *succeed*? Don't you want to stride through life, growing stronger by the day? Why *shouldn't* you go from one area of life to the next, becoming healthier, happier, more capable, more successful, more *anything you want?*

There *is* a way. But there is also a cost.

The Cost

Can you lift your head up and search the stars? Can you admit that you *have* to look if you're going to succeed?

Even if you pass this test, there is a second. Can you admit that if you didn't spy the right answer the first time, you might not spy it the second? That you need to learn how to judge truth from error? Can you accept it if the truth isn't what you thought it was, what you *hoped* it was?

If so…Then I repeat, there *are* answers.

Conclusion

Remember, the first great trial is realizing you have to *look* for answers. The obvious thing is to look for answers where you have none. But far more subtle (and difficult) is the need to look for answers where you *already* have some, but need to ask, "Am I letting a made-up map keep me from looking for a genuine one?"

I *highly* recommend *How To Actually Change Your Mind* in Eliezer Yudkowsky's *Rationality: From AI to Zombies*.to escape the chains of false knowledge.

And the second great trial is to become discerning, to get the right answer. To see a palace of glass and find the diamonds hidden in plain sight. To view the waving, warping kaleidoscope of fanciful ideas and see through their distraction to the truth. The signal amid the noise. Nate Silver's *The Signal and the Noise* and other books like it can help.

Seek truth all the days of your life, and the truth will give you power to set yourself free. Be rational. Those who seek the stars for a lifetime, one day become stars themselves.

Questions for Consideration:
• Why don't we always feel in control of our lives?
• What happened the last times you tried to improve your life?
• Why do people say "knowledge is power?"
• Why do we sometimes feel certain about things, only to later find out we were mistaken?

References
Silver, N. (2012). *The signal and the noise: why so many predictions fail--but some don't.*
Yudkowsky, E. (2015). *Rationality: From AI to Zombies.*

Chapter 5: When Should You Go With Your Gut In Everyday Life?

By Gleb Tsipursky

Caption: Puzzled woman (Parallax Dreams/Flickr)

You're walking out of a restaurant with your date when you suddenly feel a strong urge to duck your head. You realize that doing so will make you look silly in front of your date, who you really like. Do you duck or not?

This is a great time to ignore the possibility of looking foolish and go with your gut. There's a good chance that your peripheral vision picked up on something aiming at your head that you didn't have time to process consciously. Maybe some kids are playing baseball nearby and the ball is heading your way, or maybe a pine cone is falling from the tree just outside the restaurant.

The bigger point is that you should generally trust your gut in situations where you're in physical danger. Even if the object is not going to hit your head, you don't want to take that chance with the most important part of your body. The same goes for when you're crossing the street and have a sudden urge to leap away.

Why should you trust your gut in such situations? This quick, automatic reaction of the body result from the Autopilot System of thinking, also known as System 1, which is one of the two systems of thinking in our brain. It makes good decisions about 70-80% of the time, but commits certain systematic errors, which scholars call cognitive biases. This Autopilot System is great for protecting you from physical danger, as evolution optimized this part of the brain to ensure your survival, so your default reaction should be to trust it.

There are some rare occasions in which it goes awry even when dealing with physical danger. For example, you shouldn't slam on your brakes when you're skidding on the road, despite what your intuitions tell you. Our instincts will not always be spot-on with physical dangers having to do with modern life. It's important to learn about these exceptions to going with your gut so you can protect yourself from physical dangers associated with the twenty first-century life.

Also note that some psychological conditions, such as Posttraumatic Stress Disorder, can hijack the Autopilot System and make it less reliable. In these cases, where false perceptions of danger are plentiful, simply trusting the Autopilot System is unwise.

These are the times when you need to use your Intentional System, the more rational part of your brain, to override the intuitive one. It takes effort to turn it on, but it can catch and override thinking errors committed by the Autopilot System. This way, we can address the systematic mistakes made by our brains in our everyday lives.

Keep in mind that the Autopilot System and the Intentional System are simplifications of more complex processes, and that there is debate about them in the scientific community. However, for most purposes, these simplifications are very useful in helping us manage our thoughts, feelings, and behaviors.

Let's consider a less dangerous aspect of daily life. You're at an office store to get some supplies for your home office, and are choosing what white-out to get. You rarely use it and have no favorite brand, so the choices seem overwhelming. How much time and energy does it make sense to invest in this decision?

Go with your gut on this one. Since you use white-out rarely, it's not a good idea to invest time and effort into evaluating all the choices available and coming up with the best one. Just make a reasonable decision that satisfies your needs and get all the other stuff you want as well. This approach applies to all situations where you're making one-time decisions about minor matters. You'll waste a lot of time and cognitive resources optimizing rather than satisficing - making a satisfactory rather than an optimal choice.

Now, what about everyday life decisions that are not one-time but regular? For instance, say you eat cereal for breakfast every day. In that case, you definitely don't want to go with your gut and grab the first satisfactory cereal box you see.

Consider the amount of cereal you eat in a year. Say you go through a box a week. That's over 50 boxes a year! Imagine them all stacked up in a 3-stories tall pile. That's a lot of cereal. However, that's also only a year's worth. Consider how much cereal you'll eat in your lifetime. Now you're getting into skyscraper territory. Envision the nutrients you get and the amount of money it costs. Using such probabilistic thinking, this is a great area to optimize rather than satisfice.

Evaluate the factors that are important to you about cereal: taste, nutrition, cost, and anything else you can think of. Consider and rank the importance of all these elements. Then, compare all the cereals using these factors. Finally, choose one (or more if you want to vary the flavors).

Also, consider whether you can get them cheaper in bulk online than through the local grocery store, depending on the storage area in your home. For example, I eat a lot of tomato sauce and order it in bulk through Amazon, which gives me a 15% discount through their Subscribe & Save service.

The same approach applies to any life decision that you make systematically or anything which you do regularly. If you used white-out a lot, it might be worth the time to pick the best white-out. If you do journaling daily, it's a good idea to choose a nice journal and good writing implement, even if it takes more time to select them and they are more expensive. The same goes for your office chair—you'll spend a lot more money and time in the long-run addressing back problems than if you spend some upfront choosing a good chair! This strategy of decision-making, called multiple-attribute utility theory, applies to any instance where it's worthwhile for you to take the time to make a reasoned decision where you weigh multiple attributes.

However, don't spend too much time trying to get information beyond the minimal amount needed to make a good decision. Some people fall into this trap when first learning about this technique, a thinking error called information bias—trying to get information beyond that necessary to make a decision. In general, balance the need to get appropriate information with that of making a timely decision to escape the trap of "analysis paralysis."

Caption: Meme saying "I've been overthinking about overthinking again" (Tough Mudette)

The broader principle here is that we are not evolutionarily adapted for a situation where we can make systematic, long-term choices about what to get. Our Autopilot System is optimized for short-term survival. It makes good decisions most of the time, and it's great for "goon enough," one-time, everyday life decisions on minor matters.

However, for anything that is a systematic, repeating choice or something you work with regularly such as an office chair or a pen, it will sometimes steer you in the wrong direction. In those cases, it's wise to invest the time, cognitive resources, and money in using a more intentional approach to make the best decision for your long-term happiness and success.

Questions to consider:
· Where in your everyday life can you go with your gut more often?
· Where in your everyday life can you use more Intentional System thinking?
· What specific changes should you make after reading this piece?

References
Arkes, H. R. (2016). A levels of processing interpretation of dual-system theories of judgment and decision making. *Theory & Psychology*, *26*(4), 459-475.
Baron, J. (2000). *Thinking and deciding*.
Kahneman, D. (2011). *Thinking, fast and slow*.
Stanovich, K. (2011). *Rationality and the reflective mind*.

Chapter 6: When Should You Go With Your Gut In Professional Interactions?

By Gleb Tsipursky

Caption: Photo of job interview (Adabara/Pixabay)

Let's say you're interviewing a new applicant for a job and you feel something is off. You can't quite put your finger on it, but you're a bit uncomfortable with this person. She says all the right things, her resume is great, she'd be a perfect hire for this job – except your gut tells you otherwise.

Should you go with your gut?

In such situations, your default reaction should be to be suspicious of your gut. Research shows that job candidate interviews are actually poor indicators of future job performance.

Unfortunately, most employers tend to trust their guts over their heads and give jobs to people they like and perceive as part of their ingroup, rather than simply the most qualified applicant. In other situations, however, it actually does make sense to rely on gut instinct to make a decision.

Yet research on decision-making shows that most business leaders don't know when to rely on their gut and when not to. While most studies have focused on executives and managers, research shows the same problem applies to doctors, therapists and other professionals.

This is the kind of challenge I encounter when I consult with companies on how to better handle workplace relationships. Research that I and others have conducted on decision-making offers some clues on when we should – and shouldn't – listen to our guts.

The gut or the head

The reactions of our gut are rooted in the more primitive, emotional and intuitive part of our brains that ensured survival in our ancestral environment. Tribal loyalty and immediate recognition of friend or foe were especially useful for thriving in that environment.

In modern society, however, our survival is much less at risk, and our gut is more likely to compel us to focus on the wrong information to make workplace and other decisions.
For example, is the job candidate mentioned above similar to you in race, gender, socioeconomic background? Even seemingly minor things like clothing choices, speaking style and gesturing can make a big difference in determining how you evaluate another person. According to research on nonverbal communication, we like people who mimic our tone, body movements and word choices. Our guts automatically identify those people as belonging to our tribe and being friendly to us, raising their status in our eyes.

This quick, automatic reaction of our emotions represents the autopilot system of thinking, one of the two systems of thinking in our brains. It makes good decisions most of the time but also regularly makes certain systematic thinking errors that scholars refer to as cognitive biases.

The other thinking system, known as the intentional system, is deliberate and reflective. It takes effort to turn on but it can catch and override the thinking errors committed by our autopilots. This way, we can address the systematic mistakes made by our brains in our workplace relationships and other areas of life.

Keep in mind that the autopilot and intentional systems are only simplifications of more complex processes, and that there is debate about how they work in the scientific community. However, for everyday life, this systems-level approach is very useful in helping us manage our thoughts, feelings and behaviors.

In regard to tribal loyalty, our brains tend to fall for the thinking error known as the "halo effect," which causes some characteristics we like and identify with to cast a positive "halo" on the rest of the person, and its opposite the "horns effect," in which one or two negative traits change how we view the whole. Psychologists call this "anchoring," meaning we judge this person through the anchor of our initial impressions.

Overriding the gut

Now let's go back to our job interview example.

Say that the person went to the same college you did. You are more likely to hit it off. Yet, just because a person is similar to you does not mean she will do a good job. Likewise, just because someone is skilled at conveying friendliness does not mean she will do well at tasks that require technical skills rather than people skills.

The research is clear that our intuitions don't always serve us well in making the best decisions (and, for a business person, bringing in the most profit). Scholars call intuition a troublesome decision tool that requires adjustments to function properly. Such reliance on intuition is especially harmful to workplace diversity and paves the path to bias in hiring, including in terms of race, disability, gender and sex.

Despite the numerous studies showing that structured interventions are needed to overcome bias in hiring, unfortunately business leaders and HR personnel tend to over-rely on unstructured interviews and other intuitive decision-making practices. Due to the autopilot system's overconfidence bias, a tendency to evaluate our decision-making abilities as better than they are, leaders often go with their guts on hires and other business decisions rather than use analytical decision-making tools that have demonstrably better outcomes.

A good fix is to use your intentional system to override your tribal sensibilities to make a more rational, less biased choice that will more likely result in the best hire. You could note ways in which the applicant is different from you – and give them "positive points" for it – or create structured interviews with a set of standardized questions asked in the same order to every applicant.

So if your goal is to make the best decisions, avoid such emotional reasoning, a mental process in which you conclude that what you feel is true, regardless of the actual reality.

When your gut may be right

Let's take a different situation. Say you've known someone in your work for many years, collaborated with her on a wide variety of projects and have an established relationship. You already have certain stable feelings about that person, so you have a good baseline.

Imagine yourself having a conversation with her about a potential collaboration. For some reason, you feel less comfortable than usual. It's not you – you're in a good mood, well-rested, feeling fine. You're not sure why you're not feeling good about the interaction since there's nothing obviously wrong. What's going on?

Most likely, your intuitions are picking up subtle cues about something being off. Perhaps that person is squinting and not looking you in the eye or smiling less than usual. Our guts are good at picking up such signals, as they are fine-tuned to pick up signs of being excluded from the tribe.

Maybe it's nothing. Maybe that person is having a bad day or didn't get enough sleep the night before. However, that person may also be trying to pull the wool over your eyes. When people lie, they behave in ways that are similar to other indicators of discomfort, anxiety and rejection, and it's really hard to tell what's causing these signals.

Overall, this is a good time to take your gut reaction into account and be more suspicious than usual.

The gut is vital in our decision-making to help us notice when something might be amiss. Yet in most situations when we face significant decisions about workplace relationships, we need to trust our head more than our gut in order to make the best decisions.

References

Arntz, A., Rauner, M., & Van den Hout, M. (1995). "If I feel anxious, there must be danger": Ex-consequentia reasoning in inferring danger in anxiety disorders. *Behaviour Research and Therapy, 33*(8), 917-925.

Barrick, M. R., Shaffer, J. A., & DeGrassi, S. W. (2009). What you see may not be what you get: Relationships among self-presentation tactics and ratings of interview and job performance. *Journal of Applied Psychology, 94*(6), 1394-1411.

Conger, J. A., & Kanungo, R. N. (1987). Toward a behavioral theory of charismatic leadership in organizational settings. *Academy of management review, 12*(4), 637-647.

Drehmer, D. E., & Bordieri, J. E. (1985). Hiring decisions for disabled workers: The hidden bias. *Rehabilitation Psychology, 30*(3), 157.

Francisco, J. M., & Burnett, C. A. (2008). Deliberate intuition: giving intuitive insights their rightful place in the creative problem solving thinking skills model. In *Creativity and Innovation Management Journal Conference*.

Halevy, N., Bornstein, G., & Sagiv, L. (2008). "In-group love" and "out-group hate" as motives for individual participation in intergroup conflict: A new game paradigm. *Psychological science, 19*(4), 405-411.

Isaac, C., Lee, B., & Carnes, M. (2009). Interventions that affect gender bias in hiring: a systematic review. *Academic medicine: journal of the Association of American Medical Colleges, 84*(10), 1440.

Kahneman, D. (2011). *Thinking, fast and slow.*

Key, M. R. (1975). *Paralanguage and Kinesics (Nonverbal Communication).*

Klayman, J., Soll, J. B., González-Vallejo, C., & Barlas, S. (1999). Overconfidence: It depends on how, what, and whom you ask. *Organizational behavior and human decision processes, 79*(3), 216-247.

Kutschera, I., & Ryan, M. H. (2009). Implications of intuition for strategic thinking: Practical recommendations for gut thinkers. *SAM Advanced Management Journal, 74*(3), 12.

Miller, C. C., & Ireland, R. D. (2005). Intuition in strategic decision making: friend or foe in the fast-paced 21st century?. *The Academy of Management Executive, 19*(1), 19-30.

Oppenheimer, D. M., LeBoeuf, R. A., & Brewer, N. T. (2008). Anchors aweigh: A demonstration of cross-modality anchoring and magnitude priming. *Cognition, 106*(1), 13-26.

Nisbett, R. E., & Wilson, T. D. (1977). The halo effect: Evidence for unconscious alteration of judgments. *Journal of personality and social psychology, 35*(4), 250.

Patton, J. R. (2003). Intuition in decisions. *Management decision, 41*(10), 989-996.

Richerson, P. J., & Boyd, R. (2001). The evolution of subjective commitment to groups: A tribal instincts hypothesis. *Evolution and the Capacity for Commitment, 3*, 186-220.

Stanovich, K. (2011). *Rationality and the reflective mind.*

Chapter 7: When Should You Go With Your Gut In Doing Good?

By Gleb Tsipursky

Caption: Image of regretful woman (Wikimedia Commons)

I want to share my story to help you avoid the kind of regret I experienced as a deep churning in my stomach when I found out what bad decisions I made by giving to my favorite charity for many years.

Make-A-Wish Foundation helps kids with terminal diseases achieve a grand wish. For example, it could take the child and her family to Disneyland. It then shares the stories of these kids through their marketing materials. These stories are truly heartwarming. I fell for it, and donated every Giving Season, as I wanted to help kids have good lives.

However, my close friend Max Harms pointed out that Make-A-Wish Foundation makes 300 million per year telling these stories. Our brain is wired to have positive emotions from such stories, and therefore people like me donate.

By comparison, Max told me to consider the Against Malaria Foundation. It buys malaria nets that protect children in developing countries from mosquitoes carrying this deadly disease. Would not my goal of helping kids have good lives be achieved better by protecting them from death?

That question stopped me in my tracks. I had to think hard about why I gave to Make-A-Wish. I realized it was because they had heartwarming stories and great marketing that brought the stories to my attention. Our brains focus on things that come to our attention and not necessarily on things that are actually important for our goals, a thinking error called attentional bias.

What I failed to consider was the stories of children saved from malaria. I imagined a specific child, Mary, who did not get malaria because of my donation. I envisioned how Mary's mother rocked Mary to sleep. I imagined Mary's fifth birthday party, with her family all around. I imagined Mary's first day of school. I imagined her first kiss. I imagined Mary growing up, becoming an adult, getting married, and having her own kids. My last mental image was of Mary knitting in a rocking chair, enjoying her grandchildren's laughter.

It was wonderful to imagine Mary's life. By comparison to giving one positive story through Make-A-Wish, I could give Mary a lifetime of heartwarming stories. Besides, a bed net costs a few dollars, while a trip to Disneyland costs many thousands. For the same money, I can save not only Mary, but John, Ella, Sergio, Paula, Sarnur, Christian, and so many others. It was no contest.

Now I have nothing against Make-A-Wish Foundation. They do what they promised to do. It was a failure of my imagination that caused me to make bad decisions. From this experience, I learned that charities that are most effective in achieving my actual goals for donations are often not the ones with the best stories, and thus do not get funded.

Max then told me about Effective Altruism, a movement specifically set up to deal with such thinking errors. It uses data-driven strategies to promote charities that do the most good for the world. He advised me to check out GiveWell in particular, which provides research reports on the most effective charities. He also suggested The Life You Can Save, whose charity impact calculator enables you to put in your donation amount and learn immediately about the impact it makes.

I was sold! I never wanted to experience that deep churning in my stomach. So the next time you hear a great story from a charity that moves you, stop to consider the alternatives. Where else can you give your money to achieve the same ends with more impact per dollar?

I hope sharing publicly about my bad decisions helps you avoid giving regret and be truly effective in your altruism.

References

Bar-Haim, Y., Lamy, D., Pergamin, L., Bakermans-Kranenburg, M. J., & van IJzendoorn, M. H. (2007). Threat-related attentional bias in anxious and nonanxious individuals: A meta-analytic study. *Psychological Bulletin, 133*(1), 1-24.

Heath, C., & Heath, D. (2007). *Made to stick: Why some ideas survive and others die.*

Hirt, E. R., & Markman, K. D. (1995). Multiple explanation: A consider-an-alternative strategy for debiasing judgments. *Journal of Personality and Social Psychology, 69*(6), 1069.

Chapter 8: Probabilistic Thinking About the Future

By Max Harms

Your friend says to you: "I bet you $100 that in 2016 a Democrat will be elected as president of the USA."

Would you take such a wager? Why or why not?

You might think gambling is wrong. You might find it fun. You might not have enough money to want to risk it, even if you think you could win. You might simply agree with your friend. You might think the friend is trying to take advantage of you – some friend!

Or perhaps you think that unless you have insider knowledge there's absolutely no way you could make a bet, because you just can't predict which way an election will go. After all, predicting the choices of a single person is hard enough. To predict an entire election you'd need to predict the actions of millions!

Turn your mind back to Summer 2008. The Olympics were hosted in Beijing, and Usain Bolt shattered the old record for the 100 meter dash. The Dark Knight was the most popular movie in theaters. There were warnings that the world's economy was teetering on the "brink of systemic meltdown" as banks failed and global stock prices crashed. And in America there was endless debate on whether the next president would be John McCain or Barack Obama.

In this uncertain time, a young economist named Nate Silver had just set up his own blog, FiveThirtyEight, to talk about the elections. Silver was from the world of sports, and had made many predictions in baseball and other arenas. His goal was to use the same skills on politics. While some found his approach interesting, many pundits laughed him off as a nerdy outsider without a deep understanding of Washington.

And yet, he successfully predicted the outcomes for a whopping 49 out of 50 states, missing Indiana by a single percent, and successfully called the winner of all 35 Senate races that year! I don't know whether he was involved in any bets, but if he was he sure came out ahead! The mainstream media began to see him as a modern-day wizard in political forecasting.

Well, guess what? You can be a wizard, too! Nate Silver did not have any insider knowledge, no crystal ball or magic mirror. His power came from a tool accessible to anyone with a pencil and paper: math. That's right, as long as you have a paper and pencil, you have the ability to learn to be a forecasting wizard just like Silver.

So what's the secret? A special branch of statistics (with a touch of common sense) called "Bayesianism". That's what Silver used to make his successful predictions, it's what great poker players use to win millions, and it's what insurance companies use to gamble on insuring your car, home, and health.

Okay, okay. I bet I know what you're thinking. It's great that there are mathematicians out there to look into the future and predict elections, but so what? Why should I care?

The same mathematical skills that can be used to call an election can be used for your own personal life. Want to know whether you'll be employed? What about hired for a dream-job? This sort of knowledge is very useful when deciding whether to save money or spend it on a vacation. In a way, every time you make a decision you're making a bet with yourself. You're saying "I bet this will work out better than the alternatives."

Imagine that instead of betting on the outcome of an election, your friend says: "I bet you $100 that at the end of 2016 you will be unemployed." Does the bet still seem trivial? I'd wager there are plenty of areas where you would love to predict the future. Of course, it still might not be a good idea to actually bet with your friend for all the reasons we went over at the beginning. If you make that bet, your "friend" has a reason to try and get you fired, for example. But you don't have to actually gamble for you to know whether taking the bet would be a good idea or not.

To succeed in life we need to predict the future, and in many ways we're already good at it. For example, as you're reading this, try to predict the word at the end of this... sentence. Did you do it? Our basic intuition is often pretty good at seeing what's going to happen, and you don't need any math to use that. But science has shown that there are areas where our intuitions are flawed, and we can do much better by using statistics and other mental tools.

Let me make another bet about what you're thinking. You think math is hard. Perhaps you think that the sort of math that Silver and others use is beyond you? If it takes a lot of complex math to make good bets, maybe that's a good reason to not gamble!

Well, here's the good news: it doesn't have to actually be hard! Things seem complicated right up until we understand them, and then they become simple. With practice, you have the power to become a prediction wizard like Silver. It takes work, but it's also within your grasp. If you apply your skills towards your own life you can become better at avoiding surprises, making good decisions, and winning at life! The same techniques that are used to routinely predict elections can be applied to decide on the best place to live, whether to bike or drive to work, what to study in school, or even how to improve your relationships!

This is the first in a series of posts about learning to use statistics for everyday life. Don't worry, you don't have to already know any math to be able to follow along and gain skills here. As long as you can follow a system and use a calculator you can learn to predict the future! Join me next time as I begin to explain things in more detail by talking about alternate universes, and learn how to win at life by betting.

What do you think?
- What do you think about betting on future events? Is it better, worse, or the same as betting on things like dice or cards?
- Are there any domains where statistics can't be used to make better predictions than intuition?
- What can you gain from betting on your life with yourself? What can you gain from betting with others?

References
Silver, N. (2012). *The signal and the noise: why so many predictions fail--but some don't.*
Miller, C. C., & Ireland, R. D. (2005). Intuition in strategic decision making: friend or foe in the fast-paced
21st century?. *The Academy of Management Executive, 19*(1), 19-30.

Chapter 9: Probabilistic Thinking About What You Know

By Max Harms

Caption: Puzzled man (Vox Efx/Flickr)

How good is your memory? Can you remember what you had for breakfast yesterday? Can you remember the second happiest moment in your life? Can you remember your credit card number? Can you remember what city you were in ten years ago? What about your favorite book ten years ago?

Our memories come connected to a feeling of how accurate they are. I can remember what I ate this morning pretty well, but yesterday's breakfast is more of a blur. Your confidence that a memory is correct is your **credence**, the belief that something is true. I have a very high credence when I try to remember where I lived ten years ago, but a much lower credence when asked to remember what books I was reading back then.

The scale of credence is the same as the one for probability: 0% to 100%. Ideally, if I have 90% credence in ten memories, I will be misremembering only one of them. Memories in which I have 50% credence will ideally be accurate half the time.

But this is only ideally. As it turns out, we aren't the masters of our brains that we sometimes think we are. In reality most people are *too confident* in their own memories.

In the studies referenced in the video, people are made to believe false memories (and even fill in nonexistent details themselves!) by an experimenter, but false memories often occur even outside of the laboratory. Every time you remember something, the memory may change in your brain. Sometimes these changes don't make much difference, but if you rely on your memory too heavily these changes will mess you up sooner or later.

When we think about misremembering, we're often drawn to simple examples of missing an appointment or forgetting a personal item. These failures are bad, but some of the worst failures of memory are more subtle. Perhaps you misremember what a friend is interested in, and get them a gift that they don't like (but they are too polite to say so). Perhaps you forget what the weather in your hometown is actually like, and end up moving back only to be disappointed. Or perhaps you misremember something that happened to you, and end up unintentionally telling a falsehood to dozens of people without realizing your error. If it's found out, it can be not only embarrassing, but can sometimes ruin a career. Remembering something that didn't happen is often worse than forgetting something that did happen.

Want to avoid being hurt by the limits of your brain? There are several techniques you can use to succeed! The first is to write down or otherwise record things which are important. Your fragile memory is no match for a simple paper and pencil. Next, be skeptical of your own memories and the memories of other people. When you remember something, get in the habit of imagining the opposite. This keeps you from fooling yourself! For instance, if you remember that your cousin Jennifer is in medical school, quickly think "Could I be thinking of some other cousin?" and "Might she have graduated?"

Finally, practice using your memory. Studies show that people who challenge themselves with memory games or puzzles have overall better memories, are better at cognitive tasks like math, and are less likely to develop diseases like Alzheimer's. The difference in memory between people who challenge themselves and people who don't grows even larger with age.

Imagine that you have two futures in front of yourself. In one future you mix up memories and become forgetful as the years creep on. This version of yourself flinches away from challenging activities and sticks to routines that cover your mind in cobwebs.

In the other you grow wiser, more experienced, and more skilled with time. This version of you takes the time to explore new places and activities, and as a result your mind stays strong and flexible. The journey to one of these two futures starts today. Where do you want to be headed?

What do you think?

- Have you ever noticed a false memory, or a time when someone else's memory didn't match your own?
- Have you ever made a serious error because you misremembered something?
- Are there any tricks that you've developed that help you remember things?

References

Slagter, H. A., Lutz, A., Greischar, L. L., Francis, A. D., Nieuwenhuis, S., Davis, J. M., & Davidson, R. J. (2007). Mental training affects distribution of limited brain resources. *PLoS biology*, 5(6), e138.

Tronson, N. C., & Taylor, J. R. (2007). Molecular mechanisms of memory reconsolidation. *Nature*

Reviews Neuroscience, 8(4).

Willis, S. L., Tennstedt, S. L., Marsiske, M., Ball, K., Elias, J., Koepke, K. M., & Wright, E. (2006). Long-
term effects of cognitive training on everyday functional outcomes in older adults. *Jama, 296*(23), 2805-2814.

Chapter 10: Probabilistic Thinking About Coincidences

By Hunter Glenn

Caption: Shocked Man (61015/Pixabay)

Roy Cleveland Sullivan was struck by lightning seven times. Eight, actually (if you believe him)—seven are documented.

Later in life, people began to shun him during thunderstorms, for obvious reasons. Or better said, perhaps, for obvious *feelings*. Anyone can understand why people felt the way they did, but were they being reasonable? Would you stand next to Roy during a thunderstorm?

Imagine how *you* would feel if your alarm only failed to go off when it *really* mattered. Or you could never find a parking spot when you were in a rush. Or you got dumped the same day you got fired the same day you got sick. How did you get sick? Because you got a flat tire, and your phone died right then, and you had to walk to find a phone. And then it started raining...

Bad karma! The universe is out to get you! You're cursed, you have the worst luck, etc... After all, which is more likely, that these are all just coincidences, or that they *aren't* coincidences, because destiny has its hands in your life?

Well, let's check! There are seven billion people on earth. So, every day, there are seven billion different days lived. One of those seven billion days *has* to be the most improbable day of all, a day so improbable it only happens once out of every seven billion days lived.

To put that in perspective, there are about 30,000 days in the life of a 90 year old. One of those days will be the most improbable of the 30,000, a day so improbable it only happens once in 30,000 days of life, once in a 90-year lifetime. Imagine the most improbable day you'll have in your life if you live to 90, the absolute craziest! More mind-blowing than any day of your life so far. That's a one out of 30,000 kind of event.

Well, that's *nothing* compared to a one out of seven billion kind of day, and one of *those* happens once *every single day.* It's a day more improbable than the craziest day of your life, more improbable than the craziest day in the life of anyone you know. If 200,000 people lived to be 90 years old, only *one* of them would have a day this crazy!

And yet, one such day happens once a day, somewhere on earth, like winning the weird lottery.

Caption: Roulette (Meineresterampe/Pixabay)

You kinda have to feel sorry for that one person. Suddenly, for no apparent reason, life conspires against her to *blow her mind* with how ridiculously, impossibly bad (or good) a day can get. And then the next day, and for the rest of her life…? Nothing. Perfectly normal.

Nobody she talks to has ever had something like that happen to them. Some people think she must be being punished for being a bad person and avoid her, like people avoided Roy Sullivan when he kept being stuck by lightning. What would she think? Would she be able to realize it could just be chance? How would she feel? That's the kind of thing that can really mess with your head…

Just by chance, amazing, crazy things are supposed to happen. How often do one out of a million days happen on earth? 7,000 times a day. If you're 30, your life so far has about 10,000 days in it. Imagine the most amazingly improbably day of your life so far, one you might be sure can't be just chance. Well, just by chance, a day like *that* should happen on Earth 700,000 times a day.

If more than chance is at play, then maybe these days happen *more* than they're supposed to. If 700,000 people a day have a one out of 10,000 kind of day, we might say "Eh, that's just what chance would predict.". If we get more than that, *then* we can say that it can't be just chance.

Interestingly, if we saw these days not happening at all, we would *also* wonder if something more than chance was at play. Maybe destiny, or aliens, or conspiracies to make people's lives weird, or conspiracies to make people's lives normal.

Does that seem strange? Imagine a 6-sided die. Generally, it should roll a "3" about one out of six times. If instead, we got a "3" *five* out of six times, we'd know that it wasn't just chance. Probably, someone loaded the die to land on "3" a lot. But if we rolled the die a hundred times, and never *once* got a "3," we'd be suspicious *then,* too. If we rolled it another thousand times, and *still* never got a "3," we'd know that something more than chance was at play; the die was probably loaded *not* to land on "3."

So, according to chance, crazy coincidences *have* to happen a certain amount. If they happen more than they should, or if they happen *less* than they should, we can guess that it's not just chance, something else is affecting people's lives.

But we certainly can't just point to any ole crazy coincidence and say, "Look! Proof that there's a government conspiracy. There's no way this could just be the result of chance!" Well, no, because it very well *might* be the result of just chance.

Sometimes, surviving a disease is a one out of a million chance. But that just means that it is *going* to happen one out of those million times. We wouldn't point to that and say that destiny saved that person or something. One out of a million *means* that one of those million people is supposed to get better!

This should make us question testimonials of miracle cures due to prayer or other forms of spiritual intervention. After all, we don't get to see the millions who prayed and didn't get cured. We only hear about the one case where someone prayed and then got better. Yet was it due to prayer or due to chance?

Most doctors never get a one out of a million cure. If they do, it might be the craziest thing to happen in their life and they might think destiny is intervening. But doctors don't know everything (in fact, doctors' grasp of probability is surprisingly poor).

And now, you know better than them.

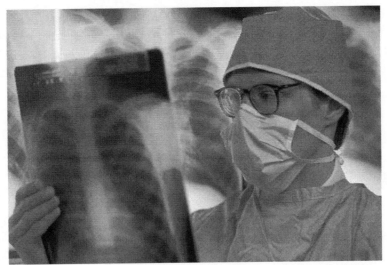

Caption: Doctor (RolandCliff/Pixabay)

So! The next time something crazy happens to you, remember:
Life is allowed to (occasionally) be crazy. Life is *supposed* to be crazy. Life is *naturally* crazy. One-out-of-a-thousand days will happen in your life every few years.

And the next time you hear about something crazy happening to someone else, remember: one-out-of-a-million days happen 7,000 times a day, somewhere on earth.

Is it destiny? Maybe. Karma? Aliens? Time Travelers? Maybe...but maybe not. It might just be chance.

Learn to look at the improbable and say "Maybe" to its face. And if your friend ever gets struck eight times by lightning, maybe you'll know not to think they're a bad person.

Questions to Consider:

- Suppose something is so rare as to only happen once every thousand days. How many of those things would have happened so far in your life?
- Why would it be weird if a one out of a thousand day *never* happened to someone?
- How many one out of a hundred days would a normal year of life have? How many have you probably had in the last year? In your whole life?
- What past events have you thought are too incredible to be just chance? Do any of them now seem like they might have just been coincidences after all?

Chapter 11: How to Protect Yourself from False Beliefs

By Gleb Tsipursky

Caption: Two faces with light bulb and brain inside (CDJ/Pixabay)

Kanisha grew up in a Democratic household in Memphis, Tennessee. As far as she remembers, her family and friends always supported leftist candidates. She watched liberal-leaning television programs. She read leftist newspapers. Her Facebook friends posted overwhelmingly liberal-friendly news articles, and Facebook's news feed algorithm edited out the articles posted by her few conservative friends. Google and other search engines also sent her similar leftist information. Kanisha lives in what is known as a filter bubble, in which she rarely sees information at odds with her views

So what's your guess on how she votes?

Even when Kanisha learns about evidence for perspectives other than her own, she generally does not give due weight to that information. For instance, when her teacher offered a balanced perspective on the pros and cons of using religion to guide public policy, Kanisha decided to Google the phrase "Why is using religion to guide public policy the right thing to do?"

Do you think the articles that came up helped her gain the most accurate perspective on this politically sensitive issue? By phrasing her Google search that way, Kanisha did not give due consideration to other perspectives. This is characteristic of Kanisha's behavior: when she hears something that makes her question her beliefs, she looks for ways to protect them, as opposed to searching for the truth.

Confirming Our Biases

Now, I don't mean to pick on Kanisha. This technology-enabled filter bubble is a characteristic of the personalization of the web. It affects many of us. This filter bubble has combined with another novel aspect of the Internet, how easily new media sources can capture our attention. Websites, bloggers, and so on tend to have lower standards for neutrality and professionalism than traditional news sources. These are key contributors to the polarization of political discourse we've seen in recent years.

I have to acknowledge that sometimes I myself am guilty of falling for the filter bubble effect. However, I fight the effect with my knowledge of cognitive biases (thinking errors made by our autopilots) and strategies for dealing with them.

When Kanisha, myself, and others ignore information that doesn't fit with our previous beliefs, we are exhibiting a thinking error called confirmation bias. Our brains tend to ignore or forget evidence that is counter to our current perspective, and will even twist ambiguous data to support our viewpoint and **confirm** our existing beliefs.

The stronger we feel about an issue, the stronger this tendency. At the extreme, confirmation bias turns into wishful thinking, when our beliefs stem from what we want to believe, instead of what is true. Confirmation bias is a big part of the polarization in our opinions, in politics and other areas of life.

Be A Proud Flip-Flopper!

So how do you deal with confirmation bias and other thinking errors? One excellent strategy is to focus on updating your beliefs. This concept has helped me and many others who attended Intentional Insights workshops, such as this videotaped one, to deal with thinking errors. To employ this strategy, it helps to practice mentally associating positive emotions such as pride and excitement with the decision to change our minds and update our beliefs based on new evidence.

Imagine how great it would be if Kanisha and everybody else associated positive emotions and felt proud of changing their minds about political issues. Politics would be so much better if everyone updated their beliefs based on new information. Right now, politicians are criticized for changing their minds with the harsh term flip-flopping. How wonderful would it be if not only the citizenry but also our politicians flip-flopped based on wherever the evidence pointed. We should all be proud flip-floppers!

Protecting Yourself From False Beliefs

Being proud of changing our minds is not intuitive, because the emotional part of the brain has a tendency to find changing our minds uncomfortable. It often persuades us to reject information that would otherwise lead us to rethink our opinions. However, we can use the rational part of our mind to train the emotional one to notice confusion, re-evaluate cached thinking and other shortcuts, revise our mental maps, and update our beliefs.

In addition to associating positive emotions with changing your mind, you can use these habits to develop more accurate beliefs:

1) Deliberately seek out contradictory evidence to your opinion on a topic, and praise yourself after giving that evidence fair consideration.

2) Consider the best possible form of arguments against your position, and be open to changing your mind if those other arguments are better than yours.

3) Focus on updating your beliefs on controversial and emotional topics, as these are harder for the human mind to manage well.

It's especially beneficial to practice changing your mind frequently. Recent research shows that those who update their beliefs more often are substantially more likely to have more accurate beliefs. So practice asking yourself systematically about whether you should change your mind based on new evidence.

Taking all of these steps and feeling good about them will help you evaluate reality accurately and thus gain agency to achieve your life goals.

Questions for Consideration
- When, if ever, has confirmation bias and associated thinking errors steered you wrong? What consequences resulted from these thinking errors?
- How can you apply the concept of updating beliefs to improve your thinking?
  What are other strategies you have found to help you change your mind and gain a more clear evaluation of reality?
- How do you think reading this post has influenced your thinking about evaluating reality? What specific steps do you plan to take as a result of reading this post to shift your thinking and behavior patterns?

References
Baum, M. A., & Groeling, T. (2008). New media and the polarization of American political discourse. *Political Communication*, *25*(4), 345-365.

Nickerson, R. S. (1998). Confirmation bias: A ubiquitous phenomenon in many guises. *Review of general psychology*, *2*(2), 175.

Tetlock, P. E., & Gardner, D. (2016). *Superforecasting: The art and science of prediction*. Random House.

Chapter 12: Free Money Is No Joke: Confessions of a (Former) Skeptic of Basic Income

By Gleb Tsipursky

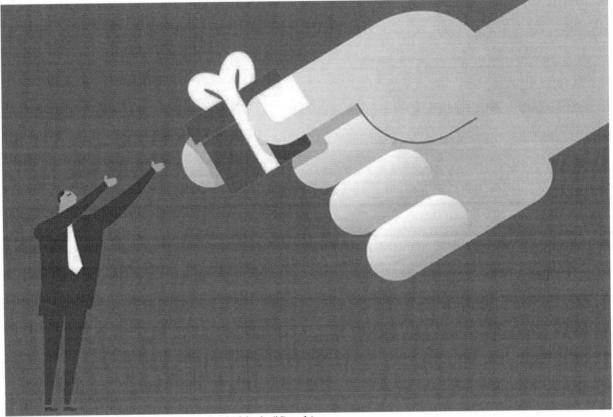

Caption: Hand giving gift to a person (Akindo/iStock)

Getting a tire replaced seems easy to me – I'd just go to the nearest tire place and get it fixed. Well, Jayleene was living from paycheck to paycheck, and didn't have the $110 to spare. She couldn't get to work, and her boss fired her. She couldn't make her rent, and was soon out on the street, all because she needed $110 at the right time.

Jayleene told me her story during my shift volunteering at a soup kitchen. Her experience was the final straw that convinced me to support basic income, the notion of giving people an unconditional living wage, supported by conservatives and liberals alike. Basic income is becoming increasingly popular around the world, with Finland, the Netherlands, Switzerland, and Canada experimenting with it.

So is the United States. In fact, there is a planned study in California funded by the well-known Y Combinator. The President of Y Combinator Sam Altman described the study thus: "In our pilot, the income will be unconditional; we're going to give it to participants for the duration of the study, no matter what. People will be able to volunteer, work, not work, move to another country—anything. We hope basic income promotes freedom, and we want to see how people experience that freedom."

Does basic income make you skeptical? I know I was pretty skeptical when I first heard about basic income. Sure, I care about people and don't want anyone to starve, to be homeless, or lack medical care. But there are nonprofits and government programs that are specifically created to take care of these needs. In fact, I myself volunteer at the soup kitchen and run fundraisers for food banks. So why give people money to do whatever they want to do with it?

I had two big concerns. One was that I simply didn't trust poor people to manage their money well, and thought they would spend it on things like alcohol, drugs, and tobacco. Another concern was that people would stop working, and just do whatever they wished to do, as opposed to being productive members of society.

However, more and more evidence appeared that contradicted my beliefs. A number of studies showed that people given cash didn't spend it on tobacco, alcohol, or similar "vice" products. Other studies demonstrated that those given a cash transfer did not do less work. Instead, the evidence indicated that people who received cash transfers improved both their income and assets, and had higher psychological and physical well-being.

Now, I could wait for more research, such as the Oakland study or another upcoming one by GiveDirectly. This nonprofit, highly rated by the best charity evaluator in the world, GiveWell, focuses on cash transfers to poor households in East Africa. GiveDirectly decided to run the largest study of basic income to date, using $30M to cover basic living costs of poor East Africans for a decade to settle questions about basic income's long-term impact. However, I could reasonably predict the future, and conclude that these new experiments will show results similar to previous ones.

Hearing Jayleene's story proved the clincher. I decided to bite the bullet, confess that my perspective was wrong, and update my beliefs based on evidence.

Freed of these limiting beliefs, I realized that basic income had other benefits. First, it's simpler to provide basic income than to fund many overlapping welfare agencies, and we can save many billions of dollars by simply giving money to the poor. Second, basic income gives people more dignity and creates less hassle for them than our current an ad-hoc system. Thirdly, poor people like Jayleene are more aware than the government of what they actually need.

For all of these reasons, I am coming out publicly to renounce my skepticism and share how the evidence convinced me to change my mind. Now, there are plenty of unresolved questions about basic income, such as how to fund a transition to it and away from using a massive system of inefficient programs. Yet that's a question of "how," not "if." I hope that sharing my story as a former skeptic of basic income will encourage a conversation about the next steps on the question of "how."

References

Evans, D., & Popova, A. (2014). Cash transfers and temptation goods: a review of global evidence. *World Bank Policy Research Working Paper* 6886, May 2014.

Macours, K., Schady, N., & Vakis, R. (2012). Cash transfers, behavioral changes, and cognitive development in early childhood: evidence from a randomized experiment. *American Economic Journal: Applied Economics*, 4(2), 247-273.

Chapter 13: This Weird Trick Set Me Free, Could It Work for You?

By Gleb Tsipursky

Caption: Hat and magic wand (Clker-Free-Vector-Images/Pixabay)

I'm very proud to be a citizen of the United States. It's one of the greatest countries in the world. America is a beacon of hope for democracy and freedom for hundreds of millions of people across the globe. Our universities consistently produce groundbreaking research, and our companies drive innovation for the global economy.

Yet I've always been uncomfortable being labeled "American." Though I'm very proud to be a citizen of the United States, the term feels restrictive and confining. It obliges me to identify with aspects of the United States with which I am not thrilled. For instance, while to some we may be the beacon of democracy, our own two-party political system leaves a lot to be desired. Democratic systems that permit more than two major parties can be more inclusive of minorities and lead to less extreme policy. In many respects, our current political system can feel stifling for many of its own citizens.

I have similar feelings of limitation with respect to other labels I assume. Some of these labels don't feel completely true to who I truly am, or impose certain perspectives on me that diverge from my own.

I recently came up with a weird trick that has made me more comfortable identifying with groups or movements that resonate with me. The trick is to simply put the word "weird" before any identity category I think about.

I'm not an "American," but a "weird American." Once I started thinking about myself as a "weird American," I was able to think calmly through which aspects of being American I identified with and which I did not, setting the latter aside from my identity. For example, I used the term "weird American" to describe myself when meeting a group of foreigners, and we had great conversations about what I meant and why I used the term. This subtle change enables my desire to identify with the label "American," but allows me to separate myself from any aspects of the label I don't support.

Beyond nationality, I've started using the term "weird" in front of other identity categories. For example, I teach classes at Ohio State University, in addition to running a nonprofit devoted to helping people reach their goals using science, Intentional Insights. I used to become deeply frustrated when students didn't prepare adequately for their classes with me. No matter how hard I tried, or whatever clever tactics I deployed, some students simply didn't care. Instead of allowing that situation to keep bothering me, I started to think of myself as a "weird professor" – one who set up an environment that helped students succeed, but didn't feel upset and frustrated by those who failed to make the most of it.

I've been applying the weird trick in my personal life, too. Thinking of myself as a "weird son" makes me feel more at ease when my mother and I don't see eye-to-eye; thinking of myself as a "weird nice guy," rather than just a nice guy, has helped me feel confident about my decisions to be firm when the occasion calls for it.

So, why does this weird trick work? It's rooted in strategies of reframing and distancing, two research-based methods for changing our thought frameworks. Reframing involves changing one's framework of thinking about a topic in order to create more beneficial modes of thinking. For instance, in reframing myself as a weird nice guy, I have been able to say "no" to requests people make of me, even though my intuitive nice guy tendency tells me I should say "yes." Distancing refers to a method of emotional management through separating oneself from an emotionally tense situation and observing it from a third-person, external perspective. Thus, if I think of myself as a weird son, I don't have nearly as much negative emotions during conflicts with my mom. It enables me to have space for calm and sound decision-making.

Overall, using the term "weird" before any identity category has helped me gain greater agency, the quality of living life intentionally to achieve my goals. It has freed me from confinements and restrictions associated with socially-imposed identity labels and allowed me to pick and choose which aspects of these labels best serve my own interests and needs. I hope being "weird" can help you reach your own goals as well!

How weird are you? Only time will tell. Consider these questions as you explore for yourself:

• Do you think using "weird" to manage your identity can help you? Why or why not?
• Where in your life, if anywhere, can you imagine identity management setting you emotionally and mentally free?
• What specific next steps will you take after reading this article?

References

Lachman, M. E., Weaver, S. L., Bandura, M., Elliot, E., & Lewkowicz, C. J. (1992). Improving memory and

   control beliefs through cognitive restructuring and self-generated strategies. *Journal of Gerontology, 47*(5), P293-P299.

Mischkowski, D., Kross, E., & Bushman, B. J. (2012). Flies on the wall are less aggressive: Self-distancing "in the heat of the moment" reduces aggressive thoughts, angry feelings and aggressive behavior. *Journal of Experimental Social Psychology, 48*(5), 1187-1191.

Chapter 14: Failing Your Way to Success!

By Gleb Tsipursky

Caption: Image of notes with "failure" and "success" written on them (Ramdlon/Pixabay)

Don't you hate finding out you made a mistake? I do. I'm proud of doing things well, and avoiding mistakes. Mistakes feel terrible to me. I remember my boss telling me about a serious mistake I made when calculating students' final course grades in my job as a professor. I was sitting at home after grading the final papers of the semester, and was already pretty tired. I just wanted to finish up all my teaching responsibilities, and go on my summer break (yes, professors love summer breaks just as much as the students). So I went on the course website, had the course management system add up all the grades, and submitted them.

I was so embarrassed when my boss told me I forgot to give students bonus grades for additional assignments. It never happened to me before. It was a truly face-palm moment.

Emotions and Mistakes

When I found out I made that mistake, my emotional self just wanted to curl up inside. I wanted to run and hide, and not deal with negative emotions associated with that mistake. This common thinking error has been studied in relation to mistakes in financial decisions and many other areas.

It's even worse when our emotional self gets aggressive and defensive in response to finding out we made a mistake. Did this ever happen to you? I know it did to me.

For instance, in the early stages of founding Intentional Insights, I did not have much practice in how to coordinate people, and made some mistakes. Because I was not watching out for this problem, I did not make sure to avoid aggressive or defensive responses to learning I was wrong. As a result, I harmed my relationships with some others also passionate about this great cause.

As an example, I was so enthusiastic about Intentional Insights that I forgot that others were not quite as passionate as myself, and misinterpreted one person's agreement to help out as a commitment to do a lot of volunteer work. When that person failed to deliver on the high expectations that I set, I grew upset, and that person was upset with my reaction – which resulted from me failing at their mind. When others told me about these mistakes, my emotional self wanted to lash out against the bearer of bad news, and not against myself for having made the mistakes. This type of thinking error is known as "shoot the messenger," meaning attributing the blame for the bad news associated with the mistake to the person who brought the message.

Did you ever experience someone with whom you shared some bad news becoming irrationally angry with you? From the other side, did you ever become angry at someone who gave you bad news? Then you know what I mean.

Such thinking errors result in many challenges for myself and others. Trying to ignore the mistake and pretend it didn't happen is not very productive for facing the truth of reality and thus gaining agency. Yet the vast majority of our social institutions and norms do not encourage acknowledging mistakes or learning from them. For example, research indicates that hundreds of thousands die from preventable medical mistakes. Yet according to a new book by Brian Goldman, an emergency room physician, medicine has a "culture of denial" that prevents doctors from sharing about and learning from their errors. Similar dynamics characterize most other professions despite the benefits associated with learning from our mistakes and from failing our way to success.

Strategies for Failing Your Way To Success

So what are some strategies for dealing with mistakes?

First, we need to overcome the negative emotions of making a mistake. It helps to remember that our mental maps of the world never match the territory of reality, and to notice our confusion as a way of indicating that we have a mistake in our evaluation of the situation, not an indication of the world being wrong (a quite unhelpful conclusion). After all, communication is frequently imperfect and our messages become garbled.

Then, apply the intentional strategy of thinking "**bad news is good news,**" one of the habits in the Rationality Habits Checklist. In other words, associate positive emotions with finding out that one made a mistake. After all, "what is true is already so," and the more effectively we overcome the negative emotions, the better we will be at facing the truth of reality, no matter how unpleasant it may be. We can then be well prepared to deal with the situation resulting from the consequence of our mistakes.

How should we do this in practice? Essentially, any time you notice yourself feeling bad after find out you made a mistake, stop and take a couple of deep breaths. Then, remember how good it is to have this knowledge, let go of stress, and then deal with the results of the mistake in the moment. Ideally we can learn to see mistakes as **opportunities** for future success.

After dealing with the consequences of the mistake, try to take advantage of the error and learn what we can from it. I've found success in using a "**Mistakes and Learning**" section as part of my daily journaling. I have a prompt in my journal where I ask myself:
• What kind of mistakes did I make recently?
• Why did I make them?
• What can I learn from them?
• How can I do better in the future?

As a result, I encourage myself to face my own mistakes, get at the reasons for making them, learn from them, and figure out how I can improve my future performance.

This process of learning from mistakes is a lifelong project. It fills me with hope, as it helps me strive to accept the truth, revise my ways of doing things, and optimize my behavior for the future. I fail my way to success!

Here are some question to ask yourself that will help you fail your way to success:
• When was the last time you noticed or were told of a mistake?
• What did you do about it?
• Do you know how to avoid that mistake in the future?
• What are your general strategies for dealing with mistakes?
• How do you deal with the negative emotions of finding out you made a mistake?
• In what ways do you learn from mistakes?
• How can you apply these strategies in your life, and how do you think you might benefit from doing so?
• What kind of plan can you make and what specific steps can you take to internalize these mental habits?

References
Galai, D., & Sade, O. (2006). The "ostrich effect" and the relationship between the liquidity and the yields
    of financial assets. *The Journal of Business*, *79*(5), 2741-2759.
Goldman, B. (2015). *The Secret Language of Doctors: Cracking the Code of Hospital Culture*.
James, J. T. (2013). A new, evidence-based estimate of patient harms associated with hospital
    care. *Journal of patient safety*, *9*(3), 122-128.

Chapter 15: How Feedback is Good For You (Even When You Feel Bad About It)

By Amy K. Watson

Caption: Picture with image of positive, negative, and neutral feedback (Pixaline/Pixabay)

What does "Performance Feedback" mean to you? People describe receiving feedback from their bosses as:

• A waste of time
• Painful
• Completely off base

- A great opportunity
- Necessary

How could all of these be said about the same experience?

Many of us have experienced feedback that is off base, unfair, and poorly timed. But what if you could find value in even the most poorly delivered evaluative comments, no matter where they come from?

For years I dismissed feedback unless it was packaged in a certain way. *Tell me I'm fantastic, and how, and why. I thought. Be specific!*

And if you see that I could improve, you have to keep in mind how much you love me and want me to succeed. I insisted. You must reiterate your faith in me. If you don't love me or have faith in me, your feedback is worthless here. Move along!

Not everyone would have such requirements, but because of the way I took critical feedback, they were necessary for me. I did not see myself as having a fragile ego. Rather, I saw myself as having standards. *Others should be mindful about how they approach human beings with their feedback. I am happy to make sure they know the standards.*

In truth, however, the way I took feedback had room for improvement. And I have been learning for many years how to process feedback so that I can get the benefit from it rather than become upset when it isn't offered according to my rules.

In 2009, when I started facilitating workshops, my co-facilitator and I would distribute feedback forms and ask participants to tell us what their experience was like. Whenever I collected the sheets after everyone left, my attention was pulled by the section where my performance was scored against my partner's.

This was my poison. I knew it would cause me pain, but I craved a message that *I was better* than my partner had been. No matter how non-competitive I might see myself in my everyday life, if you put me in a ratings race with anyone doing what I love to do, I want to *win*.

I typically scored higher in "preparation," but that didn't seem to satisfy my craving. I studied the ratings until I proved to myself that my partner had won the day in every *important* respect (which to me was any area where my partner had scored higher than me).

My emotional self used these ratings to treat me worse than I would ever treat anyone else. They seemed to reinforce a message: *I suck. Why would anybody listen to me? I'll never achieve anything. I should have stayed in bed.*

I obsessed about it for days, during which my productivity and sociability dropped away.

So much about my experience could have improved if a miracle of time travel had allowed me to read Douglas Stone and Sheila Heen's book, *Thanks for the Feedback: The Science and Art of Receiving Feedback Well*. It would have helped me to become more curious, understand and accept myself, and find a way to process feedback that didn't hurt so much. Here is what I could have learned:

Cultivate curiosity about what people are 'reading' from you.

One of the first skills the authors suggest is receiving and learning from feedback "even when it is off base, unfair, poorly delivered, and, frankly, you're not in the mood."

What could possibly be the value in trying to learn from feedback that's off base or unfair? Are Stone and Heen trying to suggest that you should change *everything* that others want you to change?

Not at all! *Still, everything you do communicates something about you, and your message will have an audience.*

Feedback is a chance to know what your "audience" is receiving, an opportunity to make adjustments so you can communicate your message more effectively. Is the information they are receiving (about either your content or about yourself) the information you want to convey? The only way you will ever know is by paying attention to your feedback and learning how to interpret the clues you get.

Start where you are–wired for taking feedback the way *you* do.

Each of us is wired to take feedback in our own particular way. According to Stone and Heen, it's not unusual for feedback to knock you off your game if:
1. you feel it isn't true *(Truth),*
2. the person delivering it is just the wrong person to say that *(Relationship),* or
3. the feedback threatens your understanding of who you are *(Identity).*

Identity is where the workshop evaluations hit me the hardest, at my sense of myself as a "really good facilitator."

You will respond to feedback in your own signature way that is characterized by how you feel and think generally and how you process feedback in particular. I was predisposed to dismiss positive feedback and to take negative feedback hard. I was also wired to recover more slowly from those hard hits.

Others might get a big boost from positive feedback (such as "well prepared") but aren't so bothered by negative feedback. Their default wiring might mean they are resistant to teaching or change because they don't take constructive critical feedback seriously enough.

By starting with a stronger understanding of your own wiring, you can develop better skills for receiving and interpreting the feedback offered to you.

Grant yourself permission to need room for improvement.

What can you do if you hate feedback that's less than glowing? Fortunately I did discover a path that led me away from the darkness of comparison and into a healthier place. As it turns out, my strategy was right in line with the recommendations in *Thanks for the Feedback.*

I found a way to focus on my own numbers and compare them to previous feedback. My curiosity about *how the numbers were changing* developed, and I took my attention off my co-facilitators' scores. This practice also developed my interest in how I might strengthen my skills in other categories.

The new approach helped so much. The drug-like attraction of comparing myself to others eased. My annoyance at my partners shifted to interest in my own development. Over time I saw my numbers improving relative to my own earlier scores. Even more importantly, as my facilitation skills improved, I learned to trust myself instead of craving external validation.

You do not have to choose between the joy of being accepted and the challenge of learning from feedback. Both are possible together. Loving yourself enough to accept feedback without fear is a wonderful practice.

For further reading about this topic, besides the already-mentioned Douglas Stone & Sheila Heen book, *Thanks for the Feedback*, I would recommend Brené Brown's *Daring Greatly*, Carol S. Dweck's *Mindset: The New Psychology Of Success*, and David Rock's *Your Brain at Work.*

Bottom Line

• How open are you to feedback? If you feel pain when receiving feedback from your boss, peers, family members, or others, a new book by Douglas Stone and Sheila Heen offers suggestions. You can develop skills for receiving feedback well–even if it's poorly delivered–by following these suggestions:
– Cultivate curiosity about what people are reading from you,
– Accept and become familiar with your default wiring for receiving feedback,
– Grant yourself permission to have room for improvement.

• How do you typically respond to feedback? Do you feel a positive or negative charge? How strong is the charge? How long does it last? If you know your typical reactions to feedback, you can predict them and even move beyond your habits.
• Try considering others' reactions to you as information to consider. What could improve for you if you did?
• What next steps will you take to improve the way you respond to feedback?

References

Brown, B. (2015). *Daring greatly: How the courage to be vulnerable transforms the way we live, love, parent, and lead.*

Dweck, C. S. (2006). *Mindset: The new psychology of success.*

Rock, D. (2009). *Your brain at work: Strategies for overcoming distraction, regaining focus, and working smarter all day long.*

Stone, D., & Heen, S. (2015). *Thanks for the Feedback: The Science and Art of Receiving Feedback Well (even when it is Off Base, Unfair, Poorly Delivered, and Frankly, You're Not in the Mood).*

Chapter 16: Defend Your Happiness Against Emotional Traps!

By Gleb Tsipursky

Caption: Sign saying "defend" (Nick Youngson/NYphotographic)

Entering that backyard was like going into a lush grove. Shady trees spread their branches around us and protected us from the summer's heat. Oh, and how beautiful the leaves would get in the fall. Can you imagine the full range of colors that would emerge – red, yellow, and orange in all the kaleidoscopic ecstasy of autumn's revel? How could this magical vision fail to deliver our heart's desire?

Walking into this backyard was the single most vivid experience of the house search undertaken by myself and my wife, Agnes Vishnevkin. I imagined myself lounging in the hammock in the peaceful shade of trees, experiencing the calm of a majestic forest. Exhausted after a long, grueling day of house hunting, this yard was the clincher for me and my wife. We excitedly told our realtor to put a bid in for the house; we couldn't wait to move in.

Little did we know, the backyard was a trap! Why was it a trap? It couldn't deliver on the emotional promises it made! Lounging around in that backyard would be rare. In reality, on my days off, I'm much more likely to go visit my friends or go out with my wife.

I was so motivated by my emotional attachment to one aspect of the house that I disregarded everything else. It was a classic thinking error, called attentional bias. This term refers to our brain's tendency to focus on whatever things in our environment that happen to push our emotional buttons, as opposed to the things that are actually important. Such emotional traps could cost us our long-term happiness when they influence our big decisions, such as getting a new car or, especially, a new home!

Fortunately, Agnes and I avoided this trap. The day after we told our agent to make the offer, we decided to re-evaluate our decision by applying the tools of probabilistic thinking and multi-attribute utility theory to our purchase.

Below is a photo of our calculations. We compared our first-choice house, labeled 170, to our second choice, 450. To avoid excessive emotional attachment to any part of the house, we wrote out the various parts of the house (first column). We then gave each a quality rating on a scale from one to three, one being the lowest and three being the highest. Then, to account for the actual usage of each part of the house, we gave a similar rating for expected usage. Next, we multiplied the quality and usage figures to give an overall weighted rating (only the overall rating is included in the chart). We separately wrote how much we thought each part of the house was worth, and how much we would use it, marked A and G, for Agnes and Gleb. Finally, we added them all up at the bottom, as you can see from this photo of my notebook.

Caption: Image of calculations (courtesy of Gleb Tsipursky)

Both of us were really surprised by the result. Our second-choice house beat out our first-choice house, and by a lot, 95 to 67.5. For instance, we realized that besides the yard, the original first choice house had a dining room that was too small for us. Also, the living room had a poor setup for the furniture we'd be bringing with us. Our original first-choice house had much worse bathroom options, and also a much poorer space for the two of us to hang out (h. o. in the photo above). While Agnes liked the kitchen in our original first choice more, it was not a factor for me, as I don't really engage with the kitchen much.

We were way off base in our initial decision-making process due to our attentional bias on the backyard and after we'd thought about it, we felt much more comfortable with our new choice. I shared my experience with others and found out that many had similar stories. We quickly called our realtor and asked her to make the bid on the second house. And we were so excited when it was finally accepted! We moved in on November 9, and haven't looked back since.

We're really happy with our new house, and I shudder to imagine what would have happened if we bought the other one. We'd have spent the long cold winter looking out the windows at the leafless, snow-covered trees in our backyard, longing for the warm weather to arrive. By contrast, this house has a lovely heated screened-in porch that we can sit in all year round, and I enjoy a view of a pine tree from my home office window.

Caption: Tree outside of author's window (Courtesy of Gleb Tsipursky)

From that episode, I learned that this type of cost-benefit analysis is really valuable when making significant decisions that impact your long-term happiness. In fact, Benjamin Franklin used a similar method when making important decisions! So, how can you use this method to avoid the emotional trap of giving in to in-the-moment feelings for the sake of your long-term happiness?

Let's go back to the car as an example. Before making a decision, sit down and assign numbers to various components of the car. First, consider how you plan to use the car – city driving, highway driving, road trips, driving in the mountains, driving by yourself, driving with family and friends, driving your date, and other uses. How much of your time will you use the car for each activity and how important is each activity to you? Assign a numerical value to each activity based on a combination of usage and importance. For instance, you might not be taking family road trips often, but it might be important for the car to be really well suited for those times, so give a higher number for that variable.

Second, based on your usage ratings, consider what aspects of the car are important to you – safety, gas mileage, comfort for the driver and passengers, trunk space, off-road capacity, coolness factor, and so on. For example, it might be important to you to impress your dates and friends with your car, so give a higher rating to the coolness factor. Or it might be very valuable to have comfort for yourself and good trunk space if you are taking long car trips. Assign a numerical value to each aspect based on your personal evaluation. Now you know what aspects are most important to you and are much less likely to be led astray by attentional bias!

Note that this does not mean you are trying to eliminate all emotion from your decisions. After all, your ratings are informed by how you feel about what you are evaluating. However, numerical ratings can help give those feelings *proper scope* in relation to other considerations, and prevent attentional bias from hijacking your decisions

Apply this method to any significant financial decision – buying a car, some furniture, vacation, a computer, a house. A smart time investment of less than half an hour could lead to a much happier future for you. Moreover, with a little imagination, this method can be applied to all important decisions, not only financial ones. In future posts, I will discuss how to quantify less tangible values to make wise decisions for your long-term happiness.

Questions to consider
• What are your strategies for making big decisions wisely?
• Has attentional bias ever led you astray when making big decisions? If so, how could you have applied the method from this article to your previous decisions in order to make better choices?
• What kind of significant financial decisions may you make soon? What kind of factors might cause attentional bias in these decisions? What specific steps can you take to avoid these problems?

References
Fox, E., Russo, R., & Dutton, K. (2002). Attentional bias for threat: Evidence for delayed disengagement from emotional faces. *Cognition & emotion, 16*(3), 355-379.
Sarin, R. K. (2001). Multi-attribute utility theory. In *Encyclopedia of Operations Research and Management Science* (pp. 526-529). Springer US.

Chapter 17: Stop Losing Money: Invest Wisely

By Peter Livingstone

Caption: Image of dollar bills (NikolayFrolochkin/Pixabay)

You're probably losing money right now, without even knowing it! Why? Well, if you have money sitting in a bank account that's giving you a return of less than 1.5%, you're losing money due to inflation. Inflation simply means that your dollar will buy less a year from now than it can buy today. In fact, you would need ten dollars today to buy what you could for one dollar in 1950.

Fortunately, you can stop losing money through successful investing, and actually make money instead of having it be eaten up by inflation. You can invest successfully by using a simple plan and avoiding common mistakes.

Let me guess what many of you are thinking. You've probably watched one of those movies about rich and powerful Wall Street investors, the so-called "masters of the universe." Maybe you've thought "I can't compete with these guys", or "I don't want to risk losing my money, so I'll just keep all my savings or retirement funds in a bank account." Perhaps you listen to the news when the Dow Jones Industrial Average drops hundreds of points and think "I couldn't stand to lose money like those folks in the stock market."

Using some simple, evidence-based methods for wise investing, you can outperform the majority of stock market investors (even those "masters of the universe"). You don't need a lot of money to start investing. If you are fortunate enough to have a workplace retirement account, such as a 401(k), you can start by contributing as little as a few dollars a month.

Even if you don't, you can get other types of investment accounts, and then make small contributions regularly. Consider doing so right now to stop losing money! Well, after you read this article, that is.

Don't Get Get Ripped Off (Hint: Avoid Actively Managed Mutual Funds)

First, let's review some long-term performance records of average investors, as well as the records of a broad United States stock market index. According to a study, the 30-year compound annual growth rate (essentially the average one-year return for the period) for average United States investors in equity (stock market) mutual funds was 3.66%. While not a terrible performance compared to today's bank savings account interest rates (about 0.06%), the annual return of the broad U.S. stock market for the same period, as represented by the S&P 500 index, was 10.35%.

To put that in perspective, if the average investor contributed just $100 per month over the 30-year period with an average return of 3.66%, that investor would have accumulated about $65,000. But, if an investor had matched the return of the S&P 500 index, that investor would have about $233,000. What a huge difference for someone nearing retirement! Wouldn't it be great to have that money in your pocket?

How can you guarantee that you can come very close to matching the performance of the broad stock market? The answer can be found by investing in a low cost index fund, a type of mutual fund or exchange traded fund which are available through most investment firms and retirement accounts. The reason many individuals are not aware of the power of investing in index funds, and leaving their money alone to grow in these funds, is that that there is very little incentive for the financial industry to make the case for such investments. After all, many stock brokers, fund managers, and financial advisors get paid through actively buying and selling individual stocks or funds by charging fees and commissions.

The goal of an index fund is simply to match the performance of a specific index of stocks, such as the S&P 500, by investing in all of the companies within that index. All funds charge some expense for the work of maintaining these investments, but the best index funds charge only about 0.05% to 0.10% of your investment, so your actual performance will be just that fraction below the index. Actively managed mutual funds, however, seek to outperform some specific index, so they charge much higher fees. The big secret is that most all of these active funds underperform the index funds. This is one case where you do not get what you pay for!

Don't Be Your Own Worst Enemy

A main reason why putting and keeping money in a low cost index fund generally outperforms more active investment styles is the avoidance of fees and commissions. Additionally, the compounding effect will increase your investment because these savings get reinvested in the fund, so the money saved each year will grow in the following years. The other big reason that most investors fail to match the return of the broad market is that they tend to try to "time" the market, thinking they can sell out before a big market drop and by in when prices are low. In reality, however, many investors get panicked when the market drops, selling out at low prices, and then feel better after prices rebound, buying back in when prices are higher. Even the most successful investors of modern times, such as Warren Buffett, believe that they cannot predict the direction of the market in order to time it, and advise that you shouldn't either.

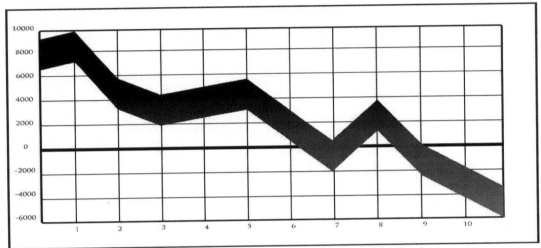

Caption: Graph of declining trend (Clker-Free-Vector-Images, Pixabay)

This is just one example of behavioral mistakes caused by cognitive biases (common thinking errors) that undermine many investors. Such cognitive biases result from the mind's two systems of thinking, the Autopilot System and the Intentional System. Learning about these systems and accounting for these biases will make you a much better investor!

Two broad cognitive biases which may contribute to buying and selling at the wrong times are the overconfidence effect and loss aversion. Overconfidence can lull us into a false sense of certainty that we know when the market will go up or down. Loss aversion is our tendency to feel worse about losses than feel good about similar-sized gains. Combined, these two biases can have the effect of leading us to sell when we see our investments drop, and then buy the same investments back when they go higher. By simply admitting that the market will go up and down, but we cannot predict when, we can begin to overcome these biases.

Don't Forget That Life Is Uncertain, But History Is A Guide

Before you start thinking that investing in an index fund is a guaranteed way of making your money grow, I must caution you that there are no guarantees in life, and anyone who tells you otherwise is a rotten liar. Yet by using probabilistic thinking, and considering some history of the market, you can make some reasonable assumptions about your chances for success. Looking back through 145 years of history in the US stock market, there have been cases of individual companies and individual stock market mutual funds losing everything, but the performance of the overall U.S. market, as measured by the S&P 500, looks much different.

Assuming the market's characteristics over the past 145 years will give us a good representation of what the future will hold, here are statistics that may give some reasonable expectations. The data was compiled by Yale Professor Robert Shiller (there are interactive calculators based on his work online, for which the following results are derived). The total average annual return for the S&P 500 (with dividends reinvested) from 1871 to 2016 was around 9.0% (not adjusted for inflation).

During this 145 year span, over every possible period of twenty years or more the index had a positive return (inflation notwithstanding), with the worst at 2% (1929-'49) and the best at 18% (1980-2000). Even for any given ten-year period during this time, the S&P 500 had a positive return 97% of the time. Over a one-year period, however, the probability of having a positive return dropped to 71%, with the worst 12 month period losing 62% (1931-'32) and the best gaining 140% (1932-'33).

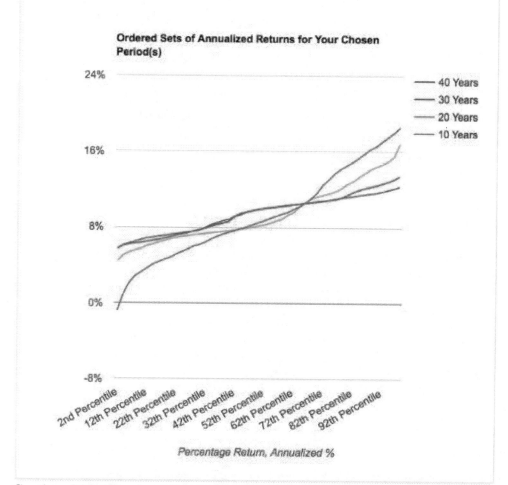

Caption: S&P 500 returns for all sets of given time periods (Robert Shiller)

How can we put this history into perspective? Let's assume you had the worst possible market timing over this 145 year history. You got an inheritance from a rich uncle in September 1929, and invested it all in a fund which matched the S&P 500 for a period of twenty years. Even though you would have been extremely unlucky to choose these exact times to get in and out of the market, you still would have returned a 2% annual compounded return. This is certainly better than stuffing cash under a mattress.

Moreover, the vast majority of people do not simply put all of their wealth into the market at one point and exit at another. Most people receive money over time, and by necessity can only invest small amounts spread out over this time. By contributing incrementally to an investment over time, your chance of picking the very worst times to enter and exit are greatly reduced, and you have a much greater chance of matching the long-term market average.

There are fancy computer models called "Monte Carlo Simulations" which calculate the probabilities of investment returns for investing and withdrawing specific amounts of money over time based on historic behavior of markets. For simplicity though, let's make some broad generalizations based on historical evidence. Assuming the characteristics of future stock market returns are close to what has been experienced in the past, over a period of investing for ten years or more (the longer the better) in a low cost index fund tracking the S&P 500, you would almost certainly have gains, most likely in the range of 5% to 13% annually, averaged over the entire period. This return would, probably, beat the majority of active funds, and the vast majority of all other investors.

Don't Just Buy The Top Performing Funds

What about those few funds and investment managers who have beaten the broad market index over many years, and why not invest with them? There has been a lot of academic research done trying to figure out how to do this, and the evidence suggests that there is no consistent, reliable way to predict who will beat the market average.

Many studies have been conducted to determine how to predict which investment funds will outperform. So far, the only factor found useful in predicting performance is costs – the lower a fund's costs, the more of your money stays in the fund and grows. By the very nature of random luck, a few high cost, actively managed funds and investment managers will perform better than the market average for any given time period, but what are the odds you or I, or even a team of market researchers, could pick them? Not very high, as the evidence shows.

Keep in mind that by investing in a low cost index fund you will not have much of a chance of making big gains quickly, and its value can drop substantially over a short period of time. However, if your goal is to save and invest over ten years or more and achieve the highest chance of positive returns, a low cost, stock market index fund is your best choice. This way, you can stop losing money, and make the best decisions to help you achieve your financial goals!

Questions to consider:

1. How much money do you have in savings that you are not very likely to need for at least ten years? Keep in mind that index funds are quite liquid, and you can get your money back in less than two weeks if you need it for some emergency.

84

2. How much can you save a little every month to invest for ten years or more?

3. Would you be comfortable knowing that the value of your investment might drop by 20%-60% sometime during that ten year period, even though there is a good chance that it will have an overall annual return of 5% or greater for the entire period? Keep this in mind – with an annual return of 7.2% your money will double in ten years.

References

Barras, L., Scaillet, O., & Wermers, R. (2010). False discoveries in mutual fund performance: Measuring luck in estimated alphas. *The journal of finance*, *65*(1), 179-216.

Fama, E. F., & French, K. R. (2010). Luck versus skill in the cross-section of mutual fund returns. *The journal of finance*, *65*(5), 1915-1947.

Kahneman, D., Knetsch, J. L., & Thaler, R. H. (1991). Anomalies: The endowment effect, loss aversion, and status quo bias. *The journal of economic perspectives*, *5*(1), 193-206.

Moore, D. A., & Healy, P. J. (2008). The trouble with overconfidence. *Psychological review*, *115*(2), 502.

Chapter 18: Don't Sink Your Money

By Peter Livingstone

Caption: Sinking Ship (Tassilo111/Pixabay)

Imagine you've gone to see a play. When you get to the box office to pay $10 for a ticket, you realize that you've lost $10 from your wallet. You've got plenty of cash left for your entertainment, so would you still pay for the ticket? Most people say they would.

Now imagine you've arrived at the box office with all of your cash still in your wallet. After buying a ticket for $10, you get to the ticket-taker and realize you've lost your ticket. Would you buy another ticket? In this case, most people say they would not.

But hold on - aren't these two cases really the same thing? In both cases, you've lost the equivalent of $10 on the way to see the play and you're making a decision to spend $10 for a ticket. Why would people be inconsistent?

What are Mental Accounting Errors?

The previous example was proposed to people in experiment conducted by the behavioral psychologists Daniel Kahneman and Amos Tversky and presented in their research on The Framing of Decisions and the Psychology of Choice. The lost ticket and the lost $10 are both examples of sunk costs - that is, the money is gone, regardless of your future decisions. The sunk cost fallacy is just one type of mental accounting error.

According to Kahneman and Tversky, the way we frame the loss is an example of mental accounting, and can explain the change in our decision. In the first case, most people do not specifically link the loss of the $10 to the ticket purchase. In the second case, however, the loss is viewed in the same mental account as purchasing another ticket. The expense required to see the show is perceived as $20, a price which most people found excessive (keep in mind this work was done in the 1970's, when $20 was worth much more than today).

Are We Rational Decision Makers?

Many people view themselves as rational decision-makers. So how could a simple reframing of a $10 loss cause people to make inconsistent decisions? According to strong evidence from the field of behavioral economics, we are inherently predisposed, under certain conditions, to consistently make irrational decisions that conflict with our goals and best interests.

These type of errors, called cognitive biases, occur repeatedly and systematically in all people to some degree. Even the leading experts in this field of science will admit to suffering from these biases, and usually describe their errors in the form of humorous anecdotes. So if the experts still make these errors, how can you and I have any chance to improve our decisions?

Before we get into fixes for financial thinking errors, let's consider how sunk costs can lead us astray in other areas of our lives. You may have read about wars between some far off countries in which citizens on either side use the justification "if we give up and stop fighting now, all of those lives lost in the war will be such a waste." From an outside perspective, this probably does not seem logical, since achieving peace would save many lives in the future, regardless of lives lost in the past. However, this may be a much more difficult view when thinking about a war involving your own country. Such justifications have probably been used with every major world conflict, as in this case with the Vietnam War. The sunk costs in these cases are, of course, human lives.

Would You Intentionally Want to Make Bad Decisions?

If, at the time of your birth, you had a choice between living a life in which you make inconsistent decisions, often conflicting with your own best interest, or having the ability to make consistent decisions in line with your values and goals, which would you chose? I don't think anyone intentionally wants to make bad decisions, so how can we learn to overcome these types of thinking errors?

This very question is much debated among the experts. It seems to be clear that simply knowing about various biases does not help one recognize, let alone mitigate, one's own errors. Within the field of cognitive psychology, the practice of debiasing (the reduction of bias with respect to judgement and decision making) can offer insights. For some in-depth debiasing methods, in an interview with Dr. Hal Arkes, Emeritus Professor of Psychology at The Ohio State University, Dr. Arkes stresses that most of us live in "overconfidence land," and that by taking a more objective "outside view" we can temper that overconfidence. Additionally, he suggests that we "show a little humility, particularly in areas in which we think we are experts."

Avoiding the Sunk Cost Fallacy

The first step in reducing our cognitive biases is to acknowledge them. Since there are about 160 different types of cognitive biases identified to date, just listing each would be overwhelming, so let's just focus on the sunk cost fallacy.

If you are making a decision with any thought of past expenditures, you could be vulnerable to the sunk cost fallacy. Keep in mind that these expenditures come in many forms, including money, time, effort, or any other resource. Can these costs be recovered as a result of your decision? If not, they are sunk costs and should not be a factor in the decision. This is a simple statement, but in practice it can be difficult to implement. If you find thoughts of sunk costs difficult to eliminate, here are some tips:

- Try reframing the decision by taking the outside view. Imagine you are coming into this decision as an outsider, new to the situation, and just try to make the best decision for the future. This may help you shed the emotional "baggage" of thinking of sunk costs as a mistake. Don't be too hard on yourself for past decisions.
- Consider that by not making a change, you are potentially giving up a better future outcome.
- Frame the decision solely as a future valuation, and ask yourself, is this worth it? You cannot recover what you've spent, but you may be able to eliminate future expenses or achieve future gains.
- Try to recall a time when you decided to make a change by stopping something, or getting rid of something. What were the benefits you gained as a result?
- Remember that some of the most successful people and companies quit or failed at many things in order to achieve a few great successes.

Lastly, if you get confused with all of the modern research into cognitive behavioral science, just remember the Law of Holes adage - **"If you find yourself in a hole, stop digging"**

References

Tetlock, P. E., & Mellers, B. A. (2002). The great rationality debate. *Psychological Science, 13*(1), 94-99.
Tversky, A., & Kahneman, D. (1981). The framing of decisions and the psychology of
        choice. *Science, 211*(4481), 453-458.

Chapter 19: 3 Decision-Making Principles I Taught My Son

By Diogo Goncalves

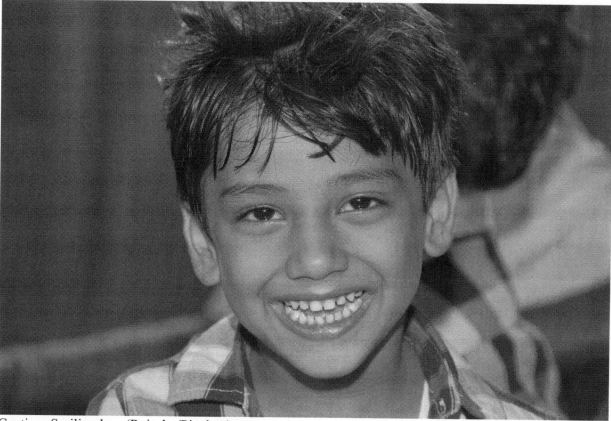

Caption: Smiling boy (Rajeshy/Pixabay)

Son, today I want to talk to you about how people make decisions.

Many choices in our lives have uncertain outcomes. Choosing between two options often involves a risk, such as whether you should spend your birthday money on a new bicycle or on a PlayStation. Each choice is like two sides of a coin: there's a risk of losing something (a loss) and an opportunity of getting something (a gain).

If you spend your birthday money on a new bicycle you'll forgo the latest PlayStation, but gain the pleasure of cruising around the neighborhood on your own bike. If you buy a PlayStation with your birthday cash, you'll lose the chance of a brand new set of wheels, but gain the pleasure of having a PlayStation to play with your friends. Both alternatives involve gains and losses.

These types of choices are affected by **three ways of thinking**, which influence the way we evaluate the expected results of our decisions, and consequently, the choices we make.

1) The first one is called **Loss Aversion**

For us humans, losing something creates stronger emotions than gaining something. In fact, the science of loss aversion says that we feel twice as bad when we lose something as we feel happy when we get that exact thing. So losing a dollar feels twice as bad as finding a dollar.

This means that if you lose a dollar and find it again the next day, you'll feel three times happier (two from canceling the loss and one from the gain) than you felt before you lost it.

2) The second one is called **Diminishing Sensitivity**

Most people really like chocolate mousse. But when you have chocolate mousse for dessert, the first spoonful of chocolate mousse tastes much better than the fifth spoonful, the fifth spoonful better than the sixth, and so on.

This means that our **sensitivity** to things becomes smaller and smaller. If I turn on a dim light in your dark room while you're sleeping, it will have a big effect. But the same dim light may be hard to see in your bright room during the day. Similarly, if your parents cut your $20 allowance by $5, you'll feel it more than you would if you had a $30 allowance, but less than you would if you had a $10 allowance, though the difference ($5) is the same in all three cases.

3) The third one is called **Reference Point**

Imagine you drink a soda with ice after having a warm soup, or after having an ice cream. The cola will seem colder after the soup than after having the ice cream. This happens because your mouth gets used to a **reference point** (warmth with the soup and coldness with the ice cream) that determines the way you experience the next thing, such as the cola.

When people think about money they also use a reference point, which is usually what you expect. Outcomes that are better than the reference point are perceived as gains, while ones that are worse are perceived as losses. So if you are used to receiving $200 from your grandmother for Christmas and she gives you only $150 this year, you'll feel like you lost something. But if you had received $100 in the past, this year's $150 will make you feel like you gained something.

These three principles revolutionized a science called economics and how we think about money. More recently, a new kind of economics emerged, has which has introduced psychology – the science of the mind – into economics. This field is called behavioral economics. Understanding its ideas can help everyone, including you, make better decisions.

Questions for Consideration
• From the three principles, what is the one you consider the most important to teach to others?
• How can we create exercises/pedagogical games that can help us to educate children having these

important principles in mind?

• How can you explain these principles most effectively to adults?

References

Erev, I., Ert, E., & Yechiam, E. (2008). Loss aversion, diminishing sensitivity, and the effect of experience
    on repeated decisions. *Journal of Behavioral Decision Making, 21*(5), 575-597.

Friedlander, M. L., & Phillips, S. D. (1984). Preventing anchoring errors in clinical judgment. *Journal of consulting and clinical psychology, 52*(3), 366.

Kahneman, D., Knetsch, J. L., & Thaler, R. H. (1991). Anomalies: The endowment effect, loss aversion, and status quo bias. *The journal of economic perspectives, 5*(1), 193-206.

Chapter 20: Your Feelings Are Not Your Fault (Mostly)

By Hunter Glenn

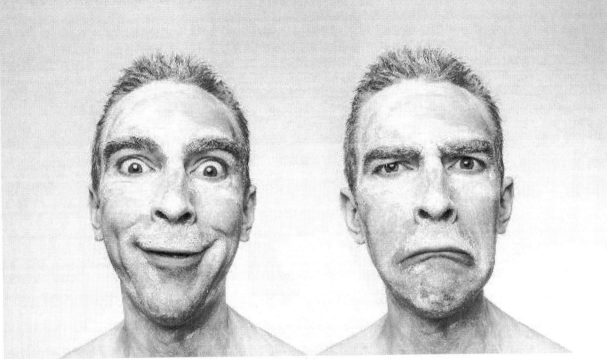

Caption: Happy and sad person (Gratisography/Pexels)

We all take responsibility for our actions; we feel guilty when we're bad, and fulfillment when we're good. Do you do the same for your feelings? Should you? I used to...
I alternated between priding myself on liking people and guilting myself for disliking them. Naturally, I rather preferred pride to guilt; I liked feeling virtuous, so I tried to force feelings of liking someone, or of respecting them, of forgiving, or of staying calm in the face of irritation. This left me frustrated when I failed, and I carried a lot of guilt for feeling the "wrong" way.

Epiphany #1

Well, there's power and there's progress in updating your beliefs. As I grew older, the thought came to me: I wasn't *asking* for my feelings, they came whether I wanted them or not! Consistent with scientific findings, I really, *really* couldn't just use my willpower to make them be whatever I wanted, not well, and not for long (the emotional part of our brain, the Autopilot System, is much more powerful than the rational part, the Intentional System). So it was hardly fair to keep telling myself the feelings were my fault!

Besides, doing so often trapped me in this loop:
1. I felt down
2. So I tried to force myself to feel better
3. I failed
4. I blamed myself for failing

Of course, this just made me feel worse, which made me try even harder, with even less success — rinse, wash, repeat — until crippling despair permeates the soul.

Research finds this loop is common. I don't think I ever suffered from depression, but I imagine if I did, it would have been hell to hold myself responsible for those feelings, to go through these cycles with even less control (and even less reason to blame myself for it all).

"Better," I thought, "if I take responsibility for what I *do* about my feelings, rather than for the feelings themselves." So, instead of holding myself 100 percent responsible for my actions, *and* 100 percent responsible for my feelings, I decided it was better to hold myself 100 percent responsible for my actions, but 0 percent responsible for my feelings.

I let my feelings off their leash and wondered where all this calm suddenly came from, as I relearned how to relax. I no longer felt like the open moments in my day had to be spent making sure my feelings had been the "right way."

I learned: Your feelings are *valid*. Your feelings are what they are. Do whatever is best to do, and let your feelings be. Let them come. And then let them pass, like the waves of the sea.

That way, my negative feelings faded sooner, more easily, than when I was trying to force them to go. I had less stress and extra energy for *doing*, once I stopped wasting it on how I was feeling.

But, my work was not yet done. If ever you've felt confident you knew what was what because you knew what *wasn't*, I hope you can learn from my error, because my learning was incomplete. Remember, I shifted from 100 percent responsibility for my feelings to no responsibility, using the Intentional System we all have.

The Problem with Epiphany #1

I still think this was mostly right. However, I wasn't *entirely* right. Because, from my earlier experiences, I knew — though I wasn't thinking of it at the time — that trying to force your feelings can work. A little. Your feelings are not *completely* decoupled from your Intentional system. Just mostly, perhaps 90%.

Epiphany #2

If you try to push your feelings more than you should, it's a slick slip down a steep slope into debilitating cycles of wasted willpower.

But. If you push — juuust a little, *juuust* enough, you can make a little headway against negative feelings.

The old idea "just have a positive attitude" sticks around because it works. Sort of. It's also a sort of hideous thing to tell someone suffering depression, or to tell someone who's already trying and failing, slipping down a cycle into despair, implying that they just aren't *trying* hard enough, so what's *wrong* with them. Don't be the one who twists that knife.

Still, if you haven't been trying at all, I can say from experience that it's worth trying a little. Take about 10 percent responsibility for your feelings, and 100 percent responsibility for your actions. Be intentional to reach your goals.

"Let it be" and "man up" are not entirely at odds with each other. Generally, "let it be" is better for your feelings, and "man up" is better for your actions. And sometimes, oh so carefully, juuust a little, just *10 percent* for your feelings, too. Perhaps something as simple as forcing yourself to smile, since it's been found that your emotions will follow your actions.

But saying "big girls don't cry" is just **not helpful.** It's more focused on what's convenient for everyone else, rather than what's healthy for the person with tears running down her face, the one who needs help more than anyone.

Now, while different people need different advice, please remember that it's much more dangerous trying to force too *much* than trying to force too little. Taking a little too much responsibility is much worse than taking too little, like drinking a little too much is worse than drinking a little less. If you tend to force too much, *relax*. Let it be. Let your feelings come, let them go. Focus on doing rather than feeling. Let yourself *not* be relaxed, *not* be calm, *not* be happy. Let feelings be what they are. When you're rested up, you can try a *little*, being careful not to take it too far all over again. If you're not trying at all, you're probably not in terrible shape. But I recommend making a little effort.

I once hurt someone I loved. She had forgiven me, and we had worked things out…but still…I felt the weight of that error. I felt pressured from every side, my will a thousand miles off, my psyche stretched thin…until it *snapped*. I didn't want to try; I didn't want to *try* to try, and it felt like I was *supposed* to feel that way.

I was wary of trying to push my feelings to be something they weren't, but I gave it a tentative attempt. Like so:
1. I imagined how I would feel if I was over it. I gave myself permission to be over it. I was not "supposed" to feel this way.
2. I then acted like I *did* feel that way. I told myself I felt that way. I pushed my feelings. Juuust a little.

It worked great! A few times that day, the negative mood approached again, but I just made a small effort to resist it … and I felt just fine — and ever since, too. I call this putting a **gossamer leash** on my feelings. With a single strand of spider silk as a leash, I gently guided my emotions where I wanted them.

I recommend the same for you:
1) – Imagine how you want to feel,
and then
2) – Step into that feeling, that persona, that role.

94

Sometimes when I do this, I get a pushback as my feelings reassert themselves. When that happens, I let it. The leash is gossamer for a reason; if an emotion pulls away, it can break free. When a bad feeling comes, push a little, see if it works, and then *let it be.*

Picture yourself doing it, see yourself stretching forward, breaking the bindings of negativity, listening to your feelings, and then letting them be. Put your feelings on a gossamer leash.

Your destiny is shaped by your actions, not by your feelings. Whatever your feelings, you can make life wonderful.

Questions for Consideration:
• Why would feeling guilty about your feelings lead to a cycle of worse feelings?
• What would happen to someone suffering from depression if they did this?
• How could letting your feelings go actually help them get better?
• When in your life would it have helped you to know about this?
• What might happen if we blame other people for how they feel?
• Whom do you know that could benefit from this notion?

References
Ehrenreich, B. (2009). *Bright-sided: How the relentless promotion of positive thinking has undermined America.*

Kabat-Zinn, J. (2012). *Mindfulness for beginners: Reclaiming the present moment—and your life.*

Lovas, M., & Holloway, P. (2009). *Axis of Influence: How Credibility and Likeability Intersect to Drive Success.*

Chapter 21: How I Escaped The Darkness of Mental Illness

By Agnes Vishnevkin

Caption: Person coming out of darkness into light (CCO Public Domain/Pxhere)

Hot tears were streaming down my face. My chest heaved up and down with heavy sobs. I couldn't stop them, no matter what I tried.

What happened?

Did I just get bad news? Was I injured? Was it a wave of emotions from a painful memory?

The answer: none of the above. What happened was my husband Gleb asked me what time I wanted to go for our nightly walk. It was a simple question, but instead of responding, I was sobbing and I had no idea why.

What's Going On?

I thought this was a one-time event. Maybe the stress in my work and personal life was getting to me.

Luckily, I had a week of vacation coming up. Instead of doing anything active during my week off, I decided just to rest. I spent a lot of time relaxing and took daily walks in a nearby park. I enjoyed the beautiful scenery and warm July weather. I hoped that time away from commitments and obligations was what my mind and body needed.

But it didn't work. Day by day, things got worse.

One evening Gleb reminded me about a small chore that I had forgotten to do. Suddenly, I felt drained and started to cry. Now, I realized that his reminder was perfectly reasonable. But I had no emotional resources to handle it. It was scary to be unable to deal with such a simple situation.

The following day I met a friend for coffee. I felt pretty good at the start of our meeting. But that didn't last long. About a half-hour later, I felt completely drained and could barely continue talking. My chest felt tight. I felt overwhelmed and distracted.

I thought I would feel better after my friend and I parted ways. I was wrong.

I continued to feel that tightness in my chest. I felt overwhelmed and anxious. It felt as if I was trying to process a huge amount of information. In reality, I was just trying to decided what to do next.

I finally decided to get some ice cream, and started browsing local shops on my phone. There were only a few places nearby, but I felt overwhelmed with the options. 10 minutes passed, and I still had not made up my mind. Finally I decided to just drive to a place near my home.

I was worried and upset that making such a simple decision caused me so much stress. It was a relief to finally have a plan of action, but I felt anxious and restless. When I started driving and got on the highway, I noticed that I had a lot of difficulty focusing on the road. I stayed in the slow lane and used what little focus I had to grip the steering wheel.

Facing The Darkness

I was forced to face the fact that the situation was getting worse and interfering with every area of my daily life.

My relationship with Gleb was starting to get strained. Many ordinary conversations either brought me to tears or caused me to lash out. Fortunately, Gleb worked really hard to adjust to this difficult situation, so we were still able to communicate with each other.

However, it was extremely difficult for me to interact with others. Even talking with my family or close friends caused me to feel extremely anxious. When I did manage to interact with someone, I ended up spending the next few hours feeling nervous and too distracted to do anything. Doing work and household tasks was becoming a big challenge, since I had to contend with unexpected bouts of crying or anxiety.

I felt scared, lost, and out of control.

I felt like I was in a tunnel, being pulled into the darkness and away from the life I worked so hard to build.

I didn't know what was happening to me or why, but one thing was clear: I was no longer reacting to everyday situations the way I used to. Something was wrong, and that something was in my mind.

I'm Sick

There's a common belief that our thoughts and feelings reflect our true selves and must be accepted without question. The mind is often described as something mysterious and distinct from our physical bodies.

Fortunately, due to my work with Intentional Insights, I knew this was not true. I recognized that what we think of as our mind resides in our brain, which is an organ just like any other. This physical brain creates and shapes our thoughts, feelings, and behaviors. And just like any other organ, our brain can be affected by illness, stress, chemical imbalance, trauma, and many other factors.

As for our thoughts and feelings, they often occur intuitively in reaction to our environment. I knew that they don't always serve our best interests. Far from reflecting our authentic selves, our thoughts and feelings are sometimes in conflict with our knowledge, values, and beliefs. Most importantly, I recognized that we can influence and change our thoughts, feelings, and behaviors.

Taking Charge of My Mind

The situation showed no signs of improvement. I knew I had to do something. I desperately wanted to find a way out and get back to the life I took for granted just a week earlier.

It was up to me to decide how to rescue myself from this dark tunnel, the scariest place I ever found myself.

I couldn't look for a solution if I didn't know the nature of the problem. I decided to spend some time to think about the facts of the situation and try to figure out what was happening. I came to the conclusion that:

1. I was experiencing some kind of problem with my mental health, and
2. The problem was serious, since it was a major impediment to my daily life

This was painful for me to accept. On the other hand, this meant I could now start looking for help.

I scheduled an appointment with a therapist specializing in cognitive behavioral therapy, a type of evidence-based treatment for a variety of mental illnesses. While I was waiting to start treatment – my first appointment was three weeks away – I worked with Gleb to come up with ideas for research-based techniques that I could start using immediately to ease my anxiety and stress.

I started building a daily regimen of meditation, deep breathing exercises, and journaling. I reflected on my experience every day and looked for opportunities to tweak my routine to make it more effective. For example, while research suggests that meditation is most effective when done at the start of the day, I found that I often felt restless and distracted in the mornings. To overcome this difficulty, I started beginning my days with mindful activities, such as exercise or cooking. Doing so helped me release some energy and regain focus, making it easier to meditate.

I continued to spend most of my days battling anxiety and sudden crying spells, but these strategies started to offer some relief. When I finally met with my therapist, she approved of my daily meditation, mindfulness, and journaling activities. I was really excited that the research-based techniques we worked out together got her endorsement! She also gave me additional suggestions, such as observing my emotional and physical state in order to be more aware of changes in my mood and energy levels.

About a month after the initial crisis, I was receiving treatment and continuing to practice my new daily routine. I was glad to have tools to help me get better. While I still felt like I was in a dark tunnel, I was slowly learning about my surroundings and finding the way back.

I didn't know how long it would take me to get out, but I was determined to keep moving, one step at a time. I finally had hope that I would recover.

Why Am I Going Public?

I had my nervous breakdown took place in the summer of 2014. Now, I am doing a lot better. However, managing my mental illness still requires constant effort. I am building a new life for myself, one that is healthier and more sustainable in the long term.

I feel like the light at the end of the tunnel is finally within my reach.

So I finally decided to share my story publicly.

I know that there are many, many people who are struggling through the darkness of mental illness. However, not everyone knows that there are many research-based strategies that can ease the burden of anxiety, depression, and other mental health challenges.

I was lucky to know about many of these tools through my work with Intentional Insights. I was also fortunate enough to have access to psychotherapy, where I learned additional valuable techniques.

It's not easy to share publicly about mental health issues. There is a lot of stigma around mental illness. I think that one way to fight it is to recognize that mental illness is very similar to other illnesses. It affects a physical organ, our brain, and it can be treated with science-based therapies.

My biggest goal for sharing my story is to empower others to fight the darkness of mental illness and find their own path toward the light.

References
Kabat-Zinn, J., & Hanh, T. N. (2009). *Full catastrophe living: Using the wisdom of your body and mind to*

face stress, pain, and illness.

Ullrich, P. M., & Lutgendorf, S. K. (2002). Journaling about stressful events: Effects of cognitive processing and emotional expression. *Annals of Behavioral Medicine, 24*(3), 244-250.

Section 2: Truth-Seeking & Other People

Chapter 22: Stop! Live the Life You Want

By Gleb Tsipursky

Caption: Stop sign with "think" painted on it (Courtesy of Cerina Gillilan)

Back when I was in high school and through the first couple of years in college, I had a clear career goal.

I planned to become a medical doctor.

Why? Looking back at it, my career goal was a result of the encouragement and expectations from my family and friends.

My family emigrated from the Soviet Union when I was 10, and we spent the next few years living in poverty. I remember my parents' early jobs in America, my dad driving a bread delivery truck and my mom cleaning other people's houses. We couldn't afford nice things. I felt so ashamed in front of other kids for not being able to get that latest cool backpack or wear cool clothes – always on the margins, never fitting in. My parents encouraged me to become a medical doctor. They gave up successful professional careers when they moved to the US, and they worked long and hard to regain financial stability. It's no wonder that they wanted me to have a career that guaranteed a high income, stability, and prestige.

My friends also encouraged me to go into medicine. This was especially so with my best friend in high school, who also wanted to become a medical doctor. He wanted to have a prestigious job and make lots of money, which sounded like a good goal to have and reinforced my parents' advice. In addition, friendly competition was a big part of what my best friend and I did – whether arguing with each other about life questions or playing poker into the wee hours of the morning. Putting in long hours to ace the biochemistry exam and get a high score on the standardized test to get into medical school was just another way for us to show each other who was top dog. I still remember the thrill of finding out that I got the higher score on the standardized test. I had won!

As you can see, it was very easy for me to go along with what my friends and family encouraged me to do.

I was in my last year of college, working through the complicated and expensive process of applying to medical schools, when I came across an essay question that stopped in me in my tracks:

"Why do you want to be a medical doctor?"

The question stopped me in my tracks. Why did I want to be a medical doctor? Well, it's what everyone around me wanted me to do. It was what my family wanted me to do. It was what my friends encouraged me to do. It would mean getting a lot of money. It would be a very safe career. It would be prestigious. So it was the right thing for me to do. Wasn't it?

Well, maybe it wasn't.

I realized that I never really stopped and thought about what I wanted to do with my life. My career is how I would spend much of my time every week for many, many years, but I never considered what kind of work I would actually want to do, not to mention whether I would want to do the work that's involved in being a medical doctor. As a medical doctor, I would work long and sleepless hours, spend my time around the sick and dying, and hold people's lives in my hands. Is that what I wanted to do?

There I was, sitting at the keyboard, staring at the blank Word document with that essay question at the top. Why did I want to be a medical doctor? I didn't have a good answer to that question.

My mind was racing, my thoughts were jumbled. What should I do? I decided to talk to someone I could trust, so I called my girlfriend to help me deal with my mini-life crisis. She was very supportive, as I thought she would be. She told me I shouldn't do what others thought I should do, but think about what would make me happy. More important than making money, she said, is having a lifestyle you enjoy, and that lifestyle can be had for much less than I might think.

Her words provided a valuable outside perspective for me. By the end of our conversation, I realized that I had no interest in doing the job of a medical doctor. And that if I continued down the path I was on, I would be miserable in my career, doing it just for the money and prestige. I realized that I was on the medical school track because others I trust – my parents and my friends – told me it was a good idea so many times that I believed it was true, regardless of whether it was actually a good thing for me to do.

Why did this happen?

I later learned that I found myself in this situation in part because of a common thinking error which scientists call the mere-exposure effect. This term refer to our brain's tendency to believe something is true and good just because we are familiar with it, regardless of whether that something is actually true and good.

Since I learned about the mere-exposure effect, I am much more suspicious of any beliefs I have that are frequently repeated by others around me, and go the extra mile to evaluate whether they are true and good for me. This means I can gain agency and intentionally take actions that help me toward my long-term goals.

So what happened next?

After my big realization about medical school and the conversation with my girlfriend, I took some time to think about my actual long-term goals. What did I – not someone else – want to do with my life? What kind of a career did I want to have? Where did I want to go?

I was always passionate about history. In grade school I got in trouble for reading history books under my desk when the teacher talked about math. As a teenager, I stayed up until 3am reading books about World War II. Even when I was on the medical school track in college I double-majored in history and biology, with history my love and joy. However, I never seriously considered going into history professionally. It's not a field where one can make much money or have great job security.

After considering my options and preferences, I decided that money and security mattered less than a profession that would be genuinely satisfying and meaningful. What's the point of making a million bucks if I'm miserable doing it, I thought to myself. I chose a long-term goal that I thought would make me happy, as opposed to simply being in line with the expectations of my parents and friends. So I decided to become a history professor.

My decision led to some big challenges with those close to me. My parents were very upset to learn that I no longer wanted to go to medical school. They really tore into me, telling me I would never be well off or have job security. Also, it wasn't easy to tell my friends that I decided to become a history professor instead of a medical doctor. My best friend even jokingly asked if I was willing to trade grades on the standardized medical school exam, since I wasn't going to use my score. Not to mention how painful it was to accept that I wasted so much time and effort to prepare for medical school only to realize that it was not the right choice for me. I really I wish this was something I realized earlier, not in my last year of college.

3 steps to prevent this from happening to you:
If you want to avoid finding yourself in a situation like this, here are 3 steps you can take:
1. Stop and think about your life purpose and your long-term goals. Write these down on a piece of paper.
2. Now review your thoughts, and see whether you may be excessively influenced by messages you get from your family, friends, or the media. If so, pay special attention and make sure that these goals are also aligned with what you want for yourself. Answer the following question: if you did not have any of those influences, what would you put down for your own life purpose and long-term goals? Recognize that your life is yours, not theirs, and you should live whatever life you choose for yourself. This approach is part of a broader strategy of dealing with common thinking errors by considering alternatives, which research shows is a very effective way for avoiding thinking errors such as the mere-exposure effect.
3. Review your answers and revise them as needed every 3 months. Avoid being attached to your previous goals. Remember, you change throughout your life, and your goals and preferences

change with you. Don't be afraid to let go of the past, and welcome the current you with arms wide open.

What do you think?
- Do you ever experience pressure to make choices that are not necessarily right for you?
- Have you ever made a big decision, but later realized that it wasn't in line with your long-term goals?
- Have you ever set aside time to think about your long-term goals? If so, what was your experience?

References

Bornstein, R. F., & Craver-Lemley, C. (2016). Mere exposure effect. *Cognitive Illusions: Intriguing Phenomena in Judgement, Thinking and Memory*, 256.

Hirt, E. R., Kardes, F. R., & Markman, K. D. (2004). Activating a mental simulation mind-set through generation of alternatives: Implications for debiasing in related and unrelated domains. *Journal of Experimental Social Psychology, 40*(3), 374-383.

Chapter 23: Are Friends the Enemies of Wise Choices?

By Charles Cassidy

Caption: Young child driving pedal car (Hadesdaiphat/Pixabay)

I recently decided to buy a petrol-guzzling car. But was it really *me* who decided? I don't like cars. They're costly on the wallet and toxic to the planet. I also live in London, a city of narrow, Victorian streets, where graceful parallel parking is a daily necessity. The only time I have ever gracefully parallel parked was in my driving test 23 years ago.

How did I end up doing something so out of character? I've always considered myself to be pretty clear on my principles. But I'd been caught in the act, exhibiting a gross ethical malfunction. Where was my virtuous character now?! An unsettling idea entered my mind. Might I not be as independently minded as I thought? The English writer George Eliot suggests I am not alone: "*There is no creature whose inward ring is so strong that it is not greatly determined by what lies outside it.*"

If my *character* and *personality* weren't in the driving seat, what else was hijacking my decision?

Am I "driving under the influence," and if so, under the influence of what?

DECISIONS, DECISIONS – HIDDEN FACTORS

Such questions have fascinated behavioral scientists for decades. One such scientist is social psychologist Professor Richard Nisbett. The well-known writer Malcolm Gladwell recently described Nisbett as the most influential thinker in his life. Nisbett claims our decisions are influenced by a combination of internal and external factors:

There are two broad classes of factors that would help explain someone's behavior – what kind of situation is the person in, and what kind of person you have. Obviously any behavior you get out of anybody is a function of "what's going on/what he's responding to" and "what's in the person."

"Internal factors" are the typical elements that we think of as having an influence on our decisions – our character traits, temperament, personal biases, previous experiences, willpower etc.

"External factors" are a little more unexpected. They are the hidden strings of the environment that guide our hands without us knowing.

So what hidden external forces might have guided my hand towards the jangling keys of a second-hand Mazda sedan? What on earth was going on here?

Caption: Man holding car key (Kaboompics/Pixabay)

EXTERNAL FORCES PART I: PEER NETWORKS

Before the arrival of virtual social networks, there were real-world social networks, composed of friends, family and colleagues. While recent media attention has been focused on filter bubbles in the online world, the power of our *real-world* social networks has been gravely overlooked.

Recent research suggests that the general behaviors of others in our networks greatly influence our individual behavior. Scientists have now identified detailed mathematical models that precisely describe how all sorts of human behaviors spread through our peer networks. Perhaps my new car and I were being pushed around by the mathematics of friendships?

First, obesity – Nicholas Christakis of Harvard Medical School and Professor James Fowler produced research in 2007 showing that if one of your friends becomes obese in a given period, your chance of becoming obese increases by 57%.

And divorce? In 2013, they went on to show that if someone you know is divorced, you are 75% more likely to be divorced. Even if a *friend* of a friend is divorced, you are 33% more likely to be divorced.

Registering my new car online, I began to wonder, are my friends secretly driving me into an early grave?

Caption: Skeleton handing rose to another skeleton (705847/Pixabay)

Fortunately, it's not only bad behavior that spreads in this fashion. The researchers also showed that if your spouse quits smoking, you are 65% less likely to smoke. Even if a friend quits, you are 36% less likely to smoke.

Some good news then, but I still found these cold numbers chilling. To learn that decisions which we view as "independently taken" are so strongly influenced by the behavior of friends and family was unnerving. So I took a moment to consider the automotive habits of my peer network.

I don't know anyone who doesn't own a car.

EXTERNAL FORCES PART II: THE IMMEDIATE SITUATION

The behavior of our established peer network is not the only hidden force at work. There is also the influence of the immediate situation we find ourselves in. I will likely strike up conversation with a stranger at a rock concert in the park on a sunny day. This is less likely at 2am in a dark alley in an unfamiliar part of town. A sinister *situation* overrides an outgoing *personality*.

In fact, one of the cornerstone principles of social psychology is that the immediate situation we find ourselves exerts a huge influence on our behavior. A famous 1973 Princeton study, sometimes known as The Good Samaritan Experiment, demonstrated this clearly. People's willingness to stop and help a stranger-in-need depended significantly more on how much of a *hurry* they happened to be in, rather than how they had scored for "religiosity" on a personality assessment. Again, a subtle element of the immediate *situation* trumps an internal *personality* trait.

Now I didn't buy my Mazda at 2am in a dark alley, but I began to wonder how else my everyday decisions were at the mercy of hidden external factors. I run a project called Evidence-Based Wisdom. We translate scientific wisdom research into understandable and helpful resources for the public. So, I am of course interested in how we might make wiser decisions in our daily lives – buying a Mazda, moving to a new city, or even deciding where to mark my cross on the ballot paper come election time.

Wisdom has typically been considered a characteristic that either you have or don't. We can all cite examples of classic wise figures – Socrates, Gandhi, Martin Luther King. Surely something as timeless and weighty as wisdom doesn't depend on trivial aspects of our immediate environment, does it?

A recent 2017 study tells quite a different story. The lead scientist was Igor Grossmann, Director of The Wisdom and Culture Lab. He is a leading light in the emerging field of wisdom research, and also a former student of Richard Nisbett.

His paper indicated that, when it comes to wise reasoning over the course of a single day, there is more variability *within* people than there is between people. This means, it's not that *some* of us are always wise and *some* are always not. It's that all of us are *sometimes* wise, and all of us are *sometimes* not.

As psychologists would say, wisdom appears to concern specific "states," rather than solely "traits." It would seem that even our wisdom varies greatly depending on the immediate situation.

If wisdom varies so much, when are we are at our wisest? A 2016 study from Grossmann's lab shows that, perhaps surprisingly, we take wiser decisions when in *company* rather than when alone.

Grossmann had already demonstrated in 2014 that we are wiser when reflecting on our own problems *as if they were someone else's problems*. Getting some distance from ourselves can help us make wiser choices, but this can be quite challenging when we are alone. This is where company can help. Grossmann explained: *"This third-person perspective on the self is likely encouraged when in the presence of friends."*

So, although the bad habits of others may be toxic to their entire network in the long term, having friends around may lead to better immediate decisions. It seems that our friends, rather than being enemies of wisdom, might in fact be its guardians.

This has turned my thinking on its head. I had previously been very much one for taking important decisions only after many hours of scribbling in my notebook, alone, in a coffee shop. I have now changed my tune, and seek out the company of trusted friends who can steer me through the perilous rocks of my own biases, towards much wiser decisions.

Had friends been present when I reached for those jangling keys, my woeful parallel parking skills would still be a secret to this day.

PRACTICAL ACTIONS

ACTION 1: Choose your peers wisely – they *will* influence your behavior, so spend time with people whose behavior you are happy to be influenced by.

ACTION 2: Take important decisions *in the presence of others*.

QUESTIONS
1. When you observe your friends' behaviors and habits, are you comfortable with the knowledge that you are likely to adopt these same behaviors and habits over time?
2. Can you think of times when you have been surprised by a decision you took? Can you think of any external factors that may have been at play?
3. If you tend to take important decisions alone, might you start to bounce ideas off of friends and colleagues to increase your chance of making a wiser call?

References

Christakis, N. A., & Fowler, J. H. (2007). The spread of obesity in a large social network over 32 years. *New England journal of medicine*, (357), 370-379.

Christakis, N. A., & Fowler, J. H. (2008). The collective dynamics of smoking in a large social network. *New England journal of medicine*, *358*(21), 2249-2258.

Darley, J. M., & Batson, C. D. (1973). " From Jerusalem to Jericho": A study of situational and dispositional variables in helping behavior. *Journal of personality and social psychology*, *27*(1), 100.

Grossmann, I. (2017). Wisdom in context. *Perspectives on Psychological Science*, *12*(2), 233-257.

Grossmann, I., Gerlach, T. M., & Denissen, J. J. (2016). Wise reasoning in the face of everyday life challenges. *Social Psychological and Personality Science*, *7*(7), 611-622.

Grossmann, I., & Kross, E. (2014). Exploring Solomon's Paradox: Self-distancing eliminates the self-other asymmetry in wise reasoning about close relationships in younger and older adults. *Psychological Science*, *25*(8), 1571-1580.

McDermott, R., Fowler, J. H., & Christakis, N. A. (2013). Breaking up is hard to do, unless everyone else is doing it too: Social network effects on divorce in a longitudinal sample. *Social Forces*, *92*(2), 491-519.

Chapter 24: Succeeding At Other Minds

By Gleb Tsipursky

Succeeding   Other Minds   Failing

Caption: Meme indicating the difference between succeeding and failing at other minds (Created for Intentional Insights by Cerina Gillilan)

Imagine you're really excited about a new idea for a collaborative project. You send an e-mail about it to a friend who you just know is going to be as excited as you. You're waiting on pins and needles for a response, checking your inbox every hour. A couple of hours pass, then a couple more. You're getting stressed and anxious, waiting on the edge of your seat for a reply. The next day goes by, and another day. You're very confused about why you haven't received a response. Why isn't your friend writing you back? Doesn't she like you? Is she upset with you? What's wrong?

Has this ever happened to you? It's happened to me many times. My Autopilot System goes into overdrive, imagining various negative scenarios and sending out stress-inducing hormones. Such catastrophizing is a common type of thinking error, one that research shows undermines mental and physical well-being.

Another thinking error in this scenario is that one's friend will share the same opinion that you do about your new idea. Studies on a cognitive bias called the "false consensus effect" indicate that our Autopilot System significantly overestimates the extent to which others agree with our opinions. This is especially true for those close to us, such as our friends and family. As a result, we make mistakes when we use our intuitions to predict the behavior of others around us, including our immediate social circle.

However, the false consensus effect applies more broadly as well. Our gut reactions tend to perceive "the public" as a whole as sharing our perspective. This problem is especially problematic when it causes us to overrate substantially the extent to which others will agree with our political opinions. Such overestimation undermines our ability to engage in healthy political discussions and contributes to political polarization. No wonder we don't do well as intuitive psychologists!

So how can we work against the false consensus effect? First, remember a previously-discussed strategy, namely that our mental maps never match the territory of reality. And our mental maps certainly do not match the mental maps of others!

To keep the latter fact in mind, here is a very useful mental habit to adopt: avoiding "failing at other minds." What does that mean in practice? Essentially, when trying to imagine how other people think about the world, take a moment to stop and remember that their perspective is inherently different from your own. This is a specific case of a broader de-biasing strategy of imagining the opposite, in this case taking the perspective of the other person. And why is this helpful? Well, our intuitive theory of mind, the way we understand the minds of others, tends to model others as ourselves. Our Autopilot System perceives others as understanding the world and having the same idea of what is true as we do. Internalizing the mental habit of avoiding failing at other minds helps remind us of this problematic tendency, and work against it. Through developing this mental habit, we can be elephant whisperers and retrain our Autopilot System to have a more intentional approach to predicting the thoughts, emotions, and behaviors of others. Thus, we can evaluate reality more clearly and gain greater agency by making more effective decisions that help us reach our goals. We can succeed at other minds!

Now, what are the strategies for most effectively learning this information, and internalizing the behaviors and mental patterns that can help you succeed? Well, educational psychology research illustrates that engaging with this information actively, personalizing it to your life, linking it to your goals, and deciding on a plan and specific next steps you will take are the best practices for this purpose. So take the time to answer the questions below to gain long-lasting benefit from reading this article:

- Are there any instances where catastrophizing has negatively influenced your well-being?
- Has the false consensus effect ever steered you wrong in personal interactions? What about in your predictions of public opinions and political engagement?
- In what ways, if any, do you think the mental habit of avoiding failing at other minds can help you have a better life and gain greater agency?
- If you think it can be beneficial for you, what kind of plan can you make and what specific steps can you take to internalize this mental habit?

References

Baron-Cohen, S., Tager-Flusberg, H., & Lombardo, M. (Eds.). (2013). *Understanding other minds: Perspectives from developmental social neuroscience.*

Bauman, K. P., & Geher, G. (2002). We think you agree: The detrimental impact of the false consensus effect on behavior. *Current Psychology, 21*(4), 293-318.

Jensen, M. P., Turner, J. A., & Romano, J. M. (2001). Changes in beliefs, catastrophizing, and coping are associated with improvement in multidisciplinary pain treatment. *Journal of consulting and clinical psychology, 69*(4), 655.

Nir, L. (2011). Motivated reasoning and public opinion perception. *Public Opinion Quarterly, 75*(3), 504-532.

Ross, L., Greene, D., & House, P. (1977). The "false consensus effect": An egocentric bias in social perception and attribution processes. *Journal of experimental social psychology, 13*(3), 279-301.

Schunk, D. H. (1989). Social cognitive theory and self-regulated learning. *Self-regulated learning and academic achievement: Theory, research, and practice*, 83-110.

Chapter 25: Advice That Works for Anyone

By Max Harms

Caption: Pin saying "Take my advice, I'm not using it" (JD Hancock/Flickr)

When was the last time you got bad advice from someone? How did it feel to be the target of advice that you knew just won't work for you, even if you might not have been able to say why? Or maybe you didn't realize the advice was bad until you tried it, and had it backfire! Of course, the person had good intentions, but does it really matter when you suffer from it?

Bad advice is everywhere. Some advice is just plain bad, but I find that most of the time the reason advice goes astray is because it's a bad fit for the person, time, or situation. We can see this in the often-contradictory pieces of advice that we're told by society. For instance, if "the pen is mightier than the sword", why is it that "actions speak louder than words."

I often advise people to give more time than they feel is necessary when setting deadlines. Studies indicate that this is useful advice for most people, but it surely can't be right for everyone.

For example, Bruce is a hopeless pessimist. He thinks negative things are the norm, a thinking error called pessimism bias, and regularly predicts other people will fail at things they attempt. His friend Julie tells him that she's writing a book. Bruce immediately thinks "she'll fail and give up within the month." This thought is automatic. He doesn't lay everything out and evaluate it intentionally–the prediction of failure comes naturally. Bruce thinks people are naturally lazy, evil, and incompetent. If things turn out well he's surprised! Do you know a Bruce in your life? Do you notice these sorts of thoughts in yourself?

If Bruce hears my advice he'll nod and say "I've been saying that people are too optimistic for ages. It figures that I was doing it wrong. I'll try to be even *more* pessimistic in the future…"

But this might be the wrong lesson for Bruce! Perhaps **most** people are too optimistic, but pessimistic Bruce is actually very accurate when it comes to predicting how much time he needs for projects. Or maybe Bruce is *too* pessimistic, and ought to be more charitable towards himself and others.

How would we know? How would we know whether we're too optimistic or too pessimistic? What advice is likely to work regardless of who you are?

Be a Scientist!

Now, before you get the wrong idea, hear me out. I don't mean that everyone should try and become a professional scientist, and I certainly don't think everyone should dress in a lab coat and goggles! What I mean is that everyone should try to **think** like a scientist. It's scientific thinking that makes someone a scientist, not their clothes, their job, or their education. Scientists have cured diseases, built spaceships, and connected the entire planet through the internet! Their three key methods aren't just useful for big technological projects. You can also apply them in your own life!

The key methods are:
1. Take Note of Your Ideas
2. Collect Data
3. Carefully Test and Update Your Beliefs

Let's say that Bruce hears the advice to be less optimistic when making plans, but he has learned to think like a scientist. What do you think this would this look like? First, I think, he'd consider the opposite. This is part of what it means to test one's ideas. It would be a good idea to do other tests as well, but to do them he'll probably need to collect some data first.

If you're trying to figure out whether to make a change in your life, one of the best tools is a big pile of data. To get one, all it takes is the habit of writing things down. If you're trying to figure out whether you're too optimistic when you set deadlines, write down all the deadlines you set and note which of them you make and which you break. Perhaps if Bruce collected this data he'd find that he's a bit too pessimistic.

I use data all the time in my personal life. I'm a data junkie. Every day I keep track of everything I'm trying to do and whether I accomplish it. All my daily to-do lists and life-logs get saved so that I can regularly go back and review. By looking at this personal data I can see that 71% of tasks that I set out for myself get accomplished according to plan, 19% get set aside because of a good reason like a last-minute change of plans, and 10% slip by because I was procrastinating, distracted, or not working hard enough. I've experienced each of these days firsthand, but it's only by keeping and sorting these notes that I'm able to look at them all together.

There's a pattern in my data, too. On a day where I miss one major task, I often miss others. These are my "bad days" where I'm low-energy or I just don't want to follow the plan that I made for myself in the past. About a fifth (20.5%) of my days are like this. I still usually get some things accomplished, but a big project will usually slip by.

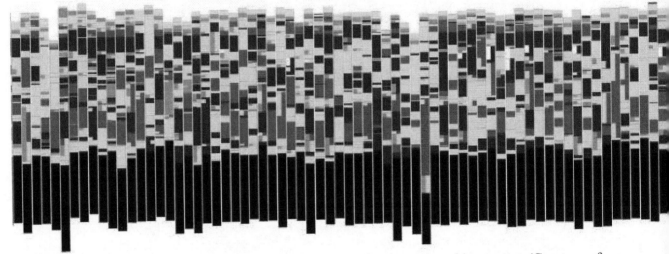

Caption: Visualization of ten weeks of the author's life from his personal tracking system (Courtesy of Max Harms)

This data allows me to know myself and be a good scientist. I don't have to rely on the vague advice that I ought to be less optimistic when making plans because I have the number. When I set deadlines for myself I take however much time I expect to need for the project and then add about 30% on top. So if I expect a project to take 10 days of work, I give myself 13, knowing that I will probably lose about a fifth of that time.

I can only do this because I think like a scientist and collect data about my life. You can do the same thing! Regular note-taking in an area of your life will lead to increased awareness and will let you predict that area in the future. For example, you can record how happy you are when you do an activity, or how stressed it makes you feel. This data will let you identify what brings you the most joy. Collecting and using data and thinking like a scientist are the foundation of many things which have been proven to make life more enjoyable.

A life that is recorded is a life that can be reflected on. Too many people let their connections with their friends slip on accident because they're not reflective enough. Too many people feel a vague confusion about what they're doing with their life. Don't let yourself fall into these common traps. Take note of who you want to spend time with, the sorts of activities you enjoy doing, and what you want to do with your life. Build a habit of studying yourself!

With the right sort of scientific thinking, you can also develop a skill at listening to advice. With enough data and knowledge about yourself, you'll be better able to tell whether a suggestion is a good fit for you, or if it's likely to backfire. Moreover, if you keep track of where good advice comes from, whether from a particularly wise friend or a good blog (hint hint), then you can come back to that source in the future to make your life even better.

What do you think?
- Where in your life do you make predictions about yourself? Have you been mistaken in your predictions before? What happened because of it?
- What sort of data could you collect to help you better understand yourself and predict your future?
- Besides meeting deadlines, what areas of your life do you think could benefit from data collection?

References

Blanton, H., Axsom, D., McClive, K. P., & Price, S. (2001). Pessimistic bias in comparative evaluations: A
    case of perceived vulnerability to the effects of negative life events. *Personality and Social Psychology Bulletin, 27*(12), 1627-1636.

Lord, C. G., Lepper, M. R., & Preston, E. (1984). Considering the opposite: a corrective strategy for social
    judgment. *Journal of personality and social psychology, 47*(6), 1231.

Chapter 26: Protect Your Relationships by Cutting Off Your Anchors

By Gleb Tsipursky

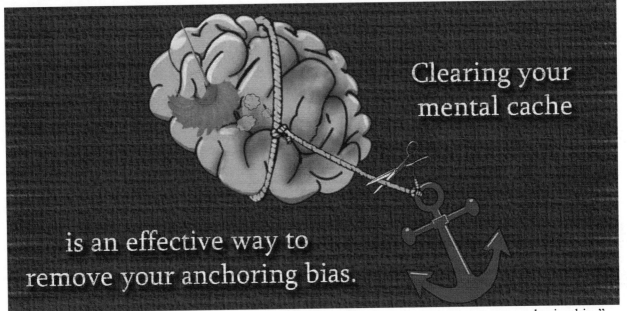

Caption: Meme saying "Clearing your mental cache is an effective way to remove your anchoring bias" (Created for Intentional Insights by Cerina Gillilan)

Communication and Long-Distance Relationships

In my early twenties, I said goodbye to my family in New York City and moved to Boston for graduate school. While I'd been living in my parents' house, I talked to my mother, father, and teenage brother all the time, and felt really good about doing so. After I moved out, I wanted to stay close, so I called my family often. However, phone calls with my brother proved a major challenge. I called him regularly but he usually did not call back. My mother encouraged me to keep calling him, and reminded him often to call me – which he rarely did. I was upset and confused by this, as you can imagine, and when I visited NYC and pressed my brother to call me, he apologized, and said he would call back when I called. He did so for a bit, but then stopped again. My mother was distraught, and I was too. Negative feelings and thoughts kept running through my head: why didn't he call me back? Didn't he love me? Didn't he care about me?

This issue festered for a couple of years, until I decided to deal with it directly. On my next extended visit to NYC, I sat down with him, and had a serious conversation. It turned out that my brother really dislikes talking on the phone. This form of communication just stresses him out. He has a much stronger preference for instant messaging as a mode of communication. Moreover, his Elephant brain developed an "ugh field," a variety of negative emotions, around communicating with me. This was due to the combination of pressure he experienced from my mother and me, and the guilt and shame that came from him failing to call.

What I Should Have Done

I really wish I knew how he felt! What I should have done was notice that he was not calling me back, and have a conversation about the problem with him right away. I should not have insisted that he call me, but instead express curiosity about why he did not. That way, I would have found out about his anxiety and stress around phone conversations. He would not have felt guilty and pressured. I would not have felt sad and confused. Everyone would have been better off!

Broader Relevance for Communication and Relationships

This story illustrates the importance of adapting one's communication style to one's audience. Much has been written about the vital role of communication in the workplace and in civic engagement, especially analyzing and targeting the preferences of your audiences to meet your communication goals. Research shows that such communication is also vital in our personal lives, such as ensuring healthy romantic relationships. Studies of family communication have likewise shown the importance of communicating well and especially being flexible about one's communication style and preferences.

Flexibility and Anchoring

Such flexibility was the missing ingredient in my communication to my brother. I had the goal of cultivating my relationship to my brother, but was trying to reach this goal in a way that was not intentional. So I decided to be more flexible and started exchanging Facebook messages with him, using Gmail chat, and other instant messaging services. We grew closer and had a much better relationship. We even worked to solve occasional problems that would come up between one of us and our parents!

Now, why did this problem occur in the first place? Well, from my background growing up, I developed a reference point, in other words a perception of what is normal and appropriate, of the phone being the "right way" to maintain and cultivate relationships with close people. I suffered from the anchoring bias, a common cognitive bias, the scientific name for thinking errors frequently made by our minds. The anchoring bias occurs when people rely too heavily on information they got early onward, and do not move away from this anchor sufficiently based on new information. I had to acknowledge that I failed at my brother's mind and forgot that my mental map does not match his mental map.

Dealing with Anchoring

So how does one deal with the anchoring bias? A useful strategy is remembering the benefit of re-examining our cached patterns. This term refers to habits of thought and feeling in our mind that we absorbed uncritically from the social environment around us, as opposed to conclusions we arrived at by our own intentional reasoning. Re-evaluating our cached patterns of thought and feeling enables us to see reality more clearly, make more effective decisions, and achieve our goals, thus helping us gain greater agency in personal relationships and other life areas.

So whenever you notice yourself confused or upset by something that you did not expect, stop and think: what is the origin of your confusion? Is it coming from some sort of cached pattern, where you think something is the only "right way" of doing things? Think about whether there are any alternative ways of achieving your desired outcome. (This is part of a broader strategy of dealing with common thinking errors by considering alternatives, which research shows is a very effective way for avoiding thinking errors.) Try listing at least 3 alternatives, and describe why each of them can be valid and right, at least for other people if not for you. Remember, relationships are a two-way street, and you need to respect the other person and their preferences in order to communicate well.

Questions for Consideration

To help you internalize this information, gain long-lasting benefit from reading this article, and use it effectively in your everyday life for improving your thinking, feeling, and behavior patterns, reflect on and answer the questions below.

- Can you identify any ugh fields you developed? How do you deal with ugh fields?
- In what ways, if any, can you be a better communicator in your professional, personal, and civic life areas?
- Are there any instances where the anchoring effect caused you to make suboptimal decisions?
- Do you think you have any cached patterns that might be harmful to your mental well-being?
- If so, what steps can you take to deal with these cached patterns?

References

Arnold, L. B. (2007). *Family communication: Theory and research.*

Gottman, J. M. (1994). *What Predicts Divorce?* Hillsdale, NJ: Lawrence Erlbaum Associates.

Gottman, J. M. (1979). *Marital Interaction: Experimental Investigations.* New York: Academic Press.

Kray, L. J., & Galinsky, A. D. (2003). The debiasing effect of counterfactual mind-sets: Increasing the search for disconfirmatory information in group decisions. *Organizational Behavior and Human Decision Processes, 91*(1), 69-81.

Tversky, A., & Kahneman, D. (1991). Loss aversion in riskless choice: A reference-dependent model. *The quarterly journal of economics, 106*(4), 1039-1061.

Chapter 27: The Problem with Debates

By Gleb Tsipursky

Caption: Photo of two people arguing with one punching another (RyanMcGuire/Pixabay)

Here's a typical scene from the meeting of a local effective altruist group. Michael thinks donating to Against Malaria Foundation will do the most good per dollar to address global poverty. Sheena believes donating to GiveDirectly does more good per dollar than AMF.

How do they resolve their disagreements? They argue, of course. I've watched scenes of Sheenas and Michaels arguing about this question until they were blue in the face. Such arguments usually result in little progress on actually determining the truth of the matter.

We all want to accomplish the broad goal of doing the most good per dollar. However, we often disagree on the best methods for doing the most good and on which organizations are most effective.

When we focus on these disagreements, it can sometimes be easy to forget the goals we share. This focus on disagreements raises the danger of what Freud called the narcissism of small differences – splintering and infighting, resulting in creating out-groups. Many social movements have splintered due to such minor disagreements, and this is a danger to watch out for within our own movement of folks determined to give effectively.

At the same time, it's important to be able to bring our differences in opinions to light and to be able to resolve them effectively. The usual method of hashing out such disagreements within our movement has been through debates, in person or online.

Yet more often than not, people on opposing sides of a debate, including within the Effective Altruism movement, end up seeking to persuade rather than focus on figuring out the best ways of giving based on evidence available. Indeed, research suggests that debates have a specific evolutionary function – not for getting at the most correct answers but to ensure that our perspective prevails within a tribal social context. No wonder debates are often compared to wars.

We may hope that those of us determined to give effectively to alleviate global poverty would strive to find the most evidence-based solutions during debates. Yet given that we are not always fully rational and strategic in our social engagements, it is easy to slip up within debate mode and orient toward winning. Heck, I know that I sometimes forget in the midst of a heated debate that I may be the one who is wrong – I'd be surprised if this didn't happen with you.

Debates, while often useful, can stir up heated emotions and result in harsh confrontations that leave all participants more set in their opinions. So while we should certainly continue to engage in debates, I propose we use additional strategies – less natural and intuitive ones. These strategies could put us in a better mindset for updating our beliefs and optimize truth discovery. One such strategy is a mode of engagement called collaborative truth-seeking. This might be a better approach in cases where debates are more likely to fail – such as when participants have deep-held beliefs, when there are strong emotional triggers around topics of discussion, or where previous debates on a specific topic have not succeeded.

Collaborative truth-seeking describes a more intentional approach drawn from the practice of rationality, in which two or more people with differing opinions engage in a process that focuses on finding out the most accurate solutions to problems, given the evidence. Collaborative truth-seeking is useful for people with shared goals and a shared sense of trust. Since we can all trust that we aim to address global poverty issues in the most effective ways possible, like-minded folks committed to effective giving are a good group with whom to use collaborative truth-seeking.

Some important features of collaborative truth-seeking, which are often not found in debates, are: focusing on a desire to change one's own mind based on evidence; a curious attitude; being sensitive to others' emotions; striving to avoid arousing emotions that will hinder updating beliefs and truth discovery; and a trust that all other participants are doing the same. These can contribute to increased social sensitivity, which, together with other attributes, correlate with accomplishing higher group performance on a variety of activities.

References

Freud, S., & Strachey, J. (1991). *Civilization, society and religion: Group psychology, civilization and its discontents and other works*.

Holland, D., Fox, G., & Daro, V. (2008). Social movements and collective identity. *Anthropological Quarterly*, *81*(1), 95-126.

Lakoff, G., & Johnson, M. (2008). *Metaphors we live by*.

Kurzban, R. (2012). *Why everyone (else) is a hypocrite: Evolution and the modular mind.*

Woolley, A. W., Chabris, C. F., Pentland, A., Hashmi, N., & Malone, T. W. (2010). Evidence for a collective intelligence factor in the performance of human groups. *Science, 330*(6004), 686-688.

Chapter 28: Collaborative Truth-Seeking

By Gleb Tsipursky

Caption: Two people engaging in conversation (Michael Coghlan/Flickr)

Collaborative truth-seeking is an opportunity for us to change our mind based on evidence. But for collaborative truth-seeking to work, we need to bring to the conversation a willingness to learn and a desire to be sensitive to others' emotions. We must also avoid arousing emotions in ourselves or others that will prevent us from working toward solutions. Mastering these traits can help us develop greater social sensitivity, which correlates with higher group performance.

Starting with Trust

The process of collaborative truth-seeking starts with establishing trust, which will help increase social sensitivity, lower barriers to updating beliefs, increase willingness to be vulnerable, and calm emotional arousal. To establish trust during collaborative truth-seeking, share weaknesses and uncertainties in your own position, describe your biases around your position, and talk about your social context and background as relevant to the discussion.

So how might the folks that I mentioned in the last post establish trust and acknowledge their biases? Let's take the example of sharing about biases and social context. Michael, who thinks Against Malaria Foundation does the most good per dollar to address global poverty, might share that he had relatives who died of deadly diseases, and is thus predisposed to favor health-oriented interventions. Sheena, who believes GiveDirectly does more good per dollar than AMF, can share that she grew up poor and was lifted out of poverty by generous philanthropic support, making her inclined to favor interventions that lift people from poverty over health interventions.

Staying in Collaborative Truth-Seeking

After establishing trust, here are techniques that can help you stay in collaborative truth-seeking mode.

Self-signal to yourself that you want to engage in collaborative truth-seeking, instead of debating by reminding yourself of this aspiration throughout the discussion. Try to empathize with the person holding a different perspective by considering how, why, and where they views originated. Recognize that they feel that their viewpoint is correct. Be prepared to calm your own and others' emotions, and watch out for defensiveness and aggressiveness in particular, in yourself and the other person.

Go slow in your discussion, and take the time to fully listen and think. Consider pausing, and have an escape route to process complex thoughts and emotions if you can't deal with them in the moment. Before you start the discussion, have a shared understanding with your collaborator(s) that all should feel free to pause and pick up the discussion later: for instance, you can say "I will take some time to think about this," and/or write things down.

Echo by paraphrasing the other person's position to indicate and check whether you've fully understood them. Be diplomatic: when you think the other person is wrong, avoid saying "you're wrong because of X" but instead to use questions, such as "what do you think X implies about your argument?" Use charity mode by being more charitable to others and their viewpoint than seems intuitive to you. Try to support your collaborator by improving the other person's points to argue against their strongest form – after all, the goal is not to win, but to figure out the best perspective on the situation, the one most strongly supported by the evidence. And on that one, be passionate about wanting to update your beliefs, maintain the most truthful perspective, and adopt the best evidence and arguments, no matter if they are yours or others.'

Be concrete by describing your points using examples as close to our sensory experiences as possible to help ensure shared understanding. Be clear to make sure the semantics are not a barrier to understanding via defining all terms. In fact, consider tabooing terms if some are emotionally arousing, and make sure you are describing the same territory of reality. For maximum clarity, use probabilistic thinking and language, to help get at the extent of disagreement and be as specific and concrete as possible. For instance, avoid saying that X is absolutely true, but say that you think there's an 80% chance it's true. Add what evidence and reasoning led you to believe so, for both you and the other participants to examine this chain of thought. Confirm your sources by looking up information when it's possible to do so (Google is your friend). Something to consider is that when people whose perspective you respect fail

125

to update their beliefs in response to your clear chain of reasoning and evidence, update a little toward their position, since that presents evidence that your position is not very convincing.

A couple of final strategies to use. First, use the reversal test to check for status quo bias. So if you are discussing whether to change a specific numeric parameter – say increase by 50% the money donated to charity X – state the reverse of your positions, for example decreasing the amount of money donated to charity X by 50 percent, and see how that impacts your perspective. Second, use CFAR's double crux technique. In this technique, two parties who hold different positions on an argument each writes the fundamental reason for their position (the crux of their position). This reason has to be the key reason, so that if it were proven incorrect, then each would have to change their perspective. Then, look for thought experiments that can test the crux. Repeat as needed. If a person identifies more than one reason as crucial, you can go through each as needed.

For example, let's take the technique of being probabilistic. Michael might state that he has 75 percent confidence that AMF is better than GiveDirectly in addressing global suffering, based on what he knows now. However, if Sheena provides him with new information – for example regarding GiveDirectly's basic income experiment and its potential consequences – he might update his perspective to say that he now has 70 percent confidence that AMF is better than GiveDirectly, due to Sheena's beliefs about the benefits of basic income support.

Conclusion

Engaging in collaborative truth-seeking goes against our natural impulses to win in a debate, and is thus more cognitively costly. It also tends to take more time and effort than just debating. It is easy to slip into debate mode even when using collaborative truth-seeking, because of the intuitive nature of debate mode. Likewise, using collaborative truth-seeking to resolve differing opinions on all issues holds the danger of creating a community oriented excessively toward sensitivity to the perspectives of others, which might result in important issues not being discussed candidly. After all, research shows the importance of having disagreement in order to make wise decisions and to figure out the truth. Of course, collaborative truth-seeking is well suited to expressing disagreements in a sensitive way, so if used appropriately, it might permit even people with emotional triggers around certain topics to express their opinions.

Taking these caveats into consideration, collaborative truth-seeking is a great tool to use to discover the truth and to update our beliefs, as it can get past the high emotional barriers to altering our perspectives that have been put up by evolution. Since we all share the same goal, effective giving venues are natural places to try out collaborative truth-seeking to answer one of the most important questions of all – how we can do good most effectively to alleviate global poverty.

References
Bostrom, N., & Ord, T. (2006). The reversal test: eliminating status quo bias in applied
    ethics. *Ethics*, *116*(4), 656-679.
Surowiecki, J. (2005). *The wisdom of crowds*.

Chapter 29: Having Trouble Resolving Disagreements? Here Are Some Effective Techniques

By Alex Weissenfels

Caption: Woman and man having trouble communicating *(Tumisu/Pixabay)*

Sara and Rafael disagree on the issue of school choice. Sara believes that students should be given vouchers and allowed to choose whether to go to a public school or a nearby private school. Rafael believes that students should not receive vouchers, but that public schools need more funding to better serve students. Every time they discuss the issue, they end up in an argument which goes nowhere. Sara thinks Rafael is being stubborn and refusing to reconsider his beliefs, while Rafael thinks that Sara is being unreasonable and not listening to his concerns. At least one of them ends up irritated at the other and uninterested in continuing the discussion, and the two of them always end the conversation on a sour note. Sara and Rafael are having trouble fostering collaborative truth-seeking. Do you, like Sarah and Rafael, find that discussions about contentious topics often deteriorate into quarrelling and frustration?

If someone appears to be upset or otherwise emotionally wound up due to a discussion, there are ways to help them wind back down. These techniques reassure a person's emotional side (or "Elephant"), making it easier for their logical side (or "Rider") to work with it.

Calming the Elephant

Having argued with many people both in person and over the Internet, I've had to learn how to put them at ease in order to have a productive conversation. Once I started practicing these techniques for calming people, the arguments and discussions I participated in became consistently constructive. Occasionally, I've even been able to help clear up other people's arguments, after listening patiently enough that everyone involved is satisfied that I understand the situation.

The first part of helping someone calm down is to listen to them talk about their point of view. Often I find that's all I really need to do. Validating their feelings and experiences (not necessarily their facts or conclusions) is the second part (you can do this while listening). The third part is to learn as much as you can about their point of view (if they seem to be repeating themselves, you can skip to part four). Part four consists of paraphrasing their point of view (while still validating their feelings) so they are satisfied you understand it and are not biased against it.

For example, in Sara and Rafael's discussion, Rafael could confirm with Sara that she is worried about her children being able to attend high quality schools. Sara could paraphrase Rafael's concerns about schools not being able to meet their fixed costs if they receive less funding due to having fewer students. The immediate effect of this validation is to make sure that both of them are aware of and appreciate each other's priorities. Such appreciation is necessary for the truth-seeking to be truly collaborative. That way, both of them can look for solutions that are acceptable to both.

Even if all you do is listen, at least one of three things will result from your discussion:
1) You are totally or partially unconvinced. But now you know why they think what they do, how they feel about it, and they accept that you know. That's logos, pathos, and ethos right there, so you have a better opportunity to demonstrate your point of view in a way they can understand and accept. They're free to be unconvinced in turn, and though there may be no consensus in a reasonable amount of time, listening makes a consensus possible where arguing doesn't, and it makes the conversation more pleasant and more constructive.

Perhaps after hearing Rafael's explanation Sara still thinks school vouchers are the best idea, but she knows why Rafael thinks they will cause problems. She will be better equipped to explain to him why she thinks that vouchers will not cause problems, or that the problems are ultimately worth dealing with.

2) You are totally or partially convinced. Now you are closer to the truth, because you see the errors or incompleteness in your own perspective. You may believe they are right, or you may believe that neither of you has the whole truth, but you're equipped to look for it together.

Maybe, after listening to Rafael, Sara no longer thinks that school vouchers are a good idea, but she is still not satisfied that merely increasing funding to public schools will result in an acceptable education for her children. She and Rafael can work together on figuring out a better solution than either of them had before.

3) They are persistently unable to explain themselves coherently, or without being disrespectful and insulting. You are completely within your rights to leave or to tell them to go away (depending on where you are). They are quite likely substituting their emotions for any substantial reasoning. Depending on how much patience and enhanced empathy you have, you may get through to them if you choose to take on that task. Unless you find it fun, like me, feel free to leave. You aren't obligated to tolerate verbal abuse in the name of listening to people.

It may turn out that no matter how many clarifying questions Sara asks, Rafael's explanation continues to be full of soundbites, buzzwords, and ad hominem attacks on people who prefer private schools. He may not be interested in being understood by Sara. Sara can walk away knowing that she was willing to listen, and Rafael will lose an opportunity to learn about Sara's perspective and contribute to a solution that he would find acceptable.

Two Key Questions

In the process of learning about someone else's point of view, there are some questions that are better for learning than others. Here are two key questions you can ask in order to more effectively seek truth during a disagreement.
- Where'd You Get That Idea? (WYGTI, pronounced "WIG-tee")
- What Are You Concerned About? (WAYCA, pronounced "WAKE-uh")

If someone states as a fact something that you think is wrong, you can ask them, "Where'd You Get That Idea?" or something along those lines. It's important that you are respectful and sincere. WYGTI is more effective than contradicting people, because they will be much more amenable to talking more about their beliefs than to being told they are wrong. In addition, explaining themselves will prompt them to think more about their train of reasoning.

WAYCA has a similar benefit, as we saw in the example with Sara and Rafael validating each other's feelings. If the disagreement is about value judgments on what should be done, you can ask someone, "What Are You Concerned About?" It bypasses a great deal of bickering if it turns out that the argument is based on differences in values or priorities. Many discussions start with an assumption that we know what each other's concerns are, which leads to people talking past each other when that assumption is incorrect. When you understand what other people care about, that is a huge step forward for the discussion. Knowing others' concerns will help you propose solutions or conclusions that address those concerns, and assuage their fears. It also makes it much more likely that they will be comfortable with admitting to flaws in their perspective.

The thing to remember about WAYCA is that what people are concerned about can't be "wrong" in the same sense that their facts can be wrong. However, with advanced technique, if someone fears something that it seems they really shouldn't fear, you can offer them an alternative perspective and inspire them with it. For example, if a person fears public speaking, that concern can't be proven "wrong". However, you can introduce something they might value, and compare its value to the risks the person is afraid of. "If you speak in public, you can make a connection with many people, and the worst that happens is you embarrass yourself. Your friends will forgive you and strangers will forget you." It also helps to trace their concerns back to more fundamental issues, in this case the fear of public embarrassment, and then introduce competing concerns for balance. For example, "You are concerned about your reputation,

129

which is rational. However, you must weigh the benefits of avoiding embarrassment against the detriments of not being able to communicate your valuable ideas to wider audiences."

It's also important to ask yourself "Where'd I Get That Idea?" and "What Am I Concerned About?" To participate effectively in a discussion, you should be aware of where your own conclusions come from and what your own priorities and values are, especially because your concerns may have influenced your conclusions.

Voicing Dissent

If you want to correct someone on something or object to a point, the best way to do that is usually to calmly raise a concern of yours and give them every opportunity to address it. If you're not satisfied with their answers, you can just tell them why and let them try again.

While it sometimes helps to accept minor assertions for the sake of argument, you're not obligated to be convinced by another person's point of view. That would defeat the point of collaborative truth-seeking. If you have any concerns about their perspective, you can express them. The following phrases should help:
- "I don't understand this part; please elaborate."
- "I was under the impression that thing worked this way, which seems to contradict this part of your reasoning. Do you think my paradigm is mistaken, or do I just misunderstand your reasoning or how the paradigm relates to it?"
  - If they are actually wrong, it's good to give them a chance to realize it first.
- You can also make suggestions: "Here's my interpretation of this evidence. Does that sound reasonable to you?"

Going back to the school choice issue, Sara can ask Rafael about his understanding of the voucher program, to make sure they are on the same page as to what it would change. After that, they will be able to have a productive discussion about the topic.

Conclusion

If you practice using these questions and phrases, and earnestly pursue an understanding of someone else's point of view, you will find that you and the other people in the discussion will learn more about how things work. Even if you don't end up on exactly the same page, you'll be much better able to work together and discuss more ideas in the future, because you'll have more respect, and trust, for each other and greater appreciation for each other's perspectives.

To help get started with practice, you can ask yourself these questions:
1. What disagreements have you had recently? Do you feel you or the other people learned anything from them?
2. Given what you just learned about collaborative truth-seeking, how might you now approach them differently?
3. If someone had asked you in those disagreements, "Where Did You Get That Idea?", or, "What Are You Concerned About?", how might you have answered?

References

Hall, K. D. (2014). *The Emotionally Sensitive Person: Finding Peace when Your Emotions Overwhelm You.*

Chapter 30: How to Talk to Professional Colleagues Who Deny the Facts

By Gleb Tsipursky

Photo conveying the image of the famous symbol: "hear no evil, see no evil, speak no evil" (Ally Aubry/Flickr)

It's the season for holiday parties at the office. They're great for building workplace camaraderie and team spirit, but when was the last time a colleague - perhaps fueled by too much alcohol - said something that showed they are looking at their professional world through rose-colored glasses.

It happens more often than you might think. A four-year study by LeadershipIQ.com found that 23 percent of CEOs got fired for denying reality, meaning refusing to recognize negative facts about the organization's performance. Other findings show that professionals at all levels suffer from the tendency to deny uncomfortable facts in business settings.

Dealing with truth denialism - in business, politics, and other life areas - is one of my areas of research. One of the strategies described there can be summarized under the acronym EGRIP (Emotions, Goals, Rapport, Information, Positive Reinforcement), which provides clear guidelines on how to deal with colleagues who deny the facts.

What Not To Do

Our intuition is to confront our colleagues with the facts and arguments, but research - and common sense, if the colleague is your supervisor - suggests that's usually exactly the wrong thing to do. When we see someone believing in something we are confident is false, we need to suspect some emotional block is at play. Research on the *confirmation bias* shows that we tend to look for and interpret information in ways that conforms to our beliefs. Studies on a phenomenon called the *backfire effect* shows when we are presented with facts that cause us to feel bad about our self-worth or worldview, we may sometimes even develop a stronger attachment to the incorrect belief.

Don't Argue, EGRIP Instead

If someone denies clear facts you can safely assume that it's their **emotions** that are leading them away from reality. While gut reactions can be helpful, they can also lead us astray in systematic and predictable ways. We need to exhibit emotional leadership and deploy the skill of empathy, meaning understanding other people's emotions, to determine what emotional blocks might cause them to stick their heads into the sand of reality.

For instance, consider the case of Mike, who was the new product development team lead in a software company for which I consulted. He set an ambitious goal for a product launch, and as more and more bugs kept creeping up, he refused to move the date. People tried to talk to him, but he hunkered down and kept insisting that the product would launch on time and work well.

Looking from the outside in, I saw that Mike tied his self-worth and sense of success to "sticking to his guns," associating strong leadership with consistency and afraid of appearing weak in his new role as team lead. In my role as a neutral consultant, he privately told me that he believed some team members were trying to undermine him by getting him to shift the schedule and admit he failed to deliver.

Understanding his fear and insecurity about being a new leader, I went on to establish shared **goals** for both of us, which is crucial for effective knowledge sharing in professional environments. I spoke with Mike about how we both share the goal of having him succeed as a leader in the long term, and secure his new position in the company. Likewise, we both shared the goal of having the new product be profitable for the company.

Third, build **rapport**. Practice mirroring, meaning rephrasing in your own words the points made by the other person, which helps build trust in business relationships. Using the empathetic listening you did previously, a vital skill in selling, to echo their emotions and show you understand how they feel. I spoke with Mike about how it must hard to be worried about the loyalty of one's team members, and the loneliness of being a new leader. We talked about what makes someone a strong leader.

At this point, start providing new **information** that might prove a bit challenging, but would not touch the actual pain point. I steered the conversation toward how research suggests one of the most important signs of being a strong leader is the ability to change your mind based on new evidence, giving examples such as Alan Mulally saving Ford Motor Company through repeated changes of course. If I had led with this information, Mike might have perceived it as threatening, but since I slipped it in naturally as part of a broader conversation after building rapport built on shared goals and empathy, he accepted it as a useful new insight.

Then, I asked him where he can best deploy this skill to show those who might try to undermine him what a strong leader he is, and at the same time make the new product as profitable as possible. Without much additional prompting, he volunteered that he can show strength by delaying the launch of the new product. I provided him with **positive reinforcement**, a research-based tactic of effective motivation, by praising his ability to exhibit the traits of a strong leader.

133

Good luck, and remember that you can use EGRIP and other similar research-based tactics not simply in professional settings, but in all situations where you want to steer others away from false beliefs.

To help facilitate your use of EGRIP, consider these questions:
- When was the last argument you had in the workplace? Can you envision how it would have gone differently if you used EGRIP?
- In what future conversations do you think you will intend to use EGRIP?
- How can you most effectively convey the tactic of EGRIP to your colleagues?

References

Aggarwal, P., Castleberry, S. B., Ridnour, R., & Shepherd, C. D. (2005). Salesperson empathy and listening: impact on relationship outcomes. *Journal of Marketing Theory and Practice, 13*(3), 16-31.

Chow, W. S., & Chan, L. S. (2008). Social network, social trust and shared goals in organizational knowledge sharing. *Information & management, 45*(7), 458-465.

Gigerenzer, G. (2007). *Gut feelings: The intelligence of the unconscious.*

Hoffman, B. G. (2012). *American icon: Alan Mulally and the fight to save Ford Motor Company.*

Kamery, R. H. (2004, July). Motivation techniques for positive reinforcement: A review. In *Allied Academies International Conference. Academy of Legal, Ethical and Regulatory Issues. Proceedings* (Vol. 8, No. 2, p. 91). Jordan Whitney Enterprises, Inc.

Klayman, J. (1995). Varieties of confirmation bias. *Psychology of learning and motivation, 32*, 385-418.

Mayer, J. D., & Geher, G. (1996). Emotional intelligence and the identification of emotion. *Intelligence, 22*(2), 89-113.

Nyhan, B., & Reifler, J. (2010). When corrections fail: The persistence of political misperceptions. *Political Behavior, 32*(2), 303-330.

Peterson, R. T., & Limbu, Y. (2009). The convergence of mirroring and empathy: Communications training in business-to-business personal selling persuasion efforts. *Journal of Business-to-business Marketing, 16*(3), 193-219.

Pittampalli, A. (2016). *Persuadable: How great leaders change their minds to change the world.*

Tedlow, R. S. (2010). *Denial: Why business leaders fail to look facts in the face--and what to do about it.*

Tsipursky, G. (2017). How Can Facts Trump Ideology? *The Human Prospect, 6.3*, 4-10.

Tversky, A., & Kahneman, D. (1974). Judgment under uncertainty: Heuristics and biases. *Science, 185*(4157), 1124-1131.

Chapter 31: How to Talk to a Science Denier without Arguing

By Gleb Tsipursky

Caption: Image of two people arguing (OpenClipart-Vectors/Pixabay)

It's the holiday season, which means plenty of opportunities for uncomfortable interactions with friends and family who are science deniers, from people who believe the moon landing was faked to those who believe vaccines cause autism or who think that humans did not cause significant global climate change. How can you deal with such science deniers effectively?

My close friend invited me to her house for Thanksgiving, where I sat across the table from her cousin Sam. Learning about my research on promoting truthfulness in our society, he proceeded to denounce what he called the "climate change hoax" as a vast attack by liberals on businesses. He told me how his dad lost his job at a factory that moved to Mexico, placing blame on government regulations - including pollution control - that made it too expensive for the plant to operate in the Columbus, OH, where Sam lives.

By the end of our conversation over that meal, he accepted the validity of the science on climate change. Sam is one of many people who updated their beliefs during conversations with me, including prominent ideologically-oriented talk show hosts. One of the strategies I use can be summarized under the acronym EGRIP (Emotions, Goals, Rapport, Information, Positive Reinforcement), which provides clear guidelines on how to deal with Sam and other people who deny the facts, in science and other life areas.

What Not To Do

Our typical response is to respond by presenting the facts and arguing about the quality of the evidence. However, studies suggest that doing so is generally not effective in changing people's minds on charged issues. Research on the *confirmation bias* shows that we tend to look for and interpret information in ways that conforms to our beliefs. Our emotions are much more powerful than our reason, and we tend to go with our guts when perceiving new information.

Moreover, research on a phenomenon called the *backfire effect* shows when we are presented with facts that cause us to feel bad about our identity and worldview, we tend to dig in our heels and refuse to accept the facts. In some cases, presenting the facts actually backfires, causing people to develop a stronger attachment to their incorrect belief.

Don't Argue, EGRIP Instead

If someone denies clear facts, you can safely assume that it's their **emotions** that are leading them away from reality. While gut reactions can be helpful, they can also lead us astray in systematic and predictable ways. We need to deploy the skill of empathy, meaning understanding other people's emotions, to determine what emotional blocks might cause them to stick their heads into the sand of reality.

In Sam's case, it was relatively easy to figure out the emotions at play through active listening: anxiety about job security, compounded by his dad's experience. I confirmed my suspicions by using curiosity to question Sam - who was in his junior year in college - about whether he was concerned that government protections would inhibit his ability to find a job, and he answered "you're damn right I'm worried about that." You will have to figure out based on the context of each individual situation the relevant emotions at play.

Next, establish shared **goals** for both of you, crucial for effective knowledge sharing. With Sam, I talked about how we both want people to secure jobs in the current uncertain economic environment, and he strongly agreed. I also said how we both want him and his friends and family - who were all around us at the Thanksgiving dinner table - to stay healthy, and he agreed as well.

Third, build **rapport**. Using the empathetic listening you did previously, a vital skill in promoting trusting relationships, echo their emotions and show you understand how they feel. In the case of Sam, I told him I understood his feelings of worry and anger. I also told him I was worried about his health and the health of other students, due to the hundreds of thousands of deaths caused by pollution. Finally, I added that we should always orient toward the facts, wherever they may lead, and added that I - along with thousands of other citizens - took the Pro-Truth Pledge as a public signal of commitment to sharing accurate information, and welcomed him to hold me accountable. He appreciated that opportunity, and it built my credibility in his eyes.

Fourth, move on to sharing **information**. Here is where you can give the facts that you held back in the beginning. Since Sam's concerns had to do with economic issues, I focused on the money rather than the science. I talked to him about how while I did not know the specifics of his dad's situation, I could truthfully state that the government sometimes makes unwise policies that result in harmful outcomes. Next, I pointed out to him how the number of clean energy jobs in Ohio is growing, and much quicker than overall job growth; given bipartisan support, this trend will likely continue. Then, I highlighted how since manufacturing jobs like the one his dad had aren't coming back, he could secure a good financial future for himself in the green energy field after college.

Likewise, he would also help protect his health and the health of his friends and family around the dinner table. As a bonus, he wouldn't have to deny scientific studies. After all, as I told him, the scientists are simply finding data, and it's government officials and business leaders who decide what to do with it. The key here is to show your conversation partner, without arousing a defensive or aggressive response, how their current truth denialism will lead to them undermining in the long term the shared goals we established earlier, a research-driven approach to addressing thinking errors.

Sam was surprised and moved by this information. He agreed that green energy might well be a good future for him. He confessed he was feeling mental strain due to denying scientific findings, and was relieved to see that believing in science did not have to mean he would not find a job. I offered **positive reinforcement** for his orientation toward the facts, praising his ability to update his beliefs. Positive reinforcement is very valuable as a research-based tactic of encouraging people to change their identity and sense of self-worth to align with truthfulness through associating positive emotions with doing so.

Think of how much better your holiday dinner could go if you use EGRIP instead of arguing!

Section 3: Truth-Seeking & Civic Life

Chapter 32: The Myth of the Irrational Voter

By Gleb Tsipursky

Caption: Photo of supporters for candidates (Elvert Barnes/Flickr)

Voters are inherently irrational. They are moved by emotions, not facts. Their biases cause them to make bad political decisions. We need to shape our political process around their irrationality, and manipulate them to get them to make more rational choices.

Or so claim many pundits, politicians, and scholars. Are they right?

These analysts make some valid points. Still, their overall depiction of the "irrational voter" is a myth.

Yes, research in psychology, cognitive neuroscience, and behavioral economics shows that we have a number of thinking errors that can cause us to make irrational decisions. We tend to think of ourselves as rational creatures who form our opinions based on logical facts. In reality, our emotions play a much larger role in influencing our beliefs than we intuitively perceive.

Politicians skilled in the psychology of persuasion can take advantage of our thinking errors to manipulate us. Unless we are paying attention, we are highly likely to be influenced by their appeals to these flawed patterns of feeling and thinking, and make biased political decisions.

Fortunately, we are not doomed to this fate of irrationality. Recent scholarship has shown that we can train ourselves to be less biased and more rational, including in our voting. Doing so requires some work to get away from our intuitive thinking errors. Yet considering how valuable our votes are – each vote is worth hundreds of thousands of dollars – it is vital for each of us to put in the effort required to make a wise decision with our vote.

For example, many people tend to vote for a candidate by their gut intuitions of whether a candidate looks presidential and other "likeability" factors. This is known as the famous "who would you rather have a beer with" test, a question that is commonly tested in the polls. However, candidates are quite strategic, and – just like candidates in job interviews – try to manage the image they project to voters of how "likeable" they are.

We have plenty of scholarship showing that an intuitive estimation at the gut level of likeability in job interviews is a very poor predictor of future job performance, and the same goes for presidential candidates. Voters using their gut intuitions – the "beer test" – are likely to be fooled. This is especially problematic for female candidates who have to walk a tightrope between appearing likeable and competent, a problem not faced by male candidates.

So do we then not allow our emotions a role in our voting decisions? No, of course not! Our emotions make us who we are as individuals.

We just need to avoid a situation where our emotions cause us to make biased decisions by allowing candidates to manipulate us. After all, we are not going to be having a beer with the candidate we elect. Since we know that evaluating candidate personalities is an area of weakness for us, we need to let our emotions play a different role.

Instead, our emotions should determine our values and consequently the policies we support. We can use our emotions to guide us on shaping our perspective on the relevant political issues and get a good read on ourselves through taking a political typology quiz.

Next, we should turn to our rational thinking to compare our positions on the issues to those of the candidates. If we are substantially closer to either of the two major party candidates, we can simply go with that, unless we have strong doubts about the fitness of that candidate for office.

If we are closest to a third party candidate, the bad news is that this candidate will almost certainly lose. So if we want our vote to make an impact in determining how billions of dollars are going to be spent, it is wise to choose a major party candidate, whoever is closest to our policy preferences. Some people also swap their vote with someone in a swing state to make an impact while ensuring a vote for their preferred candidate.

Now say your policy positions are between the two major party candidates, or you think your preferred major party candidate may not be fit for office. This is the only appropriate time to evaluate a candidate's personality. However, I strongly urge you to not trust your gut on this!

For instance, most voters tend to perceive Donald Trump as more trustworthy than Hillary Clinton, despite nonpartisan fact-checkers such as Politifact showing that Trump lies much more often than Clinton. This is because the Trump campaign has successfully manipulated many voters into believing that Clinton is less honest, in spite of the evidence that she is much more honest by comparison to Trump. The Trump campaign did so through the illusory truth effect, a thinking error in our minds that happens when statements are repeated many times and we begin to see them as true, despite these statements being false.

Research shows that we tend to be way too confident in our political evaluations when going with our gut, and this is why we need to rely on experts when evaluating candidate's personalities, such as fact-checkers, not our intuitions. Using the judgments of experts, evaluate which of the candidates will be most effective in governing the country and implementing your preferred policies if elected. Then, go with that candidate.

This simple step-by-step process can empower us to make truly rational voting decisions that align our values and emotions with our thoughts and our actions. By doing so, we can show all those politicians, scholars, and pundits that they are wrong to proclaim that voters are irrational and should be manipulated for their own good.

References

Arkes, H. R. (1991). Costs and benefits of judgment errors: Implications for debiasing. *Psychological Bulletin, 110*(3), 486-498.

Caplan, B. (2011). *The myth of the rational voter: Why democracies choose bad policies.*

Dechêne, A., Stahl, C., Hansen, J., & Wänke, M. (2010). The truth about the truth: A meta-analytic review
of the truth effect. *Personality and Social Psychology Review, 14*(2), 238-257.

Lyengar, S. (1990). The accessibility bias in politics: Television news and public opinion. *International Journal of Public Opinion Research, 2*(1), 1-15.

Larrick, R. P. (2004). Debiasing. *Blackwell handbook of judgment and decision making*, 316-338.

Morvan, C., & Jenkins, W. J. (2017). *Judgment Under Uncertainty: Heuristics and Biases.*

Ortoleva, P., & Snowberg, E. (2015). Overconfidence in political behavior. *The American Economic Review, 105*(2), 504-535.

Patton, G. W., & Kaericher, C. E. (1980). Effect of characteristics of the candidate on voter's preference. *Psychological Reports, 47*(1), 171-180.

Thaler Richard, H., & Sunstein Cass, R. (2008). *Nudge: Improving decisions about health, wealth, and happiness.*

Weiss, B., & Feldman, R. S. (2006). Looking good and lying to do it: Deception as an impression management strategy in job interviews. *Journal of Applied Social Psychology, 36*(4), 1070-1086.

Schneider, A. K., Tinsley, C. H., Cheldelin, S. I., & Amanatullah, E. T. (2010). Likeability v. competence:
The impossible choice faced by female politicians, attenuated by lawyers. *Duke Journal of Gender Law & Policy, 17*(2).

Chapter 33: The Worst Problem in Politics?

By Gleb Tsipursky

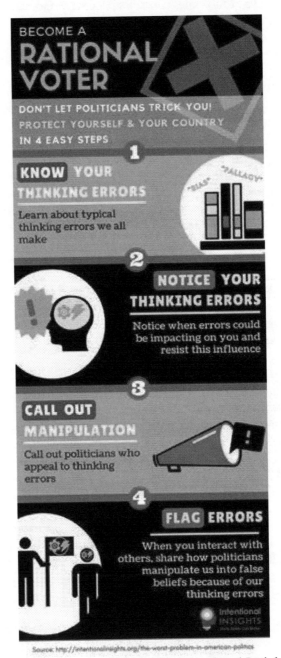

Caption: Infographic on being a rational voter (Created for Intentional Insights by Charles Cassidy)

Rationality refers to the ability to assess reality accurately and thereby make wise decisions to reach one's goals. This election has been a testament to the current inability of very many voters to make correct assessments of reality, leading them to make bad political decisions.

Research in psychology, cognitive neuroscience, and behavioral economics shows that we make such irrational assessments and poor decisions because of thinking errors in how the human mind is wired. We tend to think of ourselves as rational creatures who form our opinions based on logical facts. In reality, our emotions play a much larger role in influencing our beliefs than we intuitively perceive.

Politicians skilled in the psychology of persuasion can take advantage of our thinking errors to manipulate us. Unless we are paying attention, we are highly likely to be influenced by their appeals to these flawed patterns of feeling and thinking, and make biased political decisions.

As an example, most voters on the eve of the election perceived Donald Trump as more trustworthy than Hillary Clinton, despite nonpartisan fact-checkers such as Politifact showing that Trump lies much more often than Clinton. This false perception came from the Trump campaign successfully manipulating many voters into believing that Clinton is less honest, in spite of the evidence that she is much more honest than Trump.

The Trump campaign did so through the illusory truth effect, a thinking error in our minds that happens when false statements are repeated many times and we begin to see them as true. The illusory truth effect was used extensively by Trump throughout the campaign. Consider Trump's relentless repetition of the claim that NAFTA is the "worst deal ever signed" and cost Americans "millions of jobs." Despite the fact that experts disagree on the impact of NAFTA on the U.S. job market, Trump has successfully convinced many millions that NAFTA is terrible.

Proposing a ban on all Muslims coming to the US and more recently extreme vetting of them, as well as a particular focus on policing Muslim neighborhoods and monitoring mosques, is another example of Trump playing to our thinking errors. Concern about terrorism is one of the biggest worries for the US population. Yet it has been over a decade since any Americans died from attacks in the US committed by terrorists who were not either US citizens or legal permanent residents. This makes Trump's policy proposal irrational in the sense that it does not respond to a realistic assessment of the threat of terrorism. Instead, it appeals to the horns effect, a thinking error where negative emotions about one topic – in this case, terrorism perpetrated by radical Islamic extremists – gets spread to all Muslims, regardless of the irrationality of such thinking.

What about the proposal to monitor American Muslims – the ones who did commit some terrorist acts? Let's take a look at the numbers. In 2015, according to johnstonarchive.net, there were seven terrorist acts in the United States, with nine terrorists altogether. Six of the nine were motivated, in some part, by Muslim beliefs.

A 2011 survey estimated that the United States had 1.8 million Muslim adults. Dividing the number of Muslim adults by the six who committed terrorist acts gives you a one-in-300,000 chance that any Muslim you see would commit a terrorist act in one year. That's like picking out a terrorist randomly from the number of people in several football stadiums. Applying this sort of probabilistic thinking is a research-based way to deal with any form of fear. It allows us to see whether the anxious thoughts are

143

realistic. We can see that being Muslim is a very poor statistical indicator of whether someone is a terrorist, making fears of Muslims irrational.

The Clinton campaign appealed to human irrationality as well, if to a much lesser extent, and mostly in response to the Trump campaign's very effective strategies to appeal to irrational thinking. Consider the comment by Clinton that half of Trump's supporters belong in the "basket of deplorables" and are "irredeemable" through being sexist, racist, and homophobic. Such commentary appeals to the horns effect by associating "deplorable" with a large proportion of the US population. Yet consider someone who was convinced by Trump's rhetoric that Muslims are to be feared. This person has developed irrationally racist beliefs, yet does this make the person inherently deplorable or irredeemable? Certainly not! At least she apologized for this comment later, yet such rhetoric represents the perspectives of many liberals.

Fortunately, we are not doomed to this fate of irrationality. Recent scholarship has shown that people can grow more rational, including in our voting and more broadly in how we assess politics. Doing so requires only four things. First, we just need to learn about typical thinking errors. Second, we have to notice when they are potentially impacting us and resisting this influence. Third, we should call out those politicians who appeal to such thinking errors. Finally, we need to highlight to those we talk with who fall for such thinking errors how politicians are manipulating them into believing falsehoods

Many will claim that this unrealistic, that US citizens are inherently irrational in their politics. I beg to disagree.

Over the last few months, I have published many articles in prominent venues, and appeared on a number of TV and radio programs, to talk about how to make politics more rational. Many people emailed me expressing gratitude for the chance to learn about how politicians try to manipulate them, and asking how they can most effectively learn how to make rational political assessments.

These people ranged across the political spectrum in their views, from the most conservative to the most liberal. What they all had in common was caring about the truth first and foremost. Making politics less irrational by helping people make accurate assessments of reality is a bipartisan issue. Everyone wins by having more rational citizens, except those politicians who rely on misleading and manipulative rhetoric to sway voters.

Unfortunately, this election cycle shows how effective it can be to appeal to human irrationality. The future is dark if we do not focus our efforts on addressing this problem in our political system, which is core to all other problems. Despite the apparent polarization of American politics, we do have shared goals as a society, including economic prosperity, peaceful coexistence, safety and security. Our only hope of coming together to bridge our polarized nation and collaborate to achieve these goals is to increase rationality in the political process as a whole.

References
Burfisher, M. E., Robinson, S., & Thierfelder, K. (2001). The impact of NAFTA on the United States. *The*
    Journal of Economic Perspectives, 15(1), 125-144.
Burton, S., Cook, L. A., Howlett, E., & Newman, C. L. (2015). Broken halos and shattered horns:

overcoming the biasing effects of prior expectations through objective information disclosure. *Journal of the Academy of Marketing Science, 43*(2), 240-256.

Chapter 34: How Our Thinking Errors Cause Us To Misinterpret Politics

By Gleb Tsipursky

Caption: Image of Trump and Clinton (Wikimedia Commons)

Debate checkers usually focus on evaluating the facts of what each candidate said. While it is important to get the facts straight, focusing on the truth content of their words is not nearly enough to evaluate the actual impact of the debate on the audience. It often matters much more how candidates say things, or what they choose to leave out, than whether they stuck to the facts or not.

This results in large part from a number of typical human thinking and feeling errors, what scholars call cognitive biases. We as human beings think of ourselves as rational creatures who form our opinions based on logical facts. In reality, our emotions play a much larger of a role in influencing our beliefs than we intuitively think. We make quick and intuitive decisions based on our Autopilot System of thinking, also known as System 1, one of the two systems of thinking in our brains. It makes good decisions most of the time, but also regularly makes systematic thinking errors. The other thinking system, known as the Intentional System or System 2, is the deliberate, reflective system. It takes effort to use but it can catch and override the thinking errors committed by System 1.

Politicians skilled in the art of public speaking can take advantage of our cognitive biases to shape our opinions. They do so through making points based less on evidence, reason, and logic – the Intentional System's strengths – and instead playing to the much more powerful Autopilot System that guides our thinking. Unless we are paying very close attention, and turn on our Intentional System to catch specific

146

biases that might influence our thinking, we are highly likely to be influenced by appeals to these flawed patterns of feeling and thinking.

Both candidates made a number of such appeals. For example, Hillary Clinton stated that Donald Trump is Vladimir Putin's puppet. This invoked a bias likely to cloud the minds of the audience – the halo effect. This thinking error emerges when we see something we like or dislike, and have a reason to associate this emotional reaction with something else.

Clinton knows that many Americans do not like Putin, and the image of being someone's puppet is quite undesirable. Combining Trump with Putin and puppet is bound to create a negative emotional association. Now, a fact checker would not be able to give a straight answer on whether Trump is Putin's puppet or not – this depends on one's interpretation, and Clinton can certainly defend the perspective that she put out. Yet we can recognize that her framing of this issue is designed to appeal to our Autopilot System and create a certain impression that does not necessarily match the facts on the ground.

Trump, in turn, used repetition to drive home his claims, invoking the illusory truth effect. This flawed thinking and feeling pattern causes our brains to perceive something as true just because we hear it repeated a number of times, despite the evidence on the matter. In other words, just because something is repeated several times, we perceive it as more true, regardless of whether it is objectively true or not! Now, the previous sentence repeated the one before it, and had a similar structure. It did not provide any more actual information, but it did cause you to believe my claim more than you first did when you read the sentence. In fact, much of the advertising industry is based on using the illusory truth effect to get us to buy more goods.

In the debate, Trump's relentless repetition of the claim that NAFTA is the "worst deal ever signed" and cost Americans "millions of jobs" functions the same way. Despite the fact that experts disagree on the impact of NAFTA on the US job market, Trump has successfully convinced many millions that NAFTA is terrible. He makes similar statements about him not supporting going into Iraq, and many of his supporters are staunchly convinced that he opposed the war, despite clear evidence that he was for it before he was against it. His repetition of his claims, in opposition to clear evidence, still causes our Autopilot System to perceive them intuitively as true, and it takes effort – Intentional System effort – to fight this perception.

Turning once again to Clinton, we see her playing into a thinking error known as illusion of control. This error occurs when we perceive ourselves as having more control over a situation than we actually do. For instance, Clinton attributed the decline in the US national debt in the 1990s primarily to her husband's policies. This very much exaggerates the actual impact that any president can have on the national debt during the president's own tenure in office. This impact can only be measured later, after the policies passed by a president had time to make an impact.

Clinton also insisted – as did Trump – that her policies would add nothing to the national debt, despite independent reports by experts showing that Clinton's economic reforms would likely add billions and Trump's plan add trillions to the debt. Clinton's statements on debt, along with Trump's, showed both illusion of control and the desirability bias, the thinking error that one's idealized outcomes would come true.

Another claim often repeated by Trump ties in to his core message – America is much worse than it used to be. He conveys a rosy picture of an idealized American past, when everything was right with the world. The campaign run by Trump even has that as his central slogan: "Make America Great Again." In doing so, Trump speaks to our emotional system's tendency to view the past through rose-colored glasses, a bias known as rosy retrospection and also as declinism. In reality, the world has grown better on a whole variety of different measurements, for instance with people experiencing less violence, and having greater health, longevity, and economic well-being. Despite this reality, Trump's combination of the illusory truth effect and declinism strikes a deep chord with many people's Autopilot Systems.

These are some among many cognitive biases that the candidates used to influence our perceptions and opinions during the debate, and in public speeches as a whole. Because we are not aware of how the candidates are appealing to our Autopilot Systems, they are capable of swaying our viewpoints without our knowledge to believe falsehoods. It is vital for us to start fallacy-checking the debates and public statements more broadly in addition to fact-checking them to guard the safety of our democracy.

References

Budescu, D. V., & Bruderman, M. (1995). The relationship between the illusion of control and the desirability bias. *Journal of Behavioral Decision Making, 8*(2), 109-125.

Davidson, P. (2010). Making dollars and sense of the US government debt. *Journal of Post Keynesian Economics, 32*(4), 661-666.

Olsen, R. A. (1997). Desirability bias among professional investment managers: Some evidence from experts. *Journal of Behavioral Decision Making, 10*(1), 65-72.

Quartz, S., & Asp, A. (2015). *Cool: How the brain's hidden quest for cool drives our economy and shapes our world.*

Pinker, S. (2012). *The better angels of our nature: Why violence has declined.*

Sundar, A., Kardes, F. R., & Wright, S. A. (2015). The Influence of Repetitive Health Messages and Sensitivity to Fluency on the Truth Effect in Advertising. *Journal of Advertising, 44*(4), 375-387.

Chapter 35: Knowing Just Enough to be Dangerous: How Overconfidence Subverts Rational Politics

By Joel Lehman

Caption: Illustration of excessive confidence (Vic/Flickr)

"The fool doth think he is wise, but the wise man knows himself to be a fool."
-Shakespeare

It happens every year. It's the beginning round tryouts on the talent show American Idol, and a man confidently takes the stage, sparks in his eyes. He thinks he's destined for greatness, this is his moment. The music starts, and with anticipation quaking, he smiles full of composure, and boldly unleashes -- a cracked and cringe-worthy voice! Clearly, he can't carry a tune if his life depended on it.

The audience begins to boo, the singer's face grows red as his bravado shakes, the judges prepare their cut-throat feedback, and you wonder -- how could he have been so wrong about his ability?

But don't get too smug in your seat. This overconfident lack of self-awareness isn't unique to reality-show auditions. In general, we tend to *motivate* our reasoning so that the world appears well-aligned with our pre-existing *story* about how it should work.

Do you think you're a good driver -- at least better than average? A full *ninety-three* percent of people say they're better than average drivers. In another study, college students who performed the *worst* in tests of logic, humor, or grammar still believed they were better than most. Most of us are the heroes of our own story, even when the reality is more ordinary.

This results from the Dunning-Kruger effect, which is one of many predictable flaws in how we think. The main idea is that when we know just a little about something, we often struggle to *evaluate* just how little we know. Maybe you know a friend who read one article on a topic and now believes he's an expert. That's the Dunning-Kruger effect in action.

A similar thinking flaw is the overconfidence effect, when we take our *feeling* of certainty in knowing the right answer as evidence that we *really* do have the right answer. There's a disconnect between how likely we *really* know the answer, and how *certain* we feel inside. For example, one study shows how when people were completely confident they had the right spelling of a difficult word, they were only really right 80% of the time. You might notice the overconfidence effect when you're out with friends, and you use google on your cell phone to settle a disagreement over a simple fact, when two of your friends are absolutely certain in their opposite answers.

Okay, so maybe it's not completely surprising that we're often overconfident, but does it matter? When we are blindly optimistic about our own charisma and musical ability, it's sometimes amusing. But it's sad when the same mistaken confidence can hurt the world, especially when it comes to our beliefs about political policy.

Take, for example, the idea of raising the minimum wage. One side argues would raise the standard of living for hard-working citizens (everyone should get a living wage!), while the other argues it would actually make the poorest worse-off (higher minimum wage will destroy jobs!). A policy change like this can have huge effect, bringing serious consequences upon the lives of real people, either for good or for bad.

Generally, liberals support big boosts to minimum wage, while conservatives tend to oppose such a move. And every year, liberal and conservative politicians rehash the similar battles over taxes and government spending. These economic issues likely have better and worse answers, although in the public debate it seems we never get any closer to finding out which is which. Why should that be? And can the Dunning-Kruger effect help us to understand it?

Isn't is strange that Democrats and Republicans have near-opposite opinions about the economy, and yet neither group seemingly has any more economic expertise? Is it possible that most of the political soundbites we hear about raising (or lowering) the minimum wage, or taxes, or stimulus plans, are oversimplified noise? Why do we so often depend upon our favorite politicians to teach us about economics, when they have a vested interest, and rarely any strong qualifications? Why not take lessons from the community of experts that study economics, instead?

We might begin to suspect that the *base platforms* of the Democratic and Republican parties *pre-commit* them to particular economic policies -- no matter what evidence from economics actually suggests. Are either a Democrat running to lower the taxes on the wealthy, or a Republican running to raise taxes on the wealthy, likely to be nominated or elected? But why do individual Democrat and Republican voters each find the theory of their preferred politician and political party *so plausible*, even though those theories are *so different*?

One explanation is that it's the Dunning-Kruger effect biting us. Each of us rarely recognizes how little we actually know. We latch onto simple stories that make sense on their surface, but don't respect the complexity of the real world. We tend to parrot the "folk economics" (simple common-sense theories) of our political tribe. There's some truth that raising minimum wages could ease the lives of hard-working people struggling to raise a family. And there's also truth in the idea that a large minimum wage increase could cause struggles for small businesses. But the problem with folk economics is that both of these simple stories sound plausible, and yet undercut each other.

The problem is that there are many simple stories that could be right, but the real world works a particular way, and likely has complicated wrinkles. To uncover better stories, we need to be rooted in evidence. But most of us don't look to the evidence. Instead, we're satisfied with whatever folk economic theory appeals to how we think the world *should* work. The poet Alexander Pope anticipated the Dunning-Kruger effect in 1709 when he wrote, "A little learning is a dangerous thing." We feel certain we understand minimum wage policy and its effects, even though the economy is hugely complicated, and there is so much we personally don't comprehend.

As a result, we make poor use of what knowledge and evidence has been accumulated by the hard work of economists -- some of whom have studied questions like minimum wage their entire career. The Dunning-Kruger trap leads us as a country to again and again debate minimum wage through sound-bites and folk arguments that little resemble reality. Most of us simply don't understand economics well enough to really weigh in with any real authority, and yet the overconfidence effect leads us to feel certain anyways that our political team has the right answer.

If we stop and think, can we see through the illusion? In particular, if we find ourselves highly confident about minimum wage or another controversial policy, can we summon the self-awareness to question whether we have any *real grip* on what is scientifically known? Can we learn to investigate the possible flimsiness of the foundation of our cozy beliefs? Can we bring to light the difference between what *feels* right and what the evidence actually suggests?

One rule of thumb is to become skeptical when we're dealing with a complex issue and notice a pleasant feeling of certainty. That pleasant confident feeling might simply reveal the folk theory of whatever political tribe we belong to, and not relate to how much knowledge we actually have about the issue. The next time you listen to your favorite show with a political bent, whether it's The Daily Show or Tucker Carlson, pay attention to how good it feels to you when the host sticks it to the other side, and ask yourself if it's possible that you're getting a partisan sketch of reality, one that's designed not to cut towards truth, but to reinforce the things your political team already believes.

Indeed, the problem with the overconfidence effect is that reality is often much more complicated than we'd like to acknowledge, and requires real knowledge and expertise to understand correctly. So, if we actually want to put into place political policies that *do good* instead of those that just *feel good*, then we need to wrestle with that complexity. We also need to wrestle with the unpleasant truth that most political discussions focus on folksy Dunning-Krugerish assumptions about the world, ones that miss the heart of the matter.

To conclude, a sad facet of human nature is that we're often too sunny in gauging our competence. Having just a little bit of knowledge, like a simple folk theory, can easily delude us into a false sense of deep understanding. What's worse, this brand of overconfidence plays a big role in corrupting a rational discussion of big-impact political policies. But, each of us can strive to bring more self-awareness to situations ripe for this kind of delusion -- whenever there's a huge partisan divide over a complex issue, for example.

Of course, it's not fun to face the music: We don't know as much as we think we do. But really, there's no shame in it -- our world is astoundingly complicated, and so it's only hubris that we should really expect to understand its entirety, anyway. In the end, we're all better off the more honest we can be with ourselves, so we can hone in on the actual truth, which offers beauty more authentic than any comfortable fable.

References

Adams, P. A., & Adams, J. K. (1960). Confidence in the recognition and reproduction of words difficult to spell. *The American journal of psychology*, 544-552.

Brown, C. (1999). Minimum wages, employment, and the distribution of income. *Handbook of labor economics*, 3, 2101-2163.

Kruger, J., & Dunning, D. (1999). Unskilled and unaware of it: how difficulties in recognizing one's own incompetence lead to inflated self-assessments. *Journal of personality and social psychology*, 77(6), 1121.

Redlawsk, D. P. (2002). Hot cognition or cool consideration? Testing the effects of motivated reasoning on political decision making. *Journal of Politics*, 64(4), 1021-1044.

Rubin, P. H. (2003). Folk economics. *Southern Economic Journal*, 157-171.

Svenson, O. (1981). Are we all less risky and more skillful than our fellow drivers?. *Acta psychologica*, 47(2), 143-148.

Chapter 36: Political Precommitment Without Evidence: How Worldview Undermines Reason

By Joel Lehman

Caption: Cartoon of ostrich sticking head in the sand (Dawn Hudson/Public Domain Pictures)

"And so castles made of sand, fall in the sea, eventually."
-Jimi Hendrix

Can you recall a romantic relationship gone wrong, and notice in hindsight the clear signs of the impending breakup, even when during the actual unraveling itself you didn't notice these signs? Maybe there's a political belief you once embraced that you've now let go. Perhaps you thought Ayn Rand was the most important thinker ever, or that Communism was the one true way. Looking back, though, you wonder how you ever ignored all the opposing evidence.

How did it feel before you let those old beliefs go? And how did it feel after you replaced them with brand new ones? In both cases, you probably felt *confident* that you were right.

It's natural as we grow and mature, especially as we go from child to adult, to shift our core beliefs. But it's revealing how confident we are, even a few months before such changes. We're caught off-guard by changes in ourselves: Scientific evidence suggests that we recognize that we've changed significantly across our last decade, but are over-sure that the next decade will be different — no matter if we're 18 or 68. This effect, called "The End of History Illusion," helps explain why we may feel that we have rock-solid answers, entirely sure that those who disagree are foolishly mistaken, even though next year our answers may well have shifted drastically.

Looking back over these shifts in beliefs, we can begin to see how natural and easy it is to confuse the *feeling* of certainty for a solid foundation *truly worthy* of certainty. It's such a universal tendency, that it bears repeating: feeling certain that some belief is true is not a reliable signal that the belief actually is true. We're bad at separating our *desires* for how the world works from how the *factual evidence* suggests it does. No matter how certain I may feel that gravity is an illusion, things can only end badly for me if I jump off the edge of a cliff. The feeling's not enough — only with accumulating evidence can we have a dependable basis for confidence.

While it might seem like it's a person's right to have deluded beliefs, and that such overconfidence doesn't really harm anyone, in reality it's a serious problem when a large part of the country has broken beliefs. The reason is that beliefs have real power in a democracy, because what people believe influences who is elected and what laws and policies are instituted, or what wars are fought. Real lives hang in the balance. Political beliefs matter: unfortunately, thinking clearly about politics is a huge challenge.

Our political affiliation usually reflects some of our most deep-seated assumptions about how the world works. If we're not careful, it can *pre-commit* us to believe particular facts, no matter where the objective evidence really lies, preventing us from updating our beliefs. We can intentionally use the strategy of precommitment to manage our behaviors, such as in managing our weight, but an unaware, autopilot precommitment to certain beliefs easily undermines an accurate evaluation of reality, in politics as well as in other life areas.

Precommitment and Climate Change

Let's take on climate change as a case study. Climate change is a controversial topic in America — according to Pew Research, less than half of US adults think that the Earth is warming due to human causes. Now, as a disclaimer, because I'd alienate a large chunk of potential readers by expressing what side I land on, I'm not going to weigh in on the debate directly. This article isn't about convincing anyone about any particular political issue. The aim is to explain why it's important to have the guts to really examine the foundations of your political beliefs.

An intriguing aspect of Americans' opinions about climate change is the deep disagreement centers on what is a *purely scientific* question: is human activity warming the Earth in any significant manner? Climate change itself is not some weedy and complicated question about morality or how to best organize society. It centers instead on some concrete fact about the world. Is the Earth warming? If it is, is that warming caused to a significant extent by human activity? These clearly are well-defined questions, with right and wrong answers, that science could be applied to answer.

154

So, one might think that belief in climate change might be predicted by how much scientific knowledge a person has. That is, if there's a right answer to a scientific question, you'd think that those with more scientific knowledge would tend to get it right more often. That's usually how things work. I have more confidence that an engineer could design an airplane than a medical doctor, and more confidence that a medical doctor could set a bone fracture than an engineer.

But it turns out that what predicts a person's belief in climate change (more than how scientifically educated they are) is *their political affiliation*. Let that sink in — here we have a factual question, one that has been studied intensely by scientists. But the population is nearly evenly divided in how they feel about how that question is best answered. Where they land has little to do with how much they know about science.

So, no matter what you believe about climate change, it seems clear that something has gone wrong. It seems that one side or the other has let their political beliefs distort how they perceive reality. One hypothesis would be that the *narratives* of liberals and conservatives *predispose them* to one answer or the other. There's evidence that people choose to favor different political parties because of deep-seated differences in what they consider to be morally important and how they believe the world best functions. It's not that conservatives are smarter than liberals, or vice-versa. It's that they fundamentally *care about* different things and have different *assumptions* about the world.

For example, according to the moral foundations theory of Jonathan Haidt, conservatives tend to place more importance on values like authority, sanctity, and loyalty, while liberals tend to accentuate care and fairness. More relevant to climate change, liberals and conservatives also tend to have different views about nature. According to cultural theory, liberals are more likely to believe that nature is delicate and needs to be protected, while conservatives are more likely to view nature as not substantially impacted by human influence.

Convenience vs. Truth

From this view, it's just plain *convenient* for *both* liberals and conservatives to lean the way that they do on climate change, *irrespective* of the evidence. It's fine to have different assumptions about how things are, but any hunch should *bend* in the face of evidence. In fact, we should celebrate updating our beliefs to match reality. Whether the Earth is in fact impacted by human greenhouse gas emissions is not something an assumption can settle. Reality is what it is, and it is really harmful for our society when people rely on assumptions about politically-relevant issues when there's copious amounts of credible evidence.

Perhaps you've seen this kind of stubbornness when talking with others about climate change. Most of us have no deep understanding of climate science. While we may argue confidently about whether humans are responsible for warming the Earth, when pressed on details, discussion often devolves into parroting the line of our political tribe.

Importantly, I don't want to pretend that both sides are necessarily on even ground: "Well, climate change better fits the worldview of Democrats, and climate change skepticism better fits the worldview of Republicans, so I guess we'll have to leave it at that either side could be right." The lesson is not that we can never understand reality, because over time science *does* allow us to better understand reality. Indeed,

155

there may currently be much more evidence for one side than the other. But for anyone in the grips of an overconfident belief, being on the wrong side of evidence certainly won't *feel* that way. There's nearly always some kind of convenient escape-hatch, some shred of evidence you hold onto that supports your cherished belief, all the while fully-discounting the evidence of your "opponents."

To figure out the weight of evidence on climate change or any other issue, our best is to rely on scientific evidence. Because science is the best of all methods we've found to get closer to understanding reality and to better predict the outcomes of our actions, it's at our own risk that we hold a strong belief that opposes scientific consensus, "the collective judgment, position, and opinion of the community of scientists in a particular field of study." One can recognize scientific consensus by position statements by prestigious scientific organizations, or the result of "meta-analysis" studies (studies that summarize and analyze a wide collection of other studies). In theory, it's easy to rely on scientific evidence, but in practice it's hard, because we often *cherry-pick* what we consider as scientific evidence to support beliefs we already find comfortable to hold.

One way our psychology helps us go off the rails in this way is called the Dunning-Kruger effect: When we have little knowledge of a topic, we often reach wrong conclusions and also are overconfident in how well we understand what's going on. If we're already very sure we understand something, we're likely to think a piece of evidence is credible *only* if it agrees with our *existing* thinking. It helps to keep in mind the old adage, "A little learning is a dangerous thing," and override our strong gut instinct to distrust scientific evidence when we have only a very basic understanding of the topic.

So, for any one person who aspires to become less wrong, the important lesson is that we should be *vigilant* when we notice that we've become confident about a *controversial* belief that is both *convenient* and *comfortable* for us — we'd be likely to believe that thing anyways, so there's ample room for self-delusion. As the physicist Richard Feynman said, "The first principle is that you must not fool yourself, and you are the easiest person to fool." The challenge is to be self-aware enough to realize when we're possibly deluding ourselves. Only that way can we hope to dig ourselves out of our out-of-control overconfidence.

Here are some questions to consider as you strive to evaluate reality accurately and avoid political precommitments:
- What controversial beliefs of yours are *convenient* to your politics, and what evidence do those beliefs rest upon?
- Do you notice a strong emotional response that sometimes arises when you question a political belief?
- How has this post influenced your thinking about political beliefs and your own possible political precommitments ?

References
Baron, J. (2017). Philosophical Impediments to Citizens' Use of Science. *The Oxford Handbook of the Science of Science Communication*, 361.
Dunning, D. (2011). 5 The Dunning-Kruger Effect: On Being Ignorant of One's Own Ignorance. *Advances in experimental social psychology*, *44*, 247.
Goebbert, K., Jenkins-Smith, H. C., Klockow, K., Nowlin, M. C., & Silva, C. L. (2012). Weather, climate,

and worldviews: the sources and consequences of public perceptions of changes in local weather patterns. *Weather, Climate, and Society, 4*(2), 132-144.

Haidt, J. (2003). The moral emotions. *Handbook of affective sciences, 11,* 852-870.

Kivetz, R., & Simonson, I. (2002). Self-control for the righteous: Toward a theory of precommitment to indulgence. *Journal of Consumer Research, 29*(2), 199-217.

Nisbet, M. C. (2009). Communicating climate change: Why frames matter for public engagement. *Environment: Science and Policy for Sustainable Development, 51*(2), 12-23.

Quoidbach, J., Gilbert, D. T., & Wilson, T. D. (2013). The end of history illusion. *Science, 339*(6115), 96-98.

Verwoerd, J., de Jong, P. J., Wessel, I., & van Hout, W. J. (2013). "If I feel disgusted, I must be getting ill":

Emotional reasoning in the context of contamination fear. *Behaviour research and therapy, 51*(3), 122-127.

Chapter 37: Fear and Anger Over the Ohio State Knife Attack

By Gleb Tsipursky

Caption: Smiley faces expressing fear and anger (Open Clipart-Vectors/Pixabay)

I felt a stab of cold fear when I first learned about the Ohio State knife attack. Safely at home when the attack occurred, I saw the faces of my students and colleagues flash before my eyes. Were any of them in harm's way? As reports from friends and colleagues trickled in, I was glad to see none of them harmed, although my research assistant was right nearby and got a scare.

After the initial fear passed, I felt a growing heat of anger. Who did this and why? I checked news websites obsessively.

I learned that the attacker was a student at Ohio State, Abdul Razak Ali Artan, a Somali Muslim. He rammed his car into a crowd on campus, and then ran out waving a knife and stabbing people, before being shot and by an Ohio State police officer.

As I learned this, my thoughts immediately turned to the possibility of terrorism. The situation pattern-matched the attack at my alma mater UNC-Chapel Hill in 2006, where a former student rammed his car into a crowd of students to – in his words – "avenge the deaths of Muslims worldwide." This was part of a broader pattern of using cars to ram people, mostly perpetrated by Muslim extremists.

However, being an expert on how our brain's faulty wiring leads us to make bad decisions, I knew that such pattern-matching is a dangerous trap. We evolved in the savannah environment, where we had to make snap judgments about threats from predators, and our brain is well-adapted for that setting. It is poorly adapted to modern conditions, where threats are more complex and ambiguous, and we have much more time to investigate and determine the actual circumstances. Fortunately, learning about where our intuitions may lead us astray helps us make wise decisions about how to proceed.

Our natural instinct is to extend the fear and anger we experience from the specific individual to all individuals sharing his background, Muslim and Somali. This is a thinking error known as the horns effect, where we irrationally extend a negative perception of one member of a group to the whole group.

Some politicians already fell into this trap. For instance, Representative Peter King (R-LI) stated that "there have been significant terror problems with Somali immigrants over the past several years in the United States." Yet according to johnstonarchive.net, in 2015 there were no Somali perpetrators of terrorism in the US and in 2016 only one. This is hardly "significant terror problems."

Other politicians started criticizing Muslims. Thus, the State Treasurer of Ohio Josh Mandel Tweeted: "Looks like Radical Islamic terror came to my alma mater today." Yet we have no evidence to support Mandel's claims. What we know is that Artan expressed fear of Islamophobia in an August 2016 interview with the Ohio Student newspaper. He also expressed anger in a Facebook post right before the attack, saying "I am sick and tired of seeing my fellow Muslim brothers and sisters being killed and tortured EVERYWHERE… I can't take it anymore." These statements are not characteristic of "Radical Islamic terror," but reflect fear and anger over the treatment of Muslims.

Reactions like King's and Mandel's are natural, since they flow out of how our brains are wired, but they are not rational, as they do not reflect the reality of the situation and do not help us achieve our goals – being safe from terrorism. Instead, such expressions of fear and anger feed into the Muslim anxiety syndrome sweeping the United States and increase the irrational stigma toward Muslims and Somalis, harming relations with these communities.

Such worsening of relations makes it less likely for members of these communities to cooperate with the authorities in investigations of potential terrorism. Moreover, as we can see from Artan's words, his experience of fear and anger at the hands of Americans served as important factors for pushing him into his senseless violence.

In this case, our brain's natural patterns make us less safe, and lead to an escalating cycle of violence. We need to recognize that fear and anger we may experience toward those of Muslim and Somali background is irrational, and instead work against these instincts by being extra friendly – much more than we intuitively feel – toward these folks. Only by intentionally overcoming these instincts and working against them can we break the cycle of violence and grow safer!

References
Palmer, C. L., & Peterson, R. D. (2016). Halo effects and the attractiveness premium in perceptions of political expertise. *American Politics Research*, *44*(2), 353-382.

Chapter 38: Don't Let The Terrorists Win!

By Gleb Tsipursky

Caption: Photo of paying respect to Paris attacks (Stephanie Dreyer/Department of Defense)

After the horrible terrorist attacks on Paris, France's President Francois Hollande swore revenge against ISIS, saying we "will be merciless toward the barbarians of Islamic State group." Republican presidential candidates called for a highly aggressive military response from the United States. For example, Ted Cruz called for the US to abandon its commitment to strive for "zero tolerance for civilian casualties" when facing terrorists who "have such utter disregard for innocent life." Jeb Bush called these attacks a sign of "an organized effort to destroy Western civilization." Marco Rubio called for a "substantially increased commitment" of US ground troops in the war against ISIS.

This is exactly what ISIS wants! This terroristic state wants to be the targets of "merciless" revenge by French and other Western forces. ISIS leaders would love to see the United States publicly abandoning its commitment to trying to avoid civilian deaths in our airstrikes. US ground troops actively fighting ISIS, instead of the current situation of US Special Forces training and advising local Kurdish fighters, would be a generous gift to ISIS.

Why? Because any of these changes in government policy would radicalize other Muslims. So does rhetoric from Western political figures pitting a "Western civilization" against Islam, or promising "merciless" revenge.

What is the problem with radicalizing Muslims? Causing Muslims to grow more radical results in them contributing resources to anti-Western causes, including ISIS. There is a spectrum of radicalization, and aggressive actions we take results in some Muslims moving further along the spectrum.

Let's apply probabilistic thinking. For instance, consider what happens when there is a report in Muslim media of an airstrike by Western forces killing civilians. At any point, there are a myriad of Muslim. youths who are angry at the Western intervention into Syria. For a number of them – say a hundred – the report will be the thing that tips them over from anger to outrage, and they will decide to join ISIS.

Let's say five percent get trained in ISIS training camps as suicide bombers. That means five new suicide bombers per report of an air strike killing civilians, ready to wreak havoc on the United States and other Western countries. This same report will radicalize Muslims living in the West, making them willing to hide and otherwise support suicide bombers. It will also cause Muslims to contribute money to ISIS to fund its activities, including terrorism. This is the mix of ingredients required for the kind of mass-scale, coordinated terrorist attack that struck Paris.

By responding aggressively with airstrikes and angry rhetoric, we let the terrorists win! Even worse, by getting our ground troops directly involved in fighting ISIS, we would be taking the path to another Iraq.

So what should we do? We should not act immediately! We need to go against our intuitive emotional self's desire for revenge. Instead, we need to step back and assess the situation intentionally.

Recent research shows that after any emotionally powerful event, in politics or private life, our brains tend to assign too much weight to that event compared to what is really important to us, a thinking error called attentional bias. To fight this thinking error, we should consider what are our actual long-term goals and how to get to them in the best possible manner.

Our actual goals are to decrease the likelihood of future terrorist attacks, not increase their likelihood through an aggressive response. To achieve our goals, a good question to ask here is "what would ISIS not want us to do?"

ISIS would not want us to take quiet and covert actions that would avoid radicalizing everyday Muslims. ISIS would not want our top political figures to make powerful, courageous, and politically unpopular statements that all Muslims are not to blame for this attack, but only a small group of radicals. ISIS would not want us to reach out to Muslim leaders in our communities and around the world who condemned the Paris attacks and work together against the radicals.

Let us set aside our emotional desire for revenge, however difficult, and take the hard road that will achieve our long-term goals. Otherwise, we let the terrorists win!

References

Carraro, L., Castelli, L., & Macchiella, C. (2011). The automatic conservative: Ideology-based attentional asymmetries in the processing of valenced information. *PLoS One*, *6*(11), e26456.

Chapter 39: Was Tyre King's Shooting Justified?

By Gleb Tsipursky

Caption: Photo of Tyre King (image credit courtesy of Walton and Brown, LLP)

On September 14, the 13-year-old Tyre King was shot and killed by a police officer, Bryan Mason, in Columbus. According to the police, Tyre was shot after running from officers who were looking into an armed robbery and pulling out a BB gun that looked similar to a real weapon.

Tyre was black and Bryan white, fitting into a broader pattern of police killing of black males. Despite calls for calm from city officials, there is outrage over this shooting, with protesters calling for homicide charges against the police officer involved. Police union leaders, in turn, are defending the officer, saying he acted appropriately.

However, we have very limited information about what occurred. Definitive judgments on either side of whether the officer was justified or not should make us question the objectivity of those making such statements. Most likely, those folks are falling into confirmation bias, a typical thinking error that our minds tend to make when we let our strong personal beliefs override the evidence available.

So how can we think effectively about whether the shooting was justified? Rather than a binary yes or no approach, we can apply the principles of probabilistic thinking to gain the most accurate understanding of the situation possible based on the evidence available. Probabilistic thinking is a research-based strategy that involves placing percentage estimates on what we believe and updating our beliefs based on the evidence as it emerges.

First, let's consider Columbus police policy: officers should use deadly force only when they have a reasonable belief that they are defending themselves or others from serious injury or death. Since Tyre was not threatening anyone else at the time, we can safely assume that Bryan was defending himself when he shot Tyre. Thus our belief of whether the shooting was justified rests on whether we believe the officer perceived himself to be in immediate deadly danger.

The officer claims that after he chased Tyre into an alley, the boy pulled out his gun. Since Bryan believed it was real, he shot Tyre. If Tyre indeed did pull out his gun and hold it in a threatening manner, I would personally put a very high probability of the shooting being justified.

However, the only one who was in the alley and came out alive was the officer. In many previous cases, especially involved white officers shooting African-Americans, the accounts of the police officers involved in questionable shootings have proved false.

Imagine what would happen to Bryan if Tyre was actually not threatening him. What if Tyre was running away when he was shot? What if Tyre did not pull out his gun, but simply had it on him? What if Tyre was trying to throw the gun away to not be found with it? Not only would Bryan's career be ruined, but he would be tried and likely convicted for killing Tyre. He has a very strong incentive to lie. This lowers my percentage probability of Bryan's account being accurate.

So does other evidence. For instance, Tyre is described by those who know him as a well-behaved kid who was into sports. He also attended Bible study. Given Tyre's background and that Tyre knew it was a BB gun and that it would not do him any good at all to shoot it at the officer, I place a low probability on him actually threatening Bryan with his gun. Of course, we can't discount the possibility that Tyre panicked and did do what the officer said he did, but it seems unlikely.

Some additional evidence is an independent investigation conducted on behalf of Tyre's family by Francisco J. Diaz, MD, FCAP, a practicing medical examiner in the County of Wayne, Michigan, and a Consultant Forensic Pathologist. According to Dr. Diaz : "it is more likely than not that Tyre King was in the process of running away from the shooter." This further undermines the probability that Bryan's account is fully genuine.

More broadly, this shooting has to be understood in context of tense relations between the police and African-Americans over racial profiling. A report from the Federal Government's Bureau of Justice Statistics indicates that black people were three times as likely to be searched as whites in a traffic stop. Certain police officials wave away data suggesting unfair racial profiling by claiming that blacks are more likely to be involved in criminal activity than whites. Yet a study just released by the Center for Policing Equity corrects for racial difference in criminal activities. The study's outcomes show that African-Americans are more than three times as likely to suffer from police use of force compared to whites, for everything from mild restraint to gunshots.

Now, this does not mean that white police officers explicitly discriminate against black people. Research shows that all of us suffer from some degree of implicit bias, deeply ingrained negative attitudes associated with certain groups or markers of social identity. The large majority of white Americans – including police officers – are implicitly biased against African-Americans. These studies should further decrease our probabilistic estimate that Bryan was justified in shooting Tyre.

There are some research-based methods of debiasing which are likely to reduce implicit bias. One great technique is de-anchoring, where instead of going with our intuitive reaction, which is highly likely to be biased, we adjust our behavior based on research. For instance, if a police officer knows that black people are over three times as likely to experience police coercive force, she should think thrice before using force on someone who is black. Although further research is needed on how to deliver such training effectively, if Bryan had gone through this sort of training, I would have higher confidence in Bryan's account.

We can't discount the possibility that Tyre panicked and did do what the officer said he did. However, based on the current information available, I would put a 20% estimate on the shooting being justified. Of course, your own estimate of the weight of each piece of evidence may vary, and I am very open to updating my beliefs based on additional evidence.

How much more healthy and productive would our discourse be if we placed probabilistic estimates on our beliefs and disputed how much weight each piece of evidence should have? We can then have a much more nuanced and accurate approach to such polarizing and emotional questions.

References
Epley, N., & Gilovich, T. (2006). The anchoring-and-adjustment heuristic: Why the adjustments are insufficient. *Psychological science, 17*(4), 311-318.
Goff, P. A., Lloyd, T., Geller, A., Raphael, S., & Glaser, J. (2016). *The science of justice: race, arrests, and police use of force.* Center for Policing Equity.
Taber, C. S., & Lodge, M. (2006). Motivated skepticism in the evaluation of political beliefs. *American Journal of Political Science, 50*(3), 755-769.

Chapter 40: The Brain Science of Political Deception in the 2016 Election

By Gleb Tsipursky

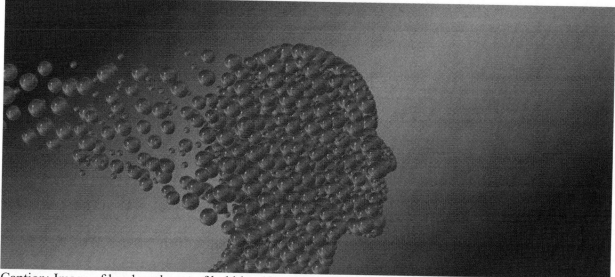

Caption: Image of head made out of bubbles (Geralt/Pixabay)

How did Donald Trump win, when he used so many misleading statements and outright deceptions? Couldn't people see through them? As an expert in brain science, I want to share why his followers fell for his lies and what can be done to address this situation in the future.

First, let's get the facts straight. Politifact.com, a well-known non-partisan website, rates only about 4 percent of statements by Trump as fully "True" and over 50 percent as either completely "False" or what they call ridiculously false – "Pants on Fire," with the rest in the middle. By comparison, Hillary Clinton rated 25 percent as fully "True" and only 12 percent as either "False" or "Pants on Fire."

The Washington Post, one of the most reputable newspapers in the country, wrote that "There's never been a presidential candidate like Donald Trump — someone so cavalier about the facts and so unwilling to ever admit error, even in the face of overwhelming evidence." In their rulings on statements made by Trump, this paper's editors evaluated 64 percent of them as Four Pinocchios, their worst rating. By contrast, statements by other politicians tend to get the worst rating 10 to 20 percent of the time.

These sentiments are representative of other prominent news media and fact-check outlets, yet according to an ABC News/Washington post poll, most voters on the eve of the election perceived Donald Trump as more trustworthy than Hillary Clinton. This false perception came from the Trump campaign building up on previous Republican criticism of Clinton, much of it misleading and some accurate, to manipulate successfully many voters into believing that Clinton is less honest, in spite of the evidence that she is much more honest than Trump. The Trump campaign did so through the illusory truth effect, a thinking error in our minds that happens when false statements are repeated many times and we begin to see them as true. In other words, just because something is stated several times, we perceive it as more accurate.

You may have noticed the last two sentences in the previous paragraph had the same meaning. The second sentence didn't provide any new information, but it did cause you to believe my claim more than you did when you read the first sentence.

The Biology of Truth Vs. Comfort

Why should the human brain be structured so that mere repetition, without any more evidence, causes us to believe a claim more strongly? The more often we are exposed to a statement, the more comfortable it seems. The fundamental error most people make is mistaking statements that make them feel comfortable for true statements.

Our brains cause us to *believe* something is true because we *feel* it is true, regardless of the evidence – a phenomenon known as emotional reasoning. This strange phenomenon can be easily explained by understanding some basic biology behind how our brain works.

When we hear a statement, the first thing that fires in our brain in a few milliseconds is our autopilot system of thinking, composed of our emotions and intuitions. Also known as System 1, the autopilot system is what the Nobel Prize-winning scientist Daniel Kahneman identified as our two systems of thinking in his 2011 *Thinking, Fast and Slow*, and represents the more ancient system of our brain. It protected us in the ancestral environment against dangerous threats such as saber-toothed tigers by making us feel bad about them and drew us toward what we needed to survive such as food and shelter by making us feel good about them. The humans who survived learned well to heed the autopilot system's guidance, and we are the children of these humans.

Unfortunately, the autopilot system is not well calibrated for the modern environment. When we hear statements that go against our current beliefs, our autopilot system perceives them as threats and causes us to feel bad about them. By contrast, statements that align with our existing beliefs cause us to feel good and we want to believe them. So if we just go with our gut reactions – our lizard brain – we will always choose statements that align with our current beliefs.

Caption: Meme saying "Lizard brain thinking is killing democracy – Please think rationally" (Made for Intentional Insights by Ed Coolidge)

Where Do We Get Our News?

Until recently, people got all their news from mainstream media, which meant they were often exposed to information that they didn't like because it did not fit their beliefs. The budget cuts and consolidation of media ownership in the last decade resulted in mainstream media getting increasingly less diverse, well described in the 2009 *Media Ownership and Concentration in America* by Eli Noam. Moreover, according to a 2016 survey by Pew Research Center, many people are increasingly getting their news mainly or only from within their own personalized social media filter bubble, which tends to exclude information that differs from their own beliefs. So their own beliefs are reinforced and it seems that everyone shares the same beliefs as them.

This trend is based on a traditional strong trust in friends as sources of reliable recommendations, according to the 2015 Nielsen Global Trust in Advertising Report. Our brains tend to spread the trust that we associate with friends to other sources of information that we see on social media. This thinking error is known as the halo effect when our assessment of one element of a larger whole as positive transfers to other elements. We can see this in research showing that people's trust in social media influencers has grown over time, nearly to the level of trust in their friends, as shown by a 2016 joint study by Twitter and analytics firm Annalect.

Even more concerning, a 2016 study from Stanford University demonstrated that over 80 percent of students, who are generally experienced social media users, could not distinguish a news story shared by a friend from a sponsored advertisement. In a particularly scary finding, many of the study's participants thought a news story was true based on irrelevant factors such as the size of the photo, as opposed to rational factors such as the credibility of the news source outlet.

The Trump team knows that many people have difficulty distinguishing sponsored stories from real news stories and that's why they were at the forefront of targeting voters with sponsored advertorials on social media. In some cases they used this tactic to motivate their own supporters, and in others they used it as a voter suppression tactic against Clinton supporters. The Trump campaign's Republican allies created fake news stories that got millions of shares on social media. The Russian propaganda machine has also used social media to manufacture fake news stories favorable to Trump and critical of Clinton.

Additionally, Trump's attacks on mainstream media and fact-checkers before the election, and even after the election, undercut the credibility of news source outlets. As a result, trust in the media amongst Republicans dropped to an all-time low of 14 percent in a September 2016 Gallup poll, a drop of over 200 percent from 2015. Fact-checking is even less credible among Republicans, with 88 percent expressing distrust in a September 2016 Rasmussen Reports poll.

All this combined in the unprecedented reliance on and sharing of fake news by Trump's supporters on social media. With the rise of the Tea Party, Republicans have tended to make many more false statements than Democrats. Lacking trust in the mainstream media and relying on social media instead, a large segment of Trump's base indiscriminately shared whatever made them feel good, regardless of whether it was true. Indeed, one fake news writer, in an interview with *The Washington Post*, said of Trump supporters: "His followers don't fact-check anything — they'll post everything, believe anything." No wonder that Trump's supporters mostly believe his statements, according to polling. By contrast, another creator of fake news, in an interview with *NPR*, described how he "tried to write fake news for liberals — but they just never take the bait" due to them practicing fact-checking and debunking.

Caption: Meme saying "People are most comfortable dealing with reality in terms of black or white, but reality tends to like shades of grey" (Made for Intentional Insights by Wayne Straight)

This fact-checking and debunking illustrates that the situation, while dismal, is not hopeless. Such truth-oriented behaviors rely on our other thinking system, the intentional system or system 2, as shown by Chip and Dan Heath in their 2013's *Decisive: How to Make Better Choices in Life and Work*. The intentional system is deliberate and reflective. It takes effort to use but it can catch and override the thinking errors committed by system 1 so that we do not adopt the belief that something is true because we feel it is true, regardless of the evidence.

Many liberals associate positive emotions with empirical facts and reason, which is why their intentional system is triggered into doing fact-checking on news stories. Trump voters mostly do not have such positive emotions around the truth, and believe in Trump's authenticity on a gut level regardless of the facts. This difference is not well recognized by the mainstream media, who treat their audience as rational thinkers and present information in a language that communicates well to liberals, but not to Trump voters.

To get more conservatives to turn on the intentional system when evaluating political discourse we need to speak to emotions and intuitions – the autopilot system, in other words. We have to get folks to associate positive emotions with the truth first and foremost, before anything else.

To do so, we should understand where these people are coming from and what they care about, validate their emotions and concerns, and only then show, using emotional language, the harm people suffer when they believe in lies. For instance, for those who care about safety and security, we can highlight how it's important for them to defend themselves against being swindled into taking actions that make the world more dangerous. Those concerned with liberty and independence would be moved by emotional language targeted toward keeping themselves free from being used and manipulated. For those focused on family values, we may speak about trust being abused.

These are strong terms that have deep emotional resonance. Many may be uncomfortable with using such tactics of emotional appeals. We have to remember the end goal of helping people orient toward the truth. This is a case where ends do justify the means. We need to be emotional to help people grow more rational – to make sure that while truth lost the battle, it will win the war.

References

Blanchette, I., & Richards, A. (2004). Reasoning about emotional and neutral materials: Is logic affected by emotion?. *Psychological Science, 15*(11), 745-752.

Fazio, L. K., Brashier, N. M., Payne, B. K., & Marsh, E. J. (2015). Knowledge does not protect against illusory truth. *Journal of Experimental Psychology: General, 144*(5), 993.

Kahneman, D. (2011). *Thinking, fast and slow.*

Noam, E. (2009). *Media ownership and concentration in America.*

Resnick, P., Garrett, R. K., Kriplean, T., Munson, S. A., & Stroud, N. J. (2013, February). Bursting your (filter) bubble: strategies for promoting diverse exposure. In *Proceedings of the 2013 conference on Computer supported cooperative work companion* (pp. 95-100). ACM.

Williams, R. (1998). *Political Scandals in the USA* (Vol. 1).

Wineburg, S., McGrew, S., Breakstone, J., & Ortega, T. (2016). Evaluating Information: The Cornerstone of Civic Online Reasoning.

Chapter 41: A Future With Trump: Truth Vs Comfort

By Hunter Glenn

Caption: Image of someone standing on edge of cliff (Jonathan Pendleton/Stocksnap)

As a country, we'd like to believe that things are looking up for us after this election. We have a new president with a new message and a new plan. Things have been bad for so long, and every time we tried something different, it just stayed the same or got worse. Now, finally, surely we've done something different enough by electing Donald Trump. So, what kind of future should we expect with President Trump?

The stakes are high. We carry a lot of baggage from our past disappointments. A lot of hope is riding on Trump to meet or exceed our expectations.

All that hope and high stakes are a warning sign, though. Does our emotional self want to believe comforting things about Donald Trump, regardless of whether they are accurate?

Well, maybe so, but optimism is a virtue. Why dwell on the negative? We should be glad the campaigning is over, the work is about to begin, and that change is around the corner.

Some question if optimism is always a good thing. Of course, it depends on what you mean. It's okay to think you won't get into a car crash and to drive worry-free – as long as you still wear a seatbelt and are just as careful as if you thought you might crash.

It's okay to vote for a candidate in the hope of that candidate winning as long as you're also prepared for the alternative. It's okay to think you're going to win a battle as long as you're prepared anyway in case you lose. The issue only comes if you think all these positive thoughts about the future and then you *let that keep you from being careful.*

Caption: Meme saying "uncomfortable truths > comfortable lies" (Made for Intentional Insights by Isabelle Giuong)

The real problem is that the higher the pressure of the situation, the more people want to believe that everything will be okay. They want to find some comforting anchor to hold on to, and then shut the rest of the world out before it convinces them that things don't look so good. This is a typical human thinking error known as the Ostrich effect. Many people stay in bad relationships because they are desperate to overlook signs their partner may be abusive.

However, our situation is not really like that of someone in an abusive relationship. It is more like we just got a new boss. Shouldn't we be optimistic about our future in the company. We don't want to cater to our fears. Instead, we should move forward. Carefully, wisely, we will move on. Yes, this is a time to prepare, to look ahead to what's coming, but also a time of much hope.

To be above fear, we must be well-prepared. If things go well, being prepared, a little extra put away, a little ahead of schedule, these can only make good times better. And if maybe things don't go so well, far, *far* better to be prepared than not.

If you ever do get in a car crash, better to have been wearing your seatbelt. If you do lose the battle, better to be in position to win the war anyway. If Trump happens to be a bad leader, better to be prepared for whatever may come. We can allow ourselves the luxury of comfortable beliefs only once we've done our due diligence, and prepared for disappointment with backup plans in case things go wrong.

We can be attentive to important political issues that may arise, and make our voice heard, rather than blindly hoping everything will be fine without our attention. We can prepare for financial mishaps that might lie ahead, or changes on the international political scene.

Truth versus comfort; it's not a real choice. Wisdom does not choose one at the expense of the other. Wisdom points us to preparation, to be ready for anything, to take comfort in our own readiness, and then look forward to the future without fear.

References

Karlsson, N., Loewenstein, G., & Seppi, D. (2009). The ostrich effect: Selective attention to information. *Journal of Risk and uncertainty, 38*(2), 95-115.

Chapter 42: How Trump Changed My Mind About Marriage

By Jeff Dubin

Caption: Image of two wedding rings (Callumramsay/Pixabay

It's not easy to admit, but I am grateful to Donald Trump for leading me to realize I was wrong about marriage. After all, I always seek to learn when I am mistaken and update my beliefs toward the truth. Sometimes, these lessons come from unexpected teachers.

As far back as I can remember, I had always been opposed to getting married, until that fateful night on November 8, 2016 when Trump was elected. I had what I thought were three compelling reasons.

MARRIAGE: FOR BETTER OR FOR WORSE

Before the recent Supreme Court ruling granting marriage equality, I thought that to get married when my lesbian and gay friends could not do so would be like choosing to patronize a "Whites Only" business. I thought that as a straight person, to get married would mean to endorse a discriminatory institution. Instead, I was boycotting marriage, just like people of good conscience in the era of open discrimination against African Americans might have refused to enter a place that admitted only whites.

Also, I felt that it made no sense to say, "'Til Death Do Us Part," when so many marriages eventually end in some other way. We all know couples whose marriage soon ended in acrimonious divorce, and whose children and other family members suffered the fallout. We cannot reliably predict the future. Why pretend that divorce or abandonment cannot possibly happen?

Then there was the apparent contradiction of saying to another person, "You're my best friend, I trust you more than anyone in the world, now SIGN THIS LEGAL CONTRACT!" I know that I consider my female partner, Charlene, to be my best friend as well as my lover. Why would you not take a best friend at their word? For either of us to demand that the other sign a legal contract, I thought, would undermine any real trust present.

Yet, there's no denying that the institution of marriage offers many benefits. These include several legal protections, such as connection in the Social Security system, eligibility for joint health insurance, decision-making power in times of severe illness, and being considered next of kin in case of death. It also tends to lead to the endorsement of one's relationship by the community. I feel close to Charlene's parents and other family members, who have been kind and welcoming toward me; likewise, my parents have already accepted her as part of the family.

REACTANCE: "I WON'T DO WHAT YOU TELL ME!"

Only recently did I realize the REAL cause of my objection to marriage: a psychological phenomenon called reactance.

Reactance is a common reaction that occurs in many of us when we feel that someone is telling us what we may or may not do. In response to real or perceived denial of a freedom, we often react by wanting to exercise that freedom.

Think of being a child and being forbidden to do something. Can you remember wanting to do that thing even more, just because it was forbidden?

Think of Marlon Brando's 1950s motorcycle gang leader, in *"The Wild One,"* who replied to the question *"What are you rebelling against?"* with, *"Whadda you got?"* Or think of Zach de la Rocha of Rage Against The Machine, screaming *"F*** YOU, I WON'T DO WHAT YOU TELL ME!"*

I try to avoid getting in fights, I'm not a punk rock singer, and I don't even have a motorcycle. Yet, I do have a very strong reactance response. If I feel that society expects me to do a thing, I tend to not want to do it, or to want to do the opposite.
Still, making decisions according to reactance, when one has the capacity to reason better, is an unwise thing to do. Suppose you were on an airplane and it lost cabin pressure, and the flight attendant told you to put on the oxygen mask. Would you rebel against authority, screaming *"F*** YOU, I WON'T DO WHAT YOU TELL ME!"*? To do so, in this instance as well as many other situations, could be a deadly mistake.

TRUMP AND MARRIAGE

On Election Day 2016, as I saw one of the worst things happen to my country and the world that I could have imagined, I thought, "I have to start making better, more responsible choices than ever before." And

I thought of President Barack Obama's paraphrase of a scripture quote, from his inauguration speech in January 2009: "*The time has come to set aside childish things.*"

So, **not** because of social pressure, but due to reasoning better than before, I decided to set aside childish thinking and make an adult decision. I suggested to my partner that we get married, and she agreed. I quickly felt the relief that you feel when you decide to do what some part of you knew all along to be the right choice. I felt a sense of freedom through no longer being held back by the obstacle that is reactance. Having a woman who loves me and treats me so well agree to be my wife was, shall we say, icing on the cake.

Caption: Photo of Jeff Dubin and fiancée Charlene (Courtesy of Jeff Dubin)

I will continue to support friends and family who are single, or widowed, or choose not to marry for all sorts of legitimate reasons. I will not pressure others, even jokingly. Ideally, I would like it if the government had nothing to do with marriage, and all relationships were honored equally. But we must live in the world that is while striving for one that is better.

As much as I despise Trump, and as much harm as I already see him doing and expect him and his post-truth political methods to do in the future, I owe him thanks for helping me to upgrade my thinking.

178

I will leave you with a few **questions to ponder:**

- When have you resisted health advice from a doctor or others–maybe to change your diet, or to exercise more, or to cut down on smoking or use of drugs–due to reactance?
- What cultural practices might be of some value to you, that you have avoided solely because of a negative feeling about tradition?

What experiences might have contributed to these reactance responses?

References

Brehm, S. S., & Brehm, J. W. (2013). *Psychological reactance: A theory of freedom and control.*

Chapter 43: The Science of Solving Alternative Facts

By Gleb Tsipursky

Caption: Photo of protest sign saying "science trumps alternative facts" (Benno Hansen/Flickr)

I shuddered, horrified to the depths of my soul when Donald Trump's senior adviser Kellyanne Conway presented the Trump administration's false claims as "alternative facts" in a January 22nd interview on NBC's "Meet The Press." She was defending the lies told by Sean Spicer, the White House Press Secretary, about Trump's inauguration. For instance, Spicer stated that Trump drew "the largest audience to ever witness an inauguration," despite the clear evidence of aerial photos(and metro usage statistics) showing that Barack Obama's inauguration drew significantly bigger crowds.

Yet are alternative facts really so bad? While I had a violent visceral reaction to hearing Conway utter the words "alternative facts," my response simply indicates an emotional distaste for deceit. I would have that response regardless of whether a Democrat or Republican used that phrase.

Many share my sentiments. Prominent columnists are condemning Conway for appealing to "alternative facts." There are calls for Sean Spicer to resign based on his lies, and internet memes featuring "alternative facts" are spreading quickly.

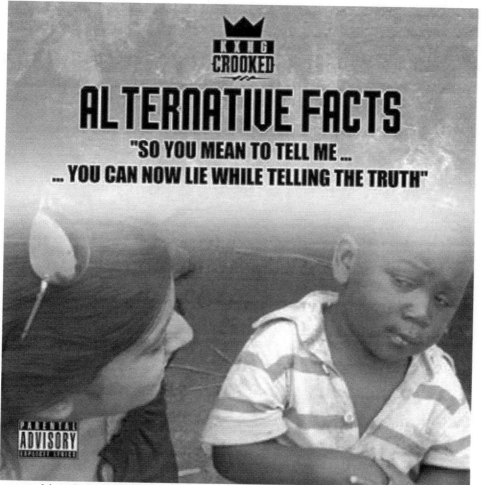

Caption: Meme making fun of alternative facts (Alternative Facts, Kxng Crooked)

However, this criticism only speaks to people who share my intuitive orientation toward truth, reason, and logic. Research shows that plenty of people resonate more with appeals to emotions rather than facts. They do not see an inherent problem when the politicians that they support lie to gain political credibility.

Their more emotionally-oriented perspective explains Trump's successful appeal to emotions such as fear and anxiety. Trump won the presidency in part through such post-truth tactics. Trump's victory was a major reason why Oxford Dictionary chose "post-truth" as its 2016 Word of the Year, defining post-truth as "relating to or denoting circumstances in which objective facts are less influential in shaping public opinion than appeals to emotion and personal belief."

How do we get across to people the dangers of post-truth political tactics, whether perpetrated by Trump or others, if they do not have a visceral concern about truth in politics? Just wagging a finger and calling out such lies, as many in the press are currently doing, will not work. This approach is characteristic of a typical thinking error, termed the "false consensus effect" in psychology, where we intuitively assume other people share our emotional predispositions and values.

The underlying challenge stems from people who respond most strongly to emotional appeals rather than facts. As an example, due to Trump's harsh and emotional criticism of mainstream media when they called him out on his deceit, trust in the mainstream media among Republicans dropped by over half from 2015 to 2016. Trump's followers resonate with his emotional appeal, trusting him at the gut level, regardless of the actual facts of reality.

As a scholar and commentator who has studied decision-making and emotions in politics extensively, I set out to learn how to reach those who do not intuitively emphasize factual truth in arriving at an opinion. Based on research in political psychology, I hypothesized that the surest way is to discover what such people care about and show them how post-truth politics will undermine what they value. The most promising avenue in my investigation has proven to be demonstrating how "alternative facts" will result in corruption and authoritarianism, one of the top fears of Americans, according to a Chapman University 2016 study.

Caption: Meme saying "uncomfortable truths > comfortable lies (Made for Intentional Insights by Isabelle Giuong)

I focused on talking to Republicans in particular, conveying the idea that if politicians can win just by telling the best lies, they do not need to care about serving the true interests of the citizenry. They could simply use emotional manipulation and lies to get and stay in power, paving the way for corruption and authoritarianism.

Indeed, without the truth about the influence of money in politics, citizens cannot evaluate who is corrupt. As Secretary of State John Kerry noted at an Anti-Corruption Summit in May 2016, "corruption tears at the entire fabric of a society." President Barack Obama has taken a series of steps to address government corruption through regulations increasing transparency in business and politics. Trump's plans to roll back regulations will reverse this transparency.

I also discussed how rhetoric that appeals to emotions and popular beliefs is a foundational feature of authoritarianism. This is the same kind of rhetoric that helped Vladimir Putin transform Russia's post-Soviet fledgling democracy into an authoritarian state, and resulted in Putin's consistently high popularity rating, something that Trump praised in a televised forum with Matt Lauer.

Trump also positively depicted Putin's "strong control over a country," and when asked on MSNBC's "Morning Joe" what he thought of Putin killing journalists who do not agree with him, Trump dismissed that question, saying that: "I think that our country does plenty of killing, too, Joe." Given that Putin began his path to authoritarian rule by undermining the Russian media, and that Trump promised to do the same in the US if elected, and is indeed carrying out this promise, the parallel is clear.

Moreover, I talked about the possibility of Trump borrowing another of Putin's favorite tactics: fraudulent elections. Imagine, I told them, Trump losing the 2020 election, and then blaming that loss on supposed millions of illegal votes, as he has already done in his false claims immediately after the election that he won the popular vote in 2016 – a lie that, according to polling, a majority of his followers believe. He continues to make these deceptive statements, most recently in his first meeting with congressional leaders on January 23, despite prominent members of his own party, such as Paul Ryan, pushing back against these lies.

Trump is surrounding himself with allies who promote similar lies. For instance, we know that Trump's pick for Attorney General has tried to suppress voting through prosecuting African-American activists for voter fraud, unsuccessfully, and more broadly promoting the false idea of widespread voter fraud among African-Americans and other minority groups. It is not at all unlikely that if he lost in 2020, he would make claims of voter fraud, and have people such as his Attorney General make up fake evidence demonstrating fraud.

Clearly, Trump has little respect for American democratic institutions. After all, back when he thought he was losing the 2016 election season, he was already making the case for the elections being rigged. If he actually lost the 2020 election, and had all the might of the presidency behind him, it is not unlikely that he would go the extra step to make up evidence to support his lies. If he succeeded in staying in power despite the will of the electorate, his actions would spell doom for American democracy.

While American political institutions are more stable than Russian ones, we should be very worried. Without intervention, our situation will only worsen. Other politicians are already learning from Trump's post-truth approach to politics. They will try to out-Trump Trump, competing based on who tells the most emotionally provocative and appealing lie, not on who will best serve the common interest.

To demonstrate the effectiveness of my approach, I went on a radio show whose host, Dwight Lilly, is a Republican activist. The reasoning I used appealed to what Lilly and his listeners cared about – corruption and authoritarianism. We had a very productive conversation where he and I agreed about the dangers of post-truth politics and the importance of not taking any claims at face value, and instead demanding credible evidence. In my post-show, informal discussion with him, Lilly said that our conversation really made him think and "that's a dangerous thing," in his words.

Caption: Meme saying "the truth is not partisan" (Made for Intentional Insights by Lexie Holliday)

Given that he has a wide following of, and represents, other Republicans with libertarian leanings, the approach I outlined seems quite promising for getting people like him and others to care about fighting post-truth politics. The key is to determine what such people do care about, and show them that "alternative facts" will, in the end, destroy what they value. Doing so will enable us to form an alliance across the political spectrum to fight for truth in politics, in letter and spirit, for the sake of preserving our democracy and preventing us from sliding down into corruption and authoritarianism.

References
Caprara, G. V., Schwartz, S., Capanna, C., Vecchione, M., & Barbaranelli, C. (2006). Personality and politics: Values, traits, and political choice. *Political psychology*, *27*(1), 1-28.
Frijda, N. H., Manstead, A. S., & Bem, S. (Eds.). (2000). *Emotions and beliefs: How feelings influence thoughts*.

Mullen, B., Atkins, J. L., Champion, D. S., Edwards, C., Hardy, D., Story, J. E., & Vanderklok, M. (1985).
    The false consensus effect: A meta-analysis of 115 hypothesis tests. *Journal of Experimental Social Psychology, 21*(3), 262-283.

Chapter 44: Towards a Post-Lies Future

By Gleb Tsipursky

Caption: Image of Trump with Pinocchio-style long nose saying "expose his venomous lies" (Meshae Studios/Flickr)

Donald Trump is our first post-truth president. And he may well be the first of many.

The Oxford Dictionaries website chose "post-truth" as its 2016 word of the year, in large part due to Trump's success in the presidential election. It defined post-truth as "relating to or denoting circumstances in which objective facts are less influential in shaping public opinion than appeals to emotion and personal belief." (Incidentally, the 2015 word of the year wasn't a word at all but the "face with tears of joy" emoji.)

Trump's political methods ultimately rely on the appeal to emotions, such as fear and anxiety, and to personal beliefs over objective truth. Moreover, his victory was secured with blatant lies and misleading rhetoric, along with a doubling down on deceptions when called on them. Glenn Kessler's highly reputable "Fact Checker" column in the *Washington Post* evaluated statements made by Trump during the campaign and assigned 64 percent of them with "Four Pinocchios" (the worst rating). By contrast, statements by other politicians get Four Pinocchios 10 to 20 percent of the time.

Trump's deceit has only continued post-election. "In addition to winning the Electoral College in a landslide, I won the popular vote if you deduct the millions of people who voted illegally," Trump tweeted on November 27, 2016, a claim he continued to support. "Serious voter fraud in Virginia, New Hampshire, and California," Trump continued, "so why isn't the media reporting on this? Serious bias— big problem!" Investigations found nothing to back up his claim, yet this didn't stop the majority of Trump voters from believing him, as reflected in a survey of 1,011 Americans conducted by Qualtrics in December.

Trump's subordinates have had no problem following his lead. Senior adviser Kellyanne Conway infamously presented the Trump administration's false claims as "alternative facts" in January 22, 2017, interview on NBC's *Meet The Press*. She was defending the lies told by White House Press Secretary Sean Spicer regarding Trump's inauguration ceremony. Spicer insisted that Trump drew "the largest audience to ever witness an inauguration," despite the clear evidence of aerial photos showing that Barack Obama's inauguration drew a significantly bigger crowd.

Some wonder if it's worth focusing on such absurd claims when there are major policy changes afoot with the new administration. However, one must consider that other politicians are highly likely to adopt Trump's successful methods. If enough of them win by doing so, we're headed for a downward spiral of deceit in our political system. Without a serious intervention to clean up the pollution of truth in politics, this spiral will lead to the end of our political order as we know it. Trump supporters will say this is the kind of disruption we need and what they sought in electing him. I would argue that our survival depends on moving from the post-truth, alternative-facts present into a post-lies future.

Caption: Meme saying "visit facts & truth: stay for more beautiful life" (Made for Intentional Insights by Jane A. Gordon)

Examining Our Vulnerability

Getting to this future requires understanding why our political system was so vulnerable to Trump. While politicians have always accused each other of lies, the mainstream media has traditionally served as mediator and fact-checker to their statements. In the past, lying parties generally didn't go against the media consensus, and either toned down or withdrew their claims. To function, this system for determining political truths has required an intangible but invaluable resource: the public's trust. And it's well documented that public trust in the media has been eroding for the last decade.

To a significant extent, such trust stemmed from the public's inability to get information from sources other than mainstream media, along with the media projecting an appearance of objectivity. However, today more and more people are getting their news from social media (from 49 percent in 2012 to 62 percent in 2016, according to a Pew Research Center poll.) Likewise, the projection of objectivity left mainstream media unable to deal effectively with a politician who lies openly and frequently.

While other politicians on the extreme Right and the extreme Left have taken advantage of these vulnerabilities to promote their agendas, they've mostly been confined to the fringes of our political system. Trump's genius rests in being the first mainstream political figure to exploit thoroughly these systemic vulnerabilities using personal magnetism and disruption.

Besides a magnetism that appealed to a certain segment of the citizenry, Trump mastered the use of social media. He bypassed the mainstream media to tweet his messages directly to voters and targeted them with sponsored advertisements on Facebook.

In a late October interview with Bloomberg Businessweek, a senior campaign official said, "we have three major voter suppression operations under way," which he described as aimed at idealistic white liberals, young women, and African Americans. In one such operation, they used Hillary Clinton's 1996 reference to certain gang members as "superpredators" who "we need to bring to heel" to create a South Park-style animation that was delivered to black voters through what Facebook terms "dark posts"—nonpublic posts whose viewership was targeted by the Trump campaign.

Such ads are very effective. A study from Stanford University found that over 80 percent of participants couldn't distinguish a news story shared by a friend from a sponsored advertisement. Moreover, many made basic mistakes in evaluating the credibility of a news story. For instance, they rated a story on Facebook as more credible if it had a larger image, rather than evaluating the reputation of the story's source. Likewise, most couldn't distinguish between the real Facebook page of a news organization and a fake page, despite the blue checkmark Facebook uses to distinguish real from fake pages. The participants were students, an age group of generally savvy social media users. Older adults are even more likely to make such mistakes.

Caption: Meme saying "don't be fooled by fake news: verify before you share" (Made for Intentional Insights by Lau Guerreiro)

Likewise, the Trump campaign's Republican allies created fake news stories that got millions of shares on social media. The Russian propaganda machine has also used social media to manufacture fake news stories favorable to Trump and critical of Clinton.

Exploiting systemic weaknesses based on trust is a particular skill set for our 45th president, and explains a significant degree of his previous economic success. For instance, the Trump Foundation relied on the trust society vests into the nonprofit sector to make illegal contributions advancing his political career and to settle legal disputes, while trust in the system of higher education was fraudulently exploited by Trump University. Other areas where he exploited systemic vulnerabilities based on trust include real estate projects, tax avoidance, and many more. Simply put, Donald Trump is highly skilled at hacking our societal structures, abusing trust in a classical use of the psychology of persuasion.

Is Post-Truth Politics Really So Bad?

It's no exaggeration to say that relying on emotions and personal opinions over facts will very likely destroy our political system. Since ancient Greece, truth in politics has been vital for a democracy to function properly. Citizens need to care about and know the reality of political affairs, at least in broad terms, to make wise decisions regarding which politicians and policies to support. Otherwise, what reason do politicians have to care about serving the true interests of the citizenry? They can simply use emotional manipulation and lies to procure and stay in power, paving the way for corruption and authoritarianism.

Caption: Meme saying "the truth is not partisan" (Made for Intentional Insights by Lexie Holliday)

Indeed, rhetoric that appeals to emotions and popular beliefs is a foundational feature of authoritarianism. It's what helped Vladimir Putin transform Russia's fledgling post-Soviet democracy into an authoritarian state, and resulted in Putin's consistently high popularity rating, something Trump praised in a televised forum with *The Today Show's* Matt Lauer.

Trump also positively depicted Putin's "strong control over a country." And when asked by former GOP congressman and MSNBC host Joe Scarborough what he thought of Putin killing journalists who don't agree with him, Trump sidestepped the question, saying, "I think that our country does plenty of killing, too, Joe." Given that Putin began his path to authoritarian rule by undermining the Russian media, and

191

that Trump promised to do the same in the United States if elected (and is indeed carrying out this promise), the parallel is clear.

Post-Truth and the Tragedy of the Commons

While American political institutions are more stable than Russian ones, we should be very worried about the truth falling victim to the tragedy of the commons. As described in Bonnie McCay and James Acheson's 1987 The *Question of the Commons: The Culture and Ecology of Communal Resources,* the tragedy occurs when a commonly shared resource is destroyed by individuals acting in their own self-interest and against the collective interest. In our case, the commonly shared good isn't a tangible resource like a forest or lake, it's a political environment that is based on appealing to objective facts. Plenty of research shows the crucial role of political trust in maintaining a stable polity (for instance, 2011's *Political Trust: Why Context Matters,* edited by Marc Hooghe and Sonja Zmerli). This intangible yet invaluable resource is being polluted and destroyed by Trump's post-truth politics.

Indeed, truth in politics is a common good just like clean air and water, and the pollution of truth will devastate our political system just as environmental pollution devastates our planet and our physical health. Fortunately, we can learn from the successes of the environmental movement. It started with small groups of motivated and informed people engaging in sustained education and advocacy. As a result of these efforts, regular citizens increasingly changed their everyday behavior through recycling, repurposing, and composting, while politicians passed pro-environmental legislation such as the Clean Air Act.

Similarly, activists for truth in politics—the pro-truth movement if you will—need to undertake educational and advocacy efforts to motivate regular citizens and politicians alike to address the pollution of truth in the political arena. Authors such as Bryan Caplan (*The Myth of the Rational Voter: Why Democracies Choose Bad Policies*) dismiss the possibility of the electorate growing more oriented toward the truth, yet recent research shows that people can train themselves to evaluate reality accurately and thus make wise decisions. This research has focused on decision making in various areas of finances, relationships, business, and elsewhere, as described in *Decisive*: *How to Make Better Choices in Life and Work* (2013) by Chip Heath and Dan Heath, and Daniel Kahneman's *Thinking, Fast and Slow* (2011).

Similar strategies apply to politics: it involves developing new mental habits such as systematically fact-checking political information and welcoming a revision of one's beliefs based on new evidence. Fortunately, once educated about the risks associated with the pollution of truth, most people easily recognize that accurate perception of reality by voters is beneficial to everyone except a few small interest groups that are devoted to deceiving the public.

Caption: Meme saying "don't be a clown, don't share fake news" (Made for Intentional Insights by Lau Guerreiro)

Rational Politics: A Case Study

As a scholar and commentator on decision making and emotions in politics, I set out to study how to reach those who don't have an intuitive concern with the truth. Based on research in political psychology, I hypothesized that the surest way is to discover what such people care about and show them how post-truth politics will undermine what they value. The most promising avenue of my investigation has proven to be demonstrating how "alternative facts" undermine what people actually care about.

For instance, I went on a radio show last fall with prominent conservative talk show host Scott Sloan. He's well known in conservative circles and had Donald Trump on his show shortly before me. Sloan is also known in the secular movement from his debate with Aron Ra over the Ark Encounter, a Christian fundamentalist theme park that opened last summer in Kentucky. In my interview with Sloan, we discussed the Ohio State University terrorist attack in November 2016 by a Muslim who rammed his car into a crowd of students and then knifed several people before being shot dead by a university policeman.

Like many conservatives, Sloan associated Muslims with terrorism and wanted to persecute them harshly. I approached the ensuing discussion by considering his emotions and goals, meeting him where he was as opposed to where I would have liked him to be. I assessed that he valued safety and security first and foremost and that he had negative feelings toward Muslims as he perceived them as a threat to safety and security.

As we began talking, I validated the host's emotions, saying it was natural and intuitive to feel anger and fear toward Muslims, as our brains naturally take shortcuts by stereotyping groups based on the actions of one member of the group. However, such stereotyping often does not serve our actual goals and values.

We discussed how in 2015 (according to johnstonarchive.net), there were seven terrorist acts in the United States, committed by a total of nine terrorists. Six of the nine were motivated, in some part, by Islamic beliefs. A 2011 Pew survey estimated that the United States had 1.8 million Muslim adults. Dividing this number by the six who committed terrorist acts gives you a one-in-300,000 chance that any Muslim you see would commit a terrorist act in a given year. That's like picking out a terrorist from the number of people in several football stadiums. So using "Muslim" as a filter for "terrorist" actually, wastes our precious resources dedicated to safety and security, and lets the real terrorists commit attacks.

I then discussed with Sloan how if we persecute Muslims, for instance through creating a Muslim registry or through heavy policing of Muslim neighborhoods, Muslim communities would be much less likely to help us root out potential terrorists in their midst. So, I concluded, for the sake of making us safer, we shouldn't antagonize Muslim communities, which so far have been quite cooperative in addressing terror concerns.

Finally, I discussed how rhetoric critical of Muslims and anti-Muslim policies will prod more Muslims to become terrorists. For instance, BBC reports that terrorist groups have used Trump's rhetoric in their recruitment tapes. This quite clearly makes us less safe and secure, I told Sloan, and so despite any negative feelings we may have toward Muslims, it's unwise to act on them. Just like if we hear criticism from our boss and want to scream in his or her face, it may not be the rational thing to do if we value our jobs. Just like we may want to take a second piece of chocolate cake, it may not be the rational thing to do if we value our health. We shouldn't go with our gut on policies and rhetoric toward Muslims if we value our security.

Caption: Meme saying "lizard brain thinking is killing democracy: please think rationally" (Made for Intentional Insights by Ed Coolidge)

In the end, Sloan agreed with my points and updated his views on Muslims—not because he felt like being nice and generous and kind toward Muslims, but because he valued his security and safety.

None of this implies that religion isn't a part of the problem. In addition to the six Muslims who committed terrorist acts in the United States in 2015, three terrorists were motivated by radical Christian and right-wing beliefs, especially the November 2015 shooting at a Planned Parenthood clinic in Colorado. Today, there are more radicals in Islam than in other religions, but the focus needs to be on radical behavior as much as religion itself.

Of course, I could have chosen to bring up my conviction that religion itself is an "alternative fact," both as a whole, and in its specific details. However, would this have been a productive use of my time on Sloan's show? It was my third interview with him, and I've had another since that conversation. By building a rapport, and not touching topics that would prevent me from being invited back on his show, I'm able to retain my channel to his conservative audience. Similarly, readers of this article may also want to consider which topics they should discuss with those who don't share their values in order to change hearts and minds—and what topics are better left for later after more low-hanging fruits are picked.

In order to save our democracy and prevent corruption and authoritarianism, reasonable people on all sides of the political spectrum need to adopt a focus on truth in letter and spirit as the most important component of our political system. We need to work tirelessly to educate everyone about the benefits of orienting toward truth. We need to use emotionally intelligent, empathetic communication in doing so, focusing on the values and emotions of those we communicate with in order to change their hearts and minds.

We also have to create incentives and consequences for politicians to be truthful, as orienting toward truth isn't conducive to winning political battles in the current environment. Such incentives would involve a combination of carrots and sticks. On the one hand, we have to catch lies and punish liars, especially those who share our own ideological perspectives, so as to minimize accusations of political bias in advocacy for truth in politics. On the other, we must praise and reward truth-telling, especially when it harms one's ideological position.

Fighting the normalization of post-truth politics and alternative facts requires us to be comfortable leaving aside easy identifications with major political movements. The pro-truth movement will require early advocates to act from the same kind of marginalized political position as early environmental activists, fighting both against the political status quo and the tendency of our brains toward lazy thinking. Yet cleaning up the pollution of truth is arguably the most important action we can take to save our democracy from sliding down into corruption and authoritarianism, and its early advocates will be the heroes of tomorrow.

References
Caplan, B. (2011). *The myth of the rational voter: Why democracies choose bad policies.*
Heath, C., & Heath, D. (2013). *Decisive: How to make better choices in life and work.*
Kahneman, D. (2011). *Thinking, fast and slow.*
McCay, B. J., & Acheson, J. M. (Eds.). (1990). *The question of the commons: The culture and ecology of communal resources.*
Tsipursky, G. (2017). How Can Facts Trump Ideology? *The Human Prospect, 6.3,* 4-10
Wineburg, S., McGrew, S., Breakstone, J., & Ortega, T. (2016). Evaluating Information: The Cornerstone of Civic Online Reasoning.
Zmerli, S. & Hooghe, M. (Eds). (2011). *Political trust: Why context matters.*

Chapter 45: How Behavioral Science Can Help Truth Triumph Over Baseless Accusations

By Gleb Tsipursky

Caption: Trump and Obama graphic (Wikimedia Commons)

Regardless of their political affiliation, most who follow politics in any depth easily dismissed Donald Trump's series of grave Twitter accusations on March 4 that Barack Obama ordered Trump Tower wiretapped before the 2016 election. Trump offered no evidence for his wiretapping claims, but instead used inflammatory language such as calling Obama "sick" and "bad," and requested that Congress conduct an investigation into the Obama administration.

Behavioral science suggests that despite Trump offering no substantive facts for his claim, the mainstream media's current coverage will get him what he craves. Fortunately, we can use the same research to reframe the narrative to help truth trump Trump's evidence-free accusations.

To understand why current coverage helps Trump get what he wants, let's consider some typical examples of how the accusations have been covered so far. CNN's story described in the first sentence how "Trump made a stunning claim" about the wiretapping, and added that he did not offer any evidence. Next, the story featured 3 screenshots of Trump's tweets, and a breakdown of the claims. Following that, the article continued with rebuttals of Trump's claims by Obama's spokesperson and US intelligence officials, and then went into an analysis of how the tweets are representative of Trump's wild and often false accusations.

The article on this topic by AP News, republished in many local newspapers and used by radio and TV stations, also started by describing Trump's "startling allegation of abuse of power," and noted that it was offered without evidence. The story continued with Obama's denial of the claim, and then went into the details of Trump's accusations, followed by a broader analysis of Trump's frequent allegations backed by "alternative facts."

Caption: Meme saying "a lie by any other name still stinks: #AlternativeFacts" (Made for Intentional Insights by Jane Gordon)

These articles offered sophisticated political observers the appropriate context for Trump's evidence-free accusations in the analytic part of each piece. Yet research on news consumption shows that most people don't usually read the analysis. Only 41% of Americans go beyond simply skimming the headline, and, among these few, most only go into the first or second paragraph.

So what do the 6 in 10 who only read headlines get from the AP News headline: *"Trump Accuses Obama of Tapping His Phones, Cites No Evidence,"* and from the CNN headline *"White House Requests Congress Investigate Whether Obama Administration Abused Power?"*

What do most of the rest get from the CNN story that starts with a thorough description of Trump's accusations?

Those who have a strong partisan perspective will likely not change their opinions, due to what psychologists term "confirmation bias," the tendency to misinterpret new information in light of our current beliefs as opposed to objective facts. However, research shows that many moderates and independents, who do not suffer from confirmation bias but are not sophisticated political observers, will also likely be swayed to believe Trump's claims.

Their engagement with the headline and the initial paragraphs, which focus on the accusations by Trump, will cause them to experience "anchoring." This well-established reasoning error results from the way in which we process information we first encounter about a topic. That initial information influences the entirety of our perspective on an issue, coloring all the content we receive moving forward, even after we get more complete information. The most information that people will retain from such coverage consist of a vague impression of Trump as unjustly wiretapped by the "bad" and "sick" Obama, a conclusion also supported by research on the availability heuristic. This fallacious thinking pattern causes us to focus on information with emotional overtones, regardless of whether it is factual or relevant.

Likewise, shallow news skimmers may be influenced by the halo effect, a phenomenon of perception in which positive associations with one aspect of an individual cause us to perceive all aspects of that individual in a positive light. Most Americans have a default positive association with the office of the President; thus they tend to give its occupant the benefit of the doubt. To that end, statements by Trump appear more believable to the public simply because he occupies an office that typically signifies credibility, and also has access to secret information unavailable to most Americans. For the same reason, Trump's request to Congress to launch an investigation will appear credible, leading people to believe there is a good reason for such an inquiry, regardless of the evidence.

These thinking errors will cause the majority of Americans to develop a mistaken impression of Trump's wiretapping claims as legitimate, despite the lack of evidence, just as so many found the baseless "birtherism" accusations launched at Obama legitimate, or the idea that George Bush was behind 9/11. Consider Trump's evidence-free but often-repeated claim that millions of illegal ballots cast for Hillary Clinton cost him the popular vote, an allegation rated false by fact-checkers, and criticized by fellow Republicans such as Paul Ryan. Nonetheless, Trump launched an investigation in February 2017 of supposed voter fraud, just as he is now asking Congress to do in regard to the Obama administration's use of investigative powers.

The consequences of Trump's evidence-free claims are stunning in their impact. A Qualtrics poll in December 2016 showed that over half of all Republicans believe that Trump won the popular vote, as do 24 percent of independents and 7 percent of Democrats. This distribution shows the impact of confirmation bias, with Republicans much more likely to believe Trump's evidence-free claims. However, Trump's tactics and the nature of media coverage lead even some independents and Trump's political opponents to buy into Trump's claims. Incidentally, the poll suggests that more sophisticated political observers are less likely to believe Trump, with only 37 percent of Republicans who had a college degree accepting Trump's baseless allegations about millions of illegal votes.

Would you be surprised if Trump's current claims about wiretapping will be rated "false" by fact-checkers just as his voter fraud claims were? Would you be surprised if the investigation of wiretapping will find nothing, just as the investigation of voter fraud has not found anything? Yet Trump keeps making such claims with no evidence, and will keep doing so, because he gets exactly what he wants–millions of people believing his baseless allegations.

Reframing the media coverage of Trump's claims, using techniques informed by behavioral science, would disincentivize Trump from making such baseless statements, instead of rewarding him. Rather than focusing on relating the details of the specific claims made by Trump, news headlines and introductory paragraphs could foreground the pattern of our President systematically making accusations lacking evidence.

For instance, in the case of this specific news item, AP News could have run the headline "Trump Delivers Another Accusation Without Evidence, This Time Against Obama." CNN could have introduced the story by focusing on Trump's pattern of making serial allegations of immoral and illegal actions by his political opponents without any evidence, focusing this time on his predecessor. Then, deeper in the article where the shallow skimmers do not reach, the story could have detailed the allegations made by Trump. This style of media coverage would make Trump less inclined to make such claims, as he would not get the impact he wants.

You can make a difference when media venues publicize Trump's evidence-free accusations by writing letters to the editor encouraging them to reframe their reporting. By doing so, you will help create appropriate incentives for all politicians–not just Trump–to make such claims only when they are supported by evidence.

References

Burton, S., Cook, L. A., Howlett, E., & Newman, C. L. (2015). Broken halos and shattered horns: overcoming the biasing effects of prior expectations through objective information disclosure. *Journal of the Academy of Marketing Science, 43*(2), 240-256.

Chapman, G. B., & Johnson, E. J. (1999). Anchoring, activation, and the construction of values. *Organizational behavior and human decision processes, 79*(2), 115-153.

Frey, D., Schulz-Hardt, S., & Stahlberg, D. (2013). Information seeking among individuals and groups and possible consequences for decision-making in business and politics. *Understanding group behavior, 2*, 211-225.

Pachur, T., Hertwig, R., & Steinmann, F. (2012). How do people judge risks: availability heuristic, affect heuristic, or both?. *Journal of Experimental Psychology: Applied, 18*(3), 314.

Chapter 46: A Behavioral Science Solution to Lies in Politics

By Gleb Tsipursky

Caption: Puzzle pieces spelling out "truth" (Geralt/Pixabay)

Deception proved a very successful strategy for political causes and individual candidates in the UK and US elections in 2016, leading Oxford Dictionary to choose post-truth politics as its 2016 word of the year. At this low point, it might seem ludicrous to many that we can solve the problem of lies in politics. However, research in behavioral science suggests that we can address political deception through a number of effective strategies, which are brought together in the Pro-Truth Pledge.

First, we need to identify why current mechanisms of preventing political deception don't work well. The traditional mechanisms for identifying the truth about politics come from mainstream media and its fact-checking. However, polling shows that trust in the mainstream media has dropped from around 50 percent to 32 percent from 2000 to 2016, and only 29 percent trust fact-checking. No wonder fewer and fewer Americans are getting their news from mainstream media and engaging with fact-checkers.

At the same time, increasing numbers are using social media to get news, 62 percent according to studies. Unfortunately, a study by Stanford University shows that most social media news consumers cannot differentiate real from fake news stories. The situation is so bad that, according to research, in the three months before the presidential election the top 20 false news stories had more Facebook shares, reactions, and comments than did the top 20 true news articles.

Given the crumbling trust in traditional media and our vulnerability to lies on social media, we should not be surprised that politicians on both sides try to manipulate voters into believing lies. After all, the incentive for politicians is to get elected, not tell the truth. To be elected, politicians need to convey the appearance of trustworthiness – what Stephen Colbert infamously called "truthiness" – as opposed to being actually trustworthy. If politicians can safely ignore fact-checking by traditional news media, and instead use social media to get their followers to believe their claims, the scale is tilted toward post-truth politics.

In the long run, this tendency leads to high political polarization and the deterioration of trust in the political system. In other democratic states – Russia, Spain, Portugal, Germany, Turkey, Italy – post-truth politics led to the rise of authoritarian and corrupt regimes. We must do all we can to prevent this outcome in the US.

Tilting the scale toward truth requires a two-pronged approach, one targeting both private citizens and public figures. Research shows that, without any intervention, people tend to reject facts that go against their beliefs, and are more likely to deceive when they see others do so and also when it benefits their in-group. However, increased risk of suffering negative consequences, being reminded about our ethics, publicity about one's honesty, and committing in advance to honesty decreases lies for ordinary citizens. For public figures, research suggests that transparent, clear information about who is truthful, and reputational rewards for socially beneficial behavior such as honesty, and penalties for dishonesty are the most vital interventions.

To solve the problem of systemic lying, a group of behavioral scientists, along with many concerned citizens, have launched the Pro-Truth Pledge project, at ProTruthPledge.org.

Caption: Pro-Truth Pledge logo (Pro-Truth Pledge website)

This pledge asks all signees to commit to a set of truth-oriented behaviors. Whenever they share a news article, signees are encouraged to add a sentence stating that they took the pledge and verify that they fact-checked the article, which serves to remind people of their ethical commitment. Pledge-takers are encouraged to share publicly with their networks about taking the pledge, asking others to hold them accountable – thus deliberately increasing the risk of negative consequences of sharing fake news. Likewise, the pledge asks signees to hold others accountable, requesting those who share fake news to retract it. Further reinforcing all the above, pledge-takers can get pledge monthly newsletters, follow the Twitter and Facebook accounts of the pledge, join a community of fellow pledge-takers online or in-person, get truth-oriented resources, and volunteer to help with the pledge.

Public figures – politicians, journalists, media figures, CEOs, academics, ministers, speakers, and others – get additional benefits, in line with the research. They have the opportunity to share a paragraph about why they took the pledge and provide links to their online presence. The paragraph is then sent around in the pledge newsletter and posted on social media, as a way of providing a reputational reward for committing to truth-oriented behavior. Public figures also get their public information listed in a database on the pledge website and can post a badge on their own website about their commitment to the pledge, providing clarity to all about which public figures are committed to truthful behavior.

These rewards for public figures will grow more substantial as the pledge gets more popular and known, creating a virtuous cycle. The more private citizens and public figures sign the pledge and the more credibility it gets, the more incentives other public figures will have to sign it. While these early adopters will be most committed to honesty, behavioral science suggests that later adopters will be more likely to do so out of a desire to gain a reputation as honest, and thus will be more likely to cheat.

To address this problem, the pledge crowd-sources the fight against lies. One of the volunteer roles for the pledge is monitoring public figure signees. If a volunteer suspects that a public figure made a false statement, the volunteer would approach the person privately and ask for clarification. The matter can be resolved by the public figure issuing a retraction – everyone makes mistakes – or the volunteer realizing that the
public figure's statement is not false. If the matter is not resolved, the volunteer would then submit the case to a mediating committee of vetted and trained Pro-Truth Pledge volunteers. They would investigate the matter and give the public figure an opportunity to issue a retraction or explain why the statement is not false.

If the public figure refuses to do so, the mediating committee then assumes that the public figure lied, meaning made a deliberately false statement, and rules the person in contempt of the pledge. This ruling triggers a substantial reputational punishment. The mediating committee issues a media advisory to all relevant media venues that the public figure is in contempt of the pledge and puts that information on the pledge website. The committee also sends an action alert to all pledge-takers who are constituents to that public figure, asking them to tweet, post, text, call, write, meet with, and otherwise lobby the public figure to retract their words. A public figure who intends to lie is much better off not taking the pledge at all.

Will the pledge work to tilt the scale toward truth? In order to tell, we'll need to evaluate whether people are taking the pledge, and also whether the pledge changes their behavior.

Rolled out in late March, the pledge has over 1000 signees so far. The pledge-takers include a number of politicians, talk show hosts, academics, and public commentators who expressed strong enthusiasm for the pledge. The pledge has already had some positive mainstream media coverage during the March for Truth events on June 3, 2017.

Caption: Interview about the Pro-Truth Pledge at the March for Truth in Columbus (Screenshot by Gleb Tsipursky)

What about behavioral change? A retired US intelligence officer described how he saw an article "that played right to [his] particular political biases" and his "first inclination was to share it as quickly and widely as possible. But then [he] remembered the pledge [he'd] signed and put the brakes on." The story turned out to be false, and "that experience has led [him] to be much more vigilant in assessing, and sharing, stories that appeal to [his] political sensibilities."

A Christian pastor and community leader, Lorenzo Neal, took the Pro-Truth Pledge. He related how he "took the Pro-Truth Pledge because I expect our political leaders at every level of government to speak truth and not deliberately spread misinformation to the people they have been elected to serve. Having taken the pledge myself, I put forth the effort to continually gather information validating stories and headlines before sharing them on my social media outlets."

John Kirbow, a US Army veteran and member Special Operations community took the pledge. He then wrote a blog post about how it impacted him. He notes that, "I've verbally or digitally passed on bad information numerous times, I am fairly sure, as a result of honest mistakes or lack of vigorous fact checking." He describes how after taking the pledge, he felt "an open commitment to a certain attitude" to "think hard when I want to play an article or statistic which I'm not completely sold on." Having taken the Pro-Truth Pledge, he found it "really does seem to change one's habits," helping push him both to correct his own mistakes with an "attitude of humility and skepticism, and of honesty and moral sincerity," and also to encourage "friends and peers to do so as well."

Michael Smith, a candidate for Congress took the pledge, and later posted on his Facebook wall a screenshot of a tweet by Donald Trump criticizing minority and disabled children. After being called out on it, he went and searched Trump's feed. He could not find the original tweet, and while Trump may have deleted that tweet, the candidate edited his own Facebook post to say that "Due to a Truth Pledge I have taken I have to say I have not been able to verify this post." He indicated that he would be more careful with future postings.

Caption: Retraction image on Facebook of Michael Smith's original post (Screenshot by Gleb Tsipursky)

The evidence so far shows that the pledge has the potential to protect our democracy from the tide of lies. Whether it will succeed depends on how many people go to the website at ProTruthPledge.org and sign it, spread the word, lobby public figures to sign it, and monitor those who do. The early results are promising.

References

Allcott, H., & Gentzkow, M. (2017). Social media and fake news in the 2016 election. *National Bureau of Economic Research* 23089.

Ariely, D., & Jones, S. (2012). *The Honest Truth about Dishonesty: How We Lie to Everyone--Especially Others.*

Ariely, D., & Wertenbroch, K. (2002). Procrastination, deadlines, and performance: Self-control by precommitment. *Psychological Science* 13 (3), 219-224.

Barrera, O., Guriev, S., Henry, E., & Zhuravskaya, E. (2017). *Facts, Alternative Facts, and Fact Checking in Times of Post-Truth Politics* (No. 12220). CEPR Discussion Papers.

Connelly, B. L., Certo, S. T., Ireland, R. D., & Reutzel, C. R. (2010). Signaling theory: A review and assessment. *Journal of Management, 37*(1), 39-67.

Correia, V., & Festinger, L. (2014). *Biased Argumentation and Critical Thinking.*

Dietz, T., Ostrom, E., & Stern, P. C. (2003). The struggle to govern the commons. *Science, 302,*1907–1912.

Dunning, D. (2011). The Dunning–Kruger effect. *Advances in Experimental Social Psychology*, 44, 247-296.

Fazio, L. K., Brashier, N. M., Payne, B. K., & Marsh, E. J. (2015). Knowledge does not protect against illusory truth. *Journal of Experimental Psychology: General, 144*(5), 993.

Frijda, N. H., Manstead, A. S. R., & Bem, S. (2010). *Emotions and Beliefs: How Feelings Influence Thoughts.*

Garrett, R. K., & Weeks, B. E. (2013, February). The promise and peril of real-time corrections to political misperceptions. In *Proceedings of the 2013 conference on Computer supported cooperative work* (pp. 1047-1058). ACM.

Gino, F., Norton, M. I., & Ariely, D. (2010). The counterfeit self. *Psychological Science, 21*(5), 712-720.

Gottfried, J., & Shearer, E. (2016). News use across social media platforms 2016. *Pew Research*

Center, 26.

Guadagno, R. E., & Cialdini, R. B. (2010). Preference for consistency and social influence: A review of current research findings. *Social Influence, 5*(3), 152-163.

Guillory, J. J., & Geraci, L. (2013). Correcting erroneous inferences in memory: The role of source credibility. *Journal of Applied Research in Memory and Cognition, 2*(4), 201-209.

Kray, L. J., & Galinsky, A. D. (2003). The debiasing effect of counterfactual mind-sets: Increasing the search for disconfirmatory information in group decisions. *Organizational Behavior and Human Decision Processes, 91*(1), 69-81.

Kruger, J., & Dunning, D. (1999). Unskilled and unaware of it: How Difficulties in Recognizing One's Own
Incompetence Lead to Inflated Self-assessments. *Journal of Personality and Social Psychology, 77*(6), 1121-1134.

Mann, H., Garcia-Rada, X., Houser, D., & Ariely. D. (2014). Everybody else is doing it: Exploring social transmission of lying behavior. *PloS One, 9*(10).

Mazar, N., Amir, O., & Ariely, D. (2008). More ways to cheat-expanding the scope of dishonesty. *Journal of Marketing Research, 45*(6), 651-653.

Mazar, N., Amir, O., & Ariely, D. (2008). The dishonesty of honest people: A theory of self-concept maintenance. *Journal of Marketing Research, 45*(6), 633-644.

Mazar, N., Amir, O., & Ariely, D. (2006). Dishonesty in everyday life and its policy implications. *Journal
of Public Policy & Marketing, 25*(1), 117-126.

McCabe, D. L., & Trevino, L. K. (1993). Academic dishonesty: Honor codes and other contextual influences. *The Journal of Higher Education, 64*(5), 522. doi:10.2307/2959991.

Myers, T. A., Maibach, E. W., Roser-Renouf, C., Akerlof, K., & Leiserowitz, A. A. (2013). The relationship
between personal experience and belief in the reality of global warming. *Nature Climate Change, 3*(4), 343-347.

Nyhan, B., & Reifler, J. (2010). When corrections fail: The persistence of political misperceptions. *Political Behavior, 32*(2), 303-330.

Ostrom, E. (2015), *Governing the Commons.*

Shu, L. L., Mazar, N., Gino, F., Ariely, D., & Bazerman, M. H. (2012). Signing at the beginning makes ethics salient and decreases dishonest self-reports in comparison to signing at the end. *Proceedings of the National Academy of Sciences, 109*(38), 15197-15200.

Swire, B., Berinsky, A. J., Lewandowsky, S., & Ecker, U. K. (2017). Processing political misinformation: Comprehending the Trump phenomenon. *Royal Society Open Science, 4*(3), 160802.

Van Vugt, M. (2009). Averting the tragedy of the commons. *Current Directions in Psychological Science, 18*(3), 169-173.

Vogler, J. (2000), *The Global Commons: Environmental and Technological Governance*, 2nd ed.

Vraga, E. K., Tully, M., & Rojas, H. (2009). Media literacy training reduces perception of bias. *Newspaper
Research Journal, 30*(4), 68-81.

Zimmerman, R. S., & Connor, C. (1989). Health promotion in context: The effects of significant others on health behavior change." *Health Education Quarterly, 16*(1), 57-75.

Chapter 47: How Can We Tell Whether Comey's Firing Was Justified?

By Gleb Tsipursky

Caption: Photo of James Comey (Wikimedia Commons)

We all want our top investigative bodies to be headed by competent officials. We also all want to ensure that these officials can freely investigate other branches of the government – including the presidential administration – without fear of retribution. How can we tell whether Donald Trump's firing of FBI Director James Comey was meant to ensure competent leadership of the FBI, as Trump claims, or to prevent Comey from digging deeper into Trump's potential connections with Russia, as many Democrats claim?

Our personal political perspectives will strongly influence us to favor one explanation or the other, regardless of the truth. According to behavioral science research, our minds tend to interpret new information in accordance with our past beliefs – a thinking error known as the confirmation bias. Fortunately, we can fight the confirmation bias in such situations by evaluating the opinions of people who both have the most information and have political motivations to support one side, but fail to do so or even support the other side.

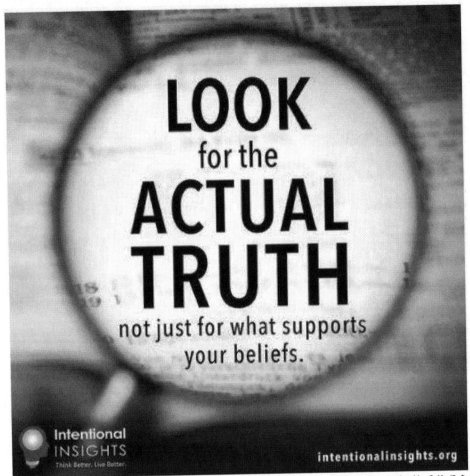

Caption: Meme saying "look for the actual truth, not just for what supports your beliefs" (Made for Intentional Insights by Lexie Holliday)

In this case, we can observe a number of prominent Republicans expressing concerns over Comey's firing. Senate Intelligence Chairman Richard Burr, a North Carolina Republican who heads the Senate's Russia investigation, stated that he was "troubled by the timing and reasoning" of Comey's firing, which "confuses an already difficult investigation for the Committee." So did a number of other influential Republican Senators, such as Bob Corker, who chairs the Senate Foreign Relations Committee and stated in response to Trump firing Comey that "It is essential that ongoing investigations are fulsome and free of political interference until their completion." Representative Justin Amash, who belongs to the conservative House Freedom Caucus, even stated that he intends to introduce legislation calling for creating an independent commission to investigate Russia's interference in the election. Pat Tiberi, a conservative member of the House, expressed potential support for a special prosecutor of the Trump and Russia connection and stated that "the White House needs to come clean."

Altogether, about 40 Republican members of Congress have expressed concerns over Comey's firing, while virtually every Democrat is calling for an independent commission or special prosecutor to evaluate Comey's firing. While some of these Republicans are known for breaking ranks at times, such as Senator John McCain, many others – such as Corker and Burr – are mainstream Republicans who generally toe the party line. This data on many of those in the know – federal lawmakers – who have clear political motivation to align with Trump firing Comey instead broke ranks provides strong evidence that the decision to fire Comey is less about incompetence and more about the Russian investigation than anything else.

Another thinking error playing a role in clouding our judgment is illusory correlation, namely an incorrect – illusory – perception of a connection between two events. Trump's administration claimed, in a memo by deputy Attorney General Rod Rosenstein that Trump referenced in his firing of Comey, that Comey lost support due to his handling of the investigation into Hillary Clinton's email server. Democrats claimed that Trump fired Comey because of Comey's investigation into the Trump-Russia connection as part of Russia's meddling in the US presidential elections.

One of these is an illusory connection, but which is it? Due to confirmation bias, Republicans will be likely to see the Trump-Russia connection as illusory. Democrats will tend to see the Clinton investigation connection as illusory.

Fortunately, we can use another technique from behavioral science to correct for this thinking error – consider the alternative. Consider a situation where Trump's true concerns lay with Comey's Clinton email server investigation. When would Trump fire Comey if this was the case? Trump would fire Comey when Trump entered office, as Trump did with a number of federal attorneys. Instead, Trump specifically made a decision to keep Comey in office when he took the presidency, despite knowing about Comey's handling of the email server. Trump specifically indicated, in a message loud and clear for the government investigative bodies, that he would not pursue any further investigation into Clinton's email server shortly after he was elected. As late as April 12, long after Trump had access to any secret information about Comey's handling of Clinton's email server and any other information relevant to Comey's pre-election activities, Trump said in an interview with Fox Business Network "I have confidence in [Comey]." Given this evidence, it seems quite unlikely that the real reason for Comey's firing is the Clinton email scandal.

What about the Trump-Russia investigation? According to Fox News, a conservative source, the day before he was fired, Comey met with the Republican and Democrat Senators on the Senate intelligence committee, Senators Richard Burr and Mark Warner. At the meeting, he discussed the inquiry into Russian hacking in the presidential election and potential involvement of Trump and members of his administration in this hacking. Burr and Warner both wanted Comey to speed up the investigation, and Comey responded that he needed more resources to conduct the investigation. Earlier, Comey allegedly made a request for more resources for this investigation from Rosenstein, whose later memo was used by Trump as a reason to fire Comey. Given the evidence of the closeness of the timing of Comey's requests for more resources and Trump firing Comey, the connection between the investigation into Russian hacking and the firing of Comey appears to be true rather than illusory.

Now, this behavioral science-based conclusion does not favor the conservative perspective, and instead favors the liberal one. Will it mean that conservatives dismiss it out of hand? To determine if this is the case, I went on the conservative radio network 700WLW to speak on this topic with the well-known radio show host Scott Sloan two days after Comey's dismissal. Sloan is known as a strong proponent of Christian and conservative values but not someone who practices post-truth politics by dismissing the truth in favor of his personal beliefs. We had a civil discussion, during which Sloan acknowledged the validity of this behavioral science-informed perspective and accepted that the evidence pointed against Trump's narrative. It is highly likely that our conversation on his radio show swayed some of his conservative audience to change their perspective as well.

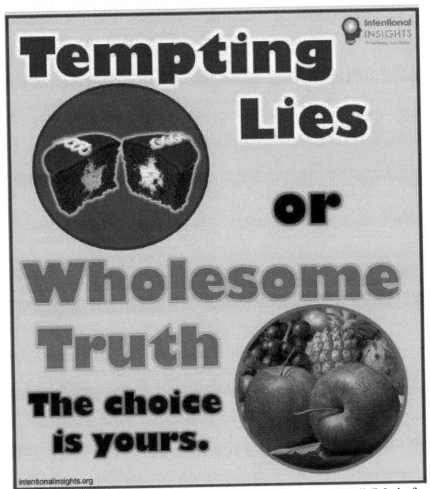

Caption: Meme saying "tempting lies or wholesome truth: the choice is yours" (Made for Intentional Insights by Jane A. Gordon)

This interview shows the benefits of using such behavioral science-based approaches to bridge the political divide and have reasonable conversations that result in people going against their current values and changing their minds to match reality. What it takes is knowing why our minds are likely to lead us astray and addressing these internal biases using science-informed strategies to do so. In this case, the evidence – once corrected for political bias – points conclusively, in a way that both reasonable conservative and liberals can agree on, to Trump firing Comey due to concerns over the FBI's investigation into Russian interference in the election.

References

Chapman, L. J. (1967). Illusory correlation in observational report. *Journal of Verbal Learning and Verbal*

    Behavior, 6(1), 151-155.

Frey, D., Schulz-Hardt, S., & Stahlberg, D. (2013). Information seeking among individuals and groups and

    possible consequences for decision-making in business and politics. *Understanding group behavior, 2,* 211-225.

Hirt, E. R., & Markman, K. D. (1995). Multiple explanation: A consider-an-alternative strategy for debiasing judgments. *Journal of Personality and Social Psychology, 69*(6), 1069.

Chapter 48: How Can Facts Trump Ideology?

By Gleb Tsipursky

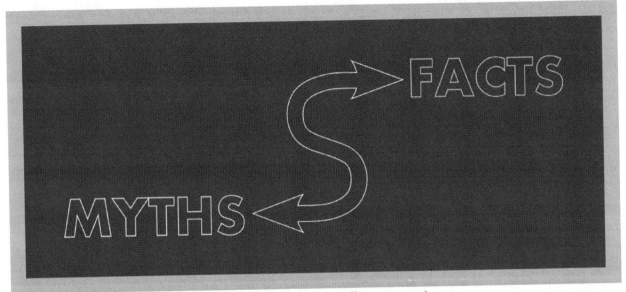

Caption:Image of arrow between facts and myths (Wikimedia commons)

Extensive evidence emerged in recent days that Donald Trump pressured and then fired FBI Director James Comey to block the FBI's investigation of Trump's administration over possible collusion with Russia. Yet a May 24 poll shows that only 24 percent of Republicans believe that this firing had to do with Comey's investigation of the administration, in comparison to 60 percent for all who took the poll. An earlier poll on May 11 shows that 24 percent of Republicans believed that Trump's actions had to do with the FBI's investigation, while 47 percent of the total poll respondents. Clearly, the evidence that emerged over these two weeks moved the general population to update their perspective to see Trump's actions as stemming from a desire to hinder the FBI's investigation. Why did the evidence fail to shift Republicans, and can we do anything to help truth trump politics?

Research on behavioral science shows that we prefer to believe whatever matches our ideological perspective, regardless of the facts. For instance, when presented with accurate information that contradicts their current political perspective, people tend to reject this information and actually feel more attaching to their current political beliefs, a phenomenon known as the backfire effect. As a scholar of behavioral science and public activist, I decided to focus on developing research-based strategies to help people whose ideological motivations push them to believe falsehoods to instead update their beliefs toward the truth.

Caption: Meme saying "look for the actual truth, not for what just supports your beliefs" (Made for Intentional Insights by Lexie Holliday)

To test and refine these research-based strategies, I have gone on radio shows with radio hosts to talk about controversial topics. As an example, two days after Donald Trump fired FBI Director James Comey, I went on the conservative radio network 700WLW to have an interview with the well-known radio show host Scott Sloan. Sloan is known as a strong proponent of Christian and conservative values, and he had a friendly chat with Trump on his show during the election campaign.

Trump has made a series of claims about why he chose to fire Comey, generally boiling down to Trump trying to ensure competent leadership of the FBI and concerns about what Trump alleged as Comey's incompetence in handling the investigation of Hillary Clinton's email server. By contrast, the Democratic leadership claimed that Trump fired Comey to prevent the latter from digging deeper into Trump's potential connections with Russia and allegations of collusion with Russia on hacking the US presidential election.

Instead of jumping into the thick of the Comey-Trump debate, at the start of our discussion I established a shared sense of goals for both of us. I noted that we all want our top investigative bodies to be headed by competent officials, and we also all want to ensure that these officials can freely investigate other branches of the government – including the presidential administration – without fear of retribution or obstruction of these investigations. Sloan agreed, establishing that common bond between us, making us allies trying to solve a common problem instead of potential enemies.

Following that, I appealed to his identity and emotions by establishing both of us as truth-oriented individuals. To do so, I talked about how all people are vulnerable to a thinking error known as the confirmation bias, a tendency of our minds to interpret new information in accordance with our past beliefs. Indeed, only 24 percent of Republicans believe that Trump fired Comey in part to disrupt the Russian investigation, while 75 percent of Democrats believed that. Then, I talked about how since Sloan and I have mutual shared goals both of ensuring competent leadership and of preventing obstruction, we need to figure out effective ways of addressing the confirmation bias. One effective way to fight the confirmation bias involves evaluating the opinions of people who both have the most information and have political motivations to support one side, but fail to do so or even support the other side. Sloan agreed that this seemed a reasonable way to address the confirmation bias.

Caption: Meme saying "our minds are most comfortable dealing with reality in binary terms, but reality is seldom, if ever, binary" (Made for Intentional Insights by Wayne Straight)

Next, I pointed out that pretty much all Democratic members of Congress and a number of prominent Republicans expressed concerns over Comey's firing, such as Senator John McCain. Sloan countered that McCain is known as a maverick who occasionally breaks ranks, and is part of a broader group of Republicans who are not fond of Trump. In my response, I highlighted that plenty of other Republicans who generally toe the party line and even supported Trump actually came out to express concerns. For example, Senate Intelligence Chairman Richard Burr, a North Carolina Republican who heads the Senate's Russia investigation, stated that he was "troubled by the timing and reasoning" of Comey's firing, which "confuses an already difficult investigation for the Committee." So did a number of other influential Republican Senators, such as Bob Corker. He chairs the Senate Foreign Relations Committee and stated in response to Trump firing Comey that "It is essential that ongoing investigations are fulsome and free of political interference until their completion."

Altogether, about 40 Republican members of Congress have expressed concerns over Comey's firing, while virtually every Democrat is calling for an independent commission or special prosecutor to evaluate Comey's firing. This data on many of those in the know – federal lawmakers – who have clear political motivation to align with Trump firing Comey instead broke ranks provides strong evidence that the decision to fire Comey is less about incompetence and more about the Russian investigation than anything else. After some further conversation, Sloan acknowledged the validity of this behavioral science-informed perspective and accepted that the evidence pointed against Trump's narrative.

When I share about such conversations, many wonder whether they are a fluke, a one-time incident. Not so. In a previous conversation with Sloan, I used similar tactics to talk about the terrorist attack at Ohio State, where I teach. In that terrorist attack on November 2016, a Somali Muslim, Abdul Razak Ali Artan, rammed his car into a crowd of students and then knifed several people before being shot dead by a university policeman.

Predictably, conservatives reacted by condemning Muslims. For instance, the State Treasurer of Ohio and current Senate candidate Josh Mandel tweeted "looks like Radical Islamic terror came to my alma mater today," despite the lack of evidence. What we know is that Artan expressed fear of Islamophobia in an August interview with the Ohio State student newspaper. He also expressed anger in a Facebook post right before the attack, saying "I am sick and tired of seeing my fellow Muslim brothers and sisters being killed and tortured EVERYWHERE… I can't take it anymore." These statements are not characteristic of "Radical Islamic terror," but reflect fear and anger over the treatment of Muslims.

Like many conservatives, Sloan associated Muslims with terrorism and wanted to persecute them. I approached the ensuing discussion by considering his emotions and goals, meeting him where he was as opposed to where I would have liked him to be. Research suggests that conservatives value safety and security first and foremost, and their negative feelings toward Muslims result from perceptions of Muslims as threats to safety and security. As we began talking, I started by validating the host's emotions, saying it was natural and intuitive to feel anger and fear toward Muslims, and I felt such emotions myself after the attack, thus creating an emotional bond between us. Then, I talked about how research shows that sometimes such gut reactions lead us astray in pursuing safety and security. For instance, our brains are wired to take shortcuts by stereotyping groups negatively based on the actions of one member of the group, a thinking error known as the horns effect.

We discussed how in 2015, there were seven terrorist acts in the United States, committed by a total of nine terrorists. Six of the nine were motivated, in some part, by Islamic beliefs. A 2011 Pew survey estimated that the United States had 1.8 million Muslim adults. Dividing this number by the six who committed terrorist acts gives you a one-in-300,000 chance that any Muslim you see would commit a terrorist act in a given year. That's like picking out a terrorist from the number of people in several football stadiums. So using "Muslim" as a filter for "terrorist" actually, wastes our precious resources dedicated to safety and security, and lets the real terrorists commit attacks.

Then, I discussed with Sloan how if we persecute Muslims, for instance through creating a Muslim registry or through heavy policing of Muslim neighborhoods, Muslim communities would be much less likely to help us root out potential terrorists in their midst. So, I concluded, for the sake of making us safer, we shouldn't antagonize Muslim communities, which so far have been quite cooperative in addressing terror concerns, according to the FBI. Finally, I discussed how rhetoric critical of Muslims and anti-Muslim policies will prod more Muslims to become terrorists. For instance, BBC reports that terrorist groups have used Trump's rhetoric in their recruitment tapes. I also pointed out the specific comments made by Artan as evidence for this point.

This quite clearly makes us less safe and secure, I told Sloan, and so despite any negative feelings we may have toward Muslims, it's unwise to act on them. Just like if we hear criticism from our boss and want to scream in his or her face, it may not be the rational thing to do if we value our jobs. Just like we may want to take a second piece of chocolate cake, it may not be the rational thing to do if we value our health. We shouldn't go with our gut on policies and rhetoric toward Muslims if we value our security. In the end, Sloan agreed with my points and updated his views on Muslims – not because he felt like being nice and generous and kind toward Muslims, but because he valued his security and safety.

Notably, Sloan retained information from our conversations and integrated them into his later commentary. For instance, afterward in his show, Sloan discussed how statistically speaking, any given Muslim has an infinitesimally small chance of being a terrorist. Neither does Sloan feel that our conversation was a "gotcha" game, as he invited me to his show four times already.

Sloan is far from unique: Bill Cunningham is another prominent conservative talk show host who had Trump on his show, is ranked 27 among "Most Important Radio Show Talk Hosts" in America by *Talkers Magazine*, and is known as a strong supporter of Trump. Cunningham's show invited me to talk about Trump's allegations that Barack Obama wiretapped Trump Tower in the 2016 presidential election.

While I intended to first connect emotionally and establish shared goals, unfortunately Cunningham did not offer me the time to do so. The show started off with a question that was somewhat unexpected for me: Cunningham asked me if it is true that the NSA tracks keywords that might cause it to passively surveil people. Certainly, I replied, based on my knowledge of the NSA's surveillance. Cunningham then asked whether Trump might then be accurate in his claim that he was surveilled. Thinking fast, I replied that if Trump had claimed that the NSA passively surveilled him, Trump might well be accurate – but this would not be newsworthy and it is not what he said.

Specifically, I cited the details of Trump's tweets, such as "Terrible! Just found out that Obama had my "wires tapped" in Trump Tower just before the victory. Nothing found. This is McCarthyism!" and also "How low has President Obama gone to tapp [sic] my phones during the very sacred election process. This is Nixon/Watergate. Bad (or sick) guy!" With the specific details of these tweets as the center of our discussion, I highlighted that Trump specifically called out Obama personally for wiretapping Trump Tower, and compared the situation to McCarthyism and Watergate. I pointed out to

Cunningham that these comparisons and the active placing of blame on Obama resulted in the storm of media coverage, and Cunningham concurred.

Then, I used a strategy from behavioral science known as consider the alternative. I asked if Trump truly had evidence of Obama ordering Trump Tower wiretapped, would Trump have simply tweeted about it as he did, without providing that evidence? He is the president, after all, and can have access to any information he wants. Next, I asked Cunningham to imagine himself in Trump's place: what would he do if he suspected Obama wiretapped his headquarters in the election. Having thought about it, Cunningham stated that he would have gathered the FBI and NSA directors in his office, and get them to give any information they had about this matter. He would not have simply tweeted about it, and then provided no further information. Thus, by the end of the interview, although it got off to a rocky start, these behavioral science strategies resulted in Cunningham acknowledging that Trump behaved inappropriately in tweeting his allegations about Obama without providing any evidence. In all cases, it is highly likely that our conversation on these radio shows swayed some of their conservative audience to change their perspectives as well, due to the credibility of Sloan and Cunningham among their listeners.

You can use these same strategies in your everyday conversation with conservatives or liberals who let their ideological perspectives cloud their evaluation of reality. What it takes is establishing shared goals with the other person, engaging emotionally by calling for a mutual orientation toward truth, and incorporating into conversations information about how our minds are likely to lead us astray, and how to address these problems. An excellent way to encourage a mutual orientation toward the truth and bridge the political divide is to get all participants in a conversation to take the Pro-Truth Pledge, a recent behavioral science instrument designed to reverse the tide of lies in our public sphere. I had interviews on both conservative and liberal shows where the hosts took the pledge, which then shaped our conversations in a highly productive manner oriented toward an accurate evaluation of reality

Caption: Meme saying "Why do we seek the truth? Because it's the right thing to do" (Made for Intentional Insights by Wayne Straight)

For example, a liberal candidate for Congress who took the Pro-Truth Pledge posted on his Facebook wall a screenshot of a tweet by Trump criticizing minority and disabled children. After being questioned on whether this was an actual tweet or photoshopped one, the candidate searched Trump's feed. He could not find the original tweet, and while Trump may have deleted that tweet, the candidate edited his own Facebook post to say that "Due to a Truth Pledge I have taken I have to say I have not been able to verify this post." He indicated that he would be more careful with future postings.

I hope these strategies empower you to help facts trump ideology!

References

Arntz, A., Rauner, M., & Van den Hout, M. (1995). "If I feel anxious, there must be danger": Ex-consequentia reasoning in inferring danger in anxiety disorders. *Behaviour Research and Therapy, 33*(8), 917-925.

Burton, S., Cook, L. A., Howlett, E., & Newman, C. L. (2015). Broken halos and shattered horns: overcoming the biasing effects of prior expectations through objective information disclosure. *Journal of the Academy of Marketing Science, 43*(2), 240-256.

Haidt, J. (2012). *The righteous mind: Why good people are divided by politics and religion.* Vintage.

Hirt, E. R., & Markman, K. D. (1995). Multiple explanation: A consider-an-alternative strategy for debiasing judgments. *Journal of Personality and Social Psychology, 69*(6), 1069.

Kunda, Z. (1990). The case for motivated reasoning. *Psychological Bulletin, 108*(3), 480.

Nickerson, R. S. (1998). Confirmation Bias: A ubiquitous phenomenon in many guises. *Review of general psychology, 2*(2), 175.

Nyhan, B. & Reifler, J. (2010) When corrections fail: The persistence of political misperceptions *Polit Behav, 32*(2) 303.

Chapter 49: Why Mainstream Media Need to Be Careful About Criticizing Conservatives

By Gleb Tsipursky

Caption: Image of newspaper saying "breaking news" (Geralt/Pixabay)

Many mainstream media outlets criticized conservatives with a broad brush over the Montana Congressional special election winner Republican Greg Gianforte assaulting a reporter, Ben Jacobs. Yet, according to behavioral science research conducted by myself and others, such criticism may end up hurting the safety of journalists, instead of advancing freedom of the press and pursuit of the truth.

First, the facts of the incident itself. According to the evidence available, Gianforte grabbed Jacobs by the neck, slammed him to the ground, and punched him. The episode was witnessed and corroborated by multiple independent witnesses, including *Fox News* and *BuzzFeed* reporters. The local sheriff – who earlier gave a financial contribution to Gianforte's campaign – charged Gianforte with misdemeanor assault.

How did conservatives respond? The assault took place on the evening of May 24, and *Fox News* – which had a reporter on scene – quickly wrote up a fair and balanced account. The *Fox News* account specifically stated that "at no point did any of us who witnessed this assault see Jacobs show any form of physical aggression toward Gianforte," which Fox News certainly did not have to do. In fact, the Fox News story contradicted the official statement offered by Gianforte's campaign, which accused Jacobs of starting the fight by grabbing Gianforte's wrist, a statement now widely seen as a lie. A conservative venue, *TheBlaze*, ran a piece critical of Gianforte's statement, and *The New York Post* ran a similar piece.

Many conservative politicians also responded in a worthy manner. Within 24 hours of the assault, Speaker of the House Paul Ryan stated that "There's never a call for physical altercations… I think he should apologize." This length of time is quite reasonable, as Ryan needed to find out the relevant facts. Steve Daines, a Montana Senator and major supporter for Gianforte, also called on Gianforte to apologize, adding "I do not condone violence in any way." Under such pressure, Gianforte rescinded his earlier deceptive official statement and instead apologized, saying "I should not have treated that reporter that way, and I'm sorry Ben Jacobs."

Certainly, some conservatives did not respond well. The conservative radio show host Rush Limbaugh practiced victim-blaming, implying that Gianforte's actions were not a big deal because "the journalist was being insolent and disrespectful." *The Daily Caller*, a prominent conservative website, ran a story about some Montana voters supporting Gianforte's actions. A former Republican congressman defended Gianforte.

Such problematic responses that appeared to condone or ignore violence against reporters do not represent the majority of conservative responses. Nonetheless, *The New York Times* ran a story entitled "A reporter was body slammed, but some conservatives want the news media to apologize." Chris Cuomo of *CNN* had harsh words for the Republican Party on the morning after the incident, asking "You know what I hear? Silence. Where is the GOP?" *The Philadelphia Inquirer* carried a piece entitled "In Trump's America, that reporter body slam didn't come out of nowhere."

Other mainstream venues downplayed condemnation by conservatives of Gianforte's behavior and emphasized those standing by him. *The Washington Post*, in its editorial responding to the incident, quoted Ryan's words supporting the right of people from Montana to elect their representative, while failing to mention that he demanded an apology. In turn, *The Atlantic* quoted a joke made by Republican Representative Mark Sanford, while conveniently forgetting that Sanford's response also condemned the culture of hostility toward the media that contributed to Gianforte's behavior.

Unfortunately, the content on these mainstream media venues fails to provide an accurate depiction of reality, which harms journalist safety. Most of the content does acknowledge – in the depths of each piece – that many conservatives condemned Gianforte's behavior. Yet behavioral science research on news consumption shows that 59 percent of Americans are casual readers who only read the headlines. Thus, many casual independent or conservative readers would fail to perceive the widespread condemnation by conservative leaders of Gianforte's assault.

This outcome harms the safety of journalists. Research shows that our minds interpret new information in accordance with our past beliefs—a thinking error known as the confirmation bias. The confirmation bias is one of several thinking errors—known in behavioral science scholarship as cognitive biases—that lead

222

to motivated reasoning, where people pre-select a certain conclusion and reach that conclusion regardless of the facts. Fortunately, we can fight the confirmation bias in such situations by evaluating the opinions of prominent influencers who have political motivations to support one side, but fail to do so or even support the other side. Such strategies have effectively changed people's perspectives even in our current polarized environment. Unfortunately, many mainstream venues failed their readership by not conveying the data needed for them to draw accurate conclusions and thus advance press freedom.

Caption: Meme saying "lizard brain thinking is killing democracy, please think rationally" (Made for Intentional Insights by Ed Coolidge)

Another problem comes from one of the strongest findings in behavioral science, which shows that human beings respond very strongly to positive reinforcement. Through the style of their coverage painting all conservatives with a broad brush, these mainstream venues fail to provide positive reinforcement to conservatives who behaved in a prosocial manner. Research suggests that optimal performance comes from a combination of internal and external motivations. External incentives according to research, are especially crucial for promoting prosocial behavior such as protecting freedom of the press.

A further issue is the equating of Trump's behavior with Gianforte's actions. Conservative venues such as *Breitbart* immediately took the opportunity to condemn such comparisons, and call out what the article depicted as media "hypocrisy" for failing to do the same when liberals used violence. As others have accurately pointed out, while Trump's actions help create a climate of hostility to the media, it is much more difficult to connect Gianforte's actions to Trump's words. Drawing such connections undermines the already-low media credibility. A much better model for reporting on this connection came from a conservative venue, *The American Conservative*. It ran a piece that accurately describes how the hostility to mainstream media among Republicans predated Trump, while acknowledging that Trump ramped up this hostility, and criticizing Gianforte for lacking anger management skills. Such reporting, by providing an accurate depiction that attributes only a small part of the blame to Trump's actions, helps protect journalists.

Next time, these mainstream venues need to provide accurate reporting to avoid undercutting their credibility, to praise prosocial behavior to create incentives and positive reinforcement, and to have all readers take away accurate impressions from their headlines. You can make a difference by writing letters to the editor and making social media posts asking journalists to commit to accurate reporting and to take the Pro-Truth Pledge for the sake of protecting the safety and freedom of the press. What you can do right now is take the pledge yourself at ProTruthPledge.org to show your own commitment to the truth and encourage those in your personal network to do so as well.

References

Baron, Alan, and Mark Galizio. "Positive and negative reinforcement: Should the distinction be preserved?." *The Behavior Analyst* 28.2 (2005): 85-98.

Bénabou, R., & Tirole, J. (2006). Incentives and prosocial behavior. *American economic review, 96*(5), 1652-1678.

Klayman, J. (1995). Varieties of confirmation bias. *Psychology of learning and motivation, 32*, 385-418.

Kreps, D. M. (1997). Intrinsic motivation and extrinsic incentives. *The American Economic Review, 87*(2), 359-364.

Kunda, Z. (1990). The case for motivated reasoning. *Psychological bulletin, 108*(3), 480.

Newman, N., Fletcher, R., Kalogeropoulos, A., Levy, D. A., & Nielsen, R. K. (2017). Reuters Institute Digital News Report 2017.

Chapter 50: The One Thing Trump Got Right On Charlottesville

By Gleb Tsipursky

Caption: Photo of car involved in car ramming attack (Wikimedia commons)

Both Democratic and Republican leaders roundly denounced President Donald Trump's statement putting "blame on both sides" about the violence at the "Unite the Right" rally in Charlottesville, NC on August 12. However, while I personally find reprehensible various forms of white nationalism, racism, and neo-Nazism, Trump's words that both sides deserve a degree of blame have some validity. A broader context provides more clarity on where Trump is right, and where he is not.

Let's start with a recap of what happened. Far-right groups – those who identify as white supremacists, neo-Nazis, Ku Klux Klan members, alt-right supporters, and others – gathered in Charlottesville to protest the removal of a statue of the Confederate general Robert E. Lee. As is typical at such events, counterprotesters gathered, and fights broke out between the groups. Such violence occurred at previous rallies, but what made the Charlottesville events uniquely horrible was what Attorney General Jeff Sessions decried as an act domestic terrorism. A man apparently holding neo-Nazi beliefs deliberately rammed his car into a crowd of counterprotesters, killing one person and injuring 19.

Immediately after the events on August 12, Trump made a statement blaming the "violence on many sides." Democrats widely condemned Trump's lack of directness about who to blame for the violence, as did many Republicans. For example, Orrin Hatch, the Senate's most senior Republican, tweeted "We should call evil by its name. My brother didn't give his life fighting Hitler for Nazi ideas to go unchallenged here at home." Another Republican Senator, Cory Gardner, tweeted similar sentiments: "Mr. President – we must call evil by its name. These were white supremacists and this was domestic terrorism." Fox News, normally supportive of Trump, reported thoroughly on Republican pressure on Trump to condemn the far-right by name.

Under such pressure, Trump made another statement on August 14, echoing the kind of language used by Hatch and Gardner in their tweets: "Racism is evil and those who cause violence in its name are criminals and thugs, including the KKK, neo-Nazis and white supremacists." However, to the consternation of his staff, he backed away from that statement on August 15 and returned to his previous stance, saying "you had a group on one side that was bad and you had a group on the other side that was also very violent," the former referring to the far-right and the latter to the counter-protesters, who he described as "charging with clubs in hands." Again, he faced criticism from prominent Republicans, such as Congressman Steve Stivers, chairman of the National Republican Congressional Committee, who tweeted "I don't understand what's so hard about this. White supremacists and Neo-Nazis are evil and shouldn't be defended." Rubio tweeted "The organizers of events which inspired & led to #charlottesvilleterroristattack are 100% to blame for a number of reasons." Fox News again had a report on the criticism by prominent Republicans of Trump's "both sides" remarks.

Is such criticism fair? Due to my personal beliefs about the despicable morality of far-right supporters, it is tempting for me to blame all the violence on them. Such temptation comes from the horns effect, a psychological thinking error where if we don't like one aspect of someone or something, the dislike will make us evaluate all other aspects more negatively as well. The horns effect helps explain why those who have implicit bias toward minority groups tend to avoid hiring or promoting them at the same rate as majority groups, and can be seen on a broader demographic level in statistics on the wage gap. It also applies in situations like the one in Charlottesville, where if we do not like something – in this case, the far-right – we are tempted to blame all bad things, such as violence, on them.

The evidence shows otherwise. After all, we know that it's not simply the far-right protesters who came with guns, sticks, shields, helmets, and torches. Some counterprotesters also had sticks, helmets, and shields. Clearly, at least some people on both sides were prepared for violence.

While the large majority of counterprotesters expressed peaceful sentiments, a minority came from the Antifa movement. Antifa refers to "anti-fascism," and unites many extreme leftists. Many Antifa members endorse violent tactics to oppose extreme conservative ideologies, and are willing to use violence against hate speech and not simply for defensive purposes only, known as Nazi punching. Indeed, video evidence of the Charlottesville events, along with firsthand accounts, demonstrates both sides participated in the violence, and both sides engaged in aggressive as well as defensive actions.

For instance, here are the words from some Antifa activists themselves: "Before the [car] attack occurred, we chased the Nazis out of their park, removing their platform." As another example, here is the report of a journalist on the scene from *The Nation*, a left-leaning publication and thus having no reason to inflate leftist violence, described the following:

A phalanx of black-helmeted white supremacists – members of the Traditionalist Workers Party, Identity Evropa, American Vanguard, and other hate warriors – commanded the steps at the southeast corner of the park, repelling attempted incursions by Wobblies, communists, and a multiracial cast of irregulars eager to fight back. Water bottles and other projectiles flew in both directions, while police tear-gas canisters thudded into an adjacent parking lot, often times lobbed back into the park by plucky leftists. As the violence boiled over the green rim of the park, the intersection of Market and 2nd Streets became the contested arena, with combatants attacking each other with fists and sticks during brief, intense skirmishes.

Engaging in "attempted incursions," throwing projectiles, and "chasing the Nazis out of the park, removing their platform" helps demonstrate that Antifa did not simply engage in defensive actions, as they were often portrayed, but also in offensive actions. This is the context in which the horrible act of domestic terrorism occurred. So Trump is right to blame both sides for violence.

However, Trump is wrong in failing to condemn strongly the act of domestic terrorism, both initially in his August 12 remarks, and in his backtracking during the August 15 remarks, where he glossed over this uniquely terrible aspect of the Charlottesville violence. After all, clashes between far-right supporters and Antifa members happen with regularity. Such clashes are deplorable, as violence has no place in our political system. There is a reason why one of the founding principles of America, our freedom of speech, is epitomized by the phrase ""I disapprove of what you say, but I will defend to the death your right to say it."

Members of both sides went beyond the line in Charlottesville, and deserve proportionate criticism – and punishment – to the extent they crossed the line. The large majority of counterprotesters were peaceful, and only a small minority were violent, while the far-right protesters were much more violent as a whole. So even before the car terrorist attack, much more of the blame lies on the far-right for the violence, but some does lie on the far-left. Commentators who fail to acknowledge this reality and say that all blame rests on the side of the far-right, as did Rubio, will lose credibility from those who care about the facts, as opposed to just scoring political points.

Of course, the much more egregious crossing of the line came from the neo-Nazi supporter who deliberately rammed his car into counterprotesters. In an ideal world – one where commentators both aimed to speak the truth and prevent future violence – their remarks would proportionately criticize both sides for the hand-to-hand violence, with more of the blame for that on the far-right. However, they need to place the brunt of censure for the violence on the domestic terrorism incident, for the extreme nature of that attack is something we should all abhor and denounce. Again, this applies only to commentary about the violence involved, rather than the morality of the two sides, where I have no doubt of the moral high ground of those who opposed the neo-Nazi and other far-right extremists.

You can make a difference in promoting a truth-oriented world by emailing and tweeting commentators who fail to appropriately apportion blame for the violence challenging them to revise their remarks and take the Pro-Truth Pledge to commit to truth in their commentary.

References
Burton, S., Cook, L. A., Howlett, E., & Newman, C. L. (2015). Broken halos and shattered horns: overcoming the biasing effects of prior expectations through objective information disclosure. *Journal of the Academy of Marketing Science, 43*(2), 240-256.

Garcia, J., Hernández, P. J., & Lopez-Nicolas, A. (2001). How wide is the gap? An investigation of gender

       wage differences using quantile regression. *Empirical economics*, *26*(1), 149-167.

Lee, C. (2012). Making race salient: Trayvon Martin and implicit bias in a not yet post-racial society. *NCL*

       Rev., *91*, 1555.

Chapter 51: Trump's Transgender Gaslighting

By Gleb Tsipursky

Caption: Photo from Incirlik Air Base Lesbian, Gay, Bisexual and Transgender committee (Airman 1st Class Kristan Campbell/Incirlik Air Base)

President Donald Trump signed a directive on Friday August 25 following up on his earlier tweets that he "will not accept or allow transgender individuals to serve in any capacity in the U.S. Military." Whatever you think about the decree, the spin from the Trump administration about it amounts to gaslighting of the transgender community.

Consider the terms of this order. It prevents any new openly transgender recruits from joining the armed forces. It also order the military to evaluate the status of currently-serving transgender soldiers and potentially get rid of them as well in line with Trump's original tweet. Transgender troops decried the order, saying it will create "complete inequality," in the words of one. The director of the LGBTQ advocacy group Palm Center said that Trump is "pull[ing] the rug out from under a group of service members who have been defending our country."

By contrast, the leader of the conservative Family Research Council praised Trump, stating that "political correctness doesn't win wars - and the president is ending policies that pretends it does." Of course, the same statements could be made - and were made - about allowing women to serve in the military.

Any reasonable person can see that the decree blatantly discriminates against transgender individuals, meaning treating them differently and worse than others. Yet the Trump administration explicitly denied this reality. According to the official briefing the press on the directive, it did not represent in any way discrimination against transgender individuals. The official stated that Trump will "continue to ensure that the rights of the LGBTQ community" are protected, and is not going back on his campaign promise in 2016 to "fight for" that community.

Why make statements that are so clearly false? There is no doubt that the directive discriminates against transgender people. So what explains the blatant lies?

This type of deception falls into the category of gaslighting, a psychological manipulation that aims to create doubt about the nature of reality. Often occurring in abusive relationships, gaslighting is so harmful that victims often report that the impact of this manipulation is worse than the original offense. It can make you doubt your reality, grow confused, vulnerable, and uncertain, and thus fail to fend off the manipulations of the perpetrator and even fall into accepting their reality, known as the gaslight effect.

Trump's administration has used gaslighting extensively as a psychological weapon. Denying reality creates confusion and uncertainty, a highly useful outcome since the victims of the gaslighting are unsure about what to do next. Should they expend their resources demonstrating the obvious truth of reality, or should they focus on addressing the problem at hand?

In this case, the transgender community is the target of Trump's gaslighting. The issue they face is whether to address the blatant lies coming from the White House about the decree, or emphasize fighting Trump's discriminatory actions.

The solution is to make the gaslighting tactic itself unacceptable. Political and social science research shows that trust is vital for healthy democracies. Citizens in a democracy have a basic expectation of their public officials being trustworthy, in their words and actions. In return, citizens comply with laws, pay taxes, and cooperate with other government initiatives. By comparison to a democracy, an autocratic state bears a much higher resource burden of policing to make its citizens comply with its laws. When political leaders act in ways that destroy trust - as the Trump administration is doing through misleading statements and outright lies - people will increasingly stop complying with laws and paying taxes.

While Trump is making short-term gains for conservatives, he is undermining the stability of our political system as a whole. No one - neither liberals nor conservatives - want the chaos and disorder that would result from the destruction of trust. All can recognize the terrible dangers posed by such denial of reality to our democracy.

Even worse, other politicians, such as New Jersey Governor Chris Christie, are adopting Trump's tactics. For instance, Christie ordered a number of state-run beaches in New Jersey closed on Friday, June 30, 2017, yet he used a closed state beach in Island Beach State Park for himself and his family on July 2, 2017. At a press conference later that same day, he was asked about being on the beach during the time of the beach shut-down order. In a classic example of gaslighting, Christie said ""I didn't get any sun today."

When Christie's spokesperson was shown the pictures, the spokesperson responded "He did not get any sun. He had a baseball hat on."

Christie's use of gaslighting to justify corruption and abuse of power points to the normalization of gaslighting within our political system. Only by coming together in a nonpartisan manner to call out such lies and commit to truth through the Pro-Truth Pledge can we hope to make gaslighting unacceptable and preserve our democracy.

References

Abramson, K. (2014). Turning up the Lights on Gaslighting. *Philosophical Perspectives*, *28*(1), 1-30.
Braithwaite, V., & Levi, M. (Eds.). (2003). *Trust and governance*.
Stern, R. (2007). *The Gaslight Effect: How to Spot and Survive the Hidden Manipulations Other People Use to Control Your Life*.

Chapter 52: Fighting the Phoenix Rally's Normalization of Post-Truth Politics

By Gleb Tsipursky

Caption: Donald Trump with fist raised (Wikimedia commons)

Donald Trump's rally speech in Phoenix on August 22 was full of falsehoods. He gave a revisionist and false history of his reaction to the Charlottesville violence to make himself look better, made false statements about media reporting, and misled the audience over his economic achievements. The speech points to the normalization of post-truth politics, when appeals to personal beliefs and emotions wins out over objective facts. To avoid this normalization, we need to borrow the successful tactics of the environmental movement.

The rally speech represents part of a broader pattern, since of Trump's statement fact-checked by *Politifact*, an astounding 49 percent are false. By comparison, his opponent in the US presidential election Hillary Clinton has 12 percent of her fact-checked statements rated false, and 14 percent for the Republican Speaker of the House Paul Ryan.

Despite Trump's extremely high rate of deception, many still believe him. As an example, 44 percent of those polled believed his falsehoods about Obama wiretapping Trump Tower during the 2016 election campaign. Thus, many will believe his Phoenix rally claims, despite the debunking by fact-checkers. Unfortunately, 29 percent of the public, and only 12 percent of Trump supporters, trust fact-checkers.

Moreover, research on debunking falsehoods shows that such debunking sometimes backfires. Called the *backfire effect*, scientists have shown that in a number of cases, people believe in falsehoods even more strongly after being presented with contradictory evidence. This situation enables Trump to pollute our politics with deception, destroying trust in our democratic political system.

Political and social science research summarized in the 2003 *Trust and Governance*, edited by Valerie Braithwaite and Margaret, shows that trust is vital for healthy democracies. Citizens in a democracy have a basic expectation of their public officials being trustworthy, in their words and actions. In return, citizens comply with laws, pay taxes, and cooperate with other government initiatives. By comparison to a democracy, an autocratic state bears a much higher resource burden of policing to make its citizens comply with its laws. In a 2002 work, *Trust and Trustworthiness*, political scientist Russell Hardin also shows the vital role of trust in creating and cultivating civil society in a democracy. When political leaders act in ways that destroy trust - as Trump is doing through misleading statements and outright lies - people will increasingly stop complying with laws, paying taxes, and engaging in civil society. Trump's actions are fatally undermining the health of our democracy.

His behavior falls within the sphere of what behavioral scientists term "tragedy of the commons," following a famous 1968 article in *Science* by Garret Hardin. Hardin demonstrated that in areas where a group of people share a common resource - the commons - without any controls on the use of this resource, individual self-interest may often lead to disaster for all involved. Because each individual may well have a strong interest in using more of the common resource than is their fair share, all suffer the consequences of depletion of that resource. Environmental pollution is a clear example where the common resource of clean air and water is abused by polluters who destroy this shared resource.

Trump is abusing the commons of trust in our political environment, and he is setting a clear example for other politicians to follow through his successful tactics. West Virginia Attorney General Patrick Morrisey and Kentucky Governor Matt Bevin are adopting the post-truth tactics of condemning media as "fake news" whenever the media report stories unfavorable to them. As an example, Bevin personally attacked a journalist who reported on Bevin's purchase of a mansion for about a million dollars under market value from a hedge fund manager, likely a bribe in return for under-the-table political favors. Such trickle-down of post-truth politics points to its normalization within our political system, thus enabling corruption and undermining our democracy.

How do we stop this pollution of truth? The modern environmental movement has been dealing successfully with a tragedy of the commons: industrial pollution. The historical consensus is that the launch of the modern environmental movement came with the publication of Rachel Carson's *Silent Spring* in 1962. This and other similar publications brought about an awakening of the public to the danger posed by environmental pollution to individual and community health, and led to the coordinated movement of activists - Republican and Democrat - fighting for the environment.

As a result, environmental problems drew much wider public attention. Consider the 1969 fire on the Cuyahoga river in Cleveland. The river has had a long history of pollution, and in June 1969, oil-covered debris caught fire, causing $100,000 worth of damage to two railroad bridges. This event drew national attention and became a major story in *Time*. Cleveland's mayor testified before Congress to urge greater attention to pollution by the federal government. Notably, the Cuyahoga river had experienced many other fires due to industrial pollution, such as one in 1952 that resulted in over $1.3 million in damages - ten times that incurred in 1969. However, this much bigger and more destructive fire inspired little national attention, or efforts to change the situation, as compared to the fire of 1969.

The marked difference in the reaction to the two fires stemmed from the launch of the modern environmental movement, combining the coordinated actions of activists to seek out and highlight these problems with heightened public attention awareness of the danger of environmental pollution. We can do the same for the pollution of truth by launching a nonpartisan pro-truth movement. Such a movement would require a coordinated group of activists holding public figures accountable for deception as well as publicly highlighting the danger that post-truth politics poses to the health of our democracy.

While the 1960s required the publication of books to raise awareness and launch a movement, our contemporary digital environment provides easier tools. The Pro-Truth Pledge project at ProTruthPledge.org allows private citizens and public figures to take a pledge to commit to twelve truth-oriented behaviors. This site both offers a coordination venue for those determined to roll back the tide of lies and protect our democracy, and raises awareness of the dangers of political deception. Hundreds of private citizens across the US and dozens of public figures have already taken the pledge, including household names such as Peter Singer and Steven Pinker as well as over twenty Democratic and Republican politicians.

Moreover, we can take the most successful tactics from the environmental movement on addressing the tragedy of the commons and apply them to the pro-truth movement. Research on the environmental movement's efforts to address environmental degradation suggests that the commons can still be maintained through a number of strategies, such as providing credible information about the environment and through providing appropriate incentives for participants. All of these have been built into the Pro-Truth Pledge. Those who take it provide credible information of their commitment to truth-oriented behavior, especially due to the accountability mechanisms built into the pledge. Likewise, the pledge offers the incentive of a positive reputation boost, since those who take it can put pledge badges on their website, social media, and business cards, and reputation has been shown by scholars as crucial to addressing tragedies of the commons.

By launching a pro-truth movement uniting people across the political divide, we can avoid the normalization of post-truth politics. Doing so will help ensure that the kind of falsehoods uttered by Trump at the Phoenix rally get a response equivalent to the 1969 fire on the Cuyahoga river, rather than the 1952 one. Whether the pro-truth movement takes off depends on how many people choose to take the pledge and join the effort to protect the health of our democracy from the pollution of truth.

References
Braithwaite, V., & Levi, M. (Eds.). (2003). *Trust and governance.*
Change, R. (2000). *The global commons: environmental and technological governance.*
Hardin, G. (1968). The tragedy of the commons. *Science. 162*(3859), 1243-1248.
Hardin, R. (2002). *Trust and trustworthiness.*

Milinski, M., Semmann, D., & Krambeck, H. J. (2002). Reputation helps solve the 'tragedy of the commons'. *Nature, 415*(6870), 424-426.

Nyhan, B., & Reifler, J. (2015). The roles of information deficits and identity threat in the prevalence of misperceptions. *Manuscript submitted for publication.*

Peter, C., & Koch, T. (2016). When Debunking Scientific Myths Fails (and When It Does Not) The Backfire Effect in the Context of Journalistic Coverage and Immediate Judgments as Prevention Strategy. *Science Communication, 38*(1), 3-25.

Silveira, S. J. (2000). The American environmental movement: surviving through diversity. *BC Envtl. Aff. L. Rev., 28*, 497.

Van Vugt, M. (2009). Averting the tragedy of the commons: Using social psychological science to protect the environment. *Current Directions in Psychological Science, 18*(3), 169-173.

Chapter 53: A Pro-Truth Movement

By Gleb Tsipursky

Caption: Image of a Pro-Truth Pledge shirt (Pro-Truth Pledge website)

Donald Trump's rally speech in Phoenix on August 22 was full of falsehoods. He gave a revisionist and false history of his reaction to the Charlottesville violence to make himself look better, made false statements about media reporting and misled the audience over his economic achievements. The speech points to the normalization of post-truth politics, when appeals to personal beliefs and emotions wins out over objective facts. To avoid this normalization, we need to borrow the successful tactics of the environmental movement.

The rally speech represents part of a broader pattern: Of Trump's statements fact-checked by *Politifact*, an astounding 49 percent are false. By comparison, his Democratic opponent in the U.S. presidential election, Hillary Clinton, has 12 percent of her fact checked statements rated false; 14 percent of Republican Speaker of the House Paul Ryan's are.

Despite Trump's extremely high rate of deception, many still believe him. As an example, 44 percent of those polled believed his falsehoods about Obama wiretapping Trump Tower during the 2016 election campaign. Thus, many will believe his Phoenix rally claims, despite the debunking by fact checkers. Unfortunately, 29 percent of the public, and only 12 percent of Trump supporters, trust fact checkers. Moreover, research on debunking falsehoods shows such debunking sometimes backfires. Called the *backfire effect*, scientists have shown in a number of cases people believe in falsehoods even more strongly after being presented with contradictory evidence. This situation enables Trump to pollute our politics with deception, destroying trust in our democratic political system.

Political and social science research summarized in the 2003 *Trust and Governance*, edited by Valerie Braithwaite and Margaret Levi, shows trust is vital for healthy democracies. Citizens in a democracy have a basic expectation of their public officials being trustworthy, in their words and actions. In return, citizens comply with laws, pay taxes and cooperate with other government initiatives. By comparison to a democracy, an autocratic state bears a much higher resource burden of policing to make its citizens comply with its laws. In his 2002 work, *Trust and Trustworthiness*, political scientist Russell Hardin also shows the vital role of trust in creating and cultivating civil society in a democracy. When political leaders act in ways that destroy trust—as Trump is doing through misleading statements and outright lies—people will increasingly stop complying with laws, paying taxes and engaging in civil society. Trump's actions are fatally undermining the health of our democracy.

His behavior falls within the sphere of what behavioral scientists term "tragedy of the commons," following a famous 1968 article in *Science* by Garret Hardin. Hardin demonstrated that in areas where a group of people share a common resource—the commons—without any controls on the use of this resource, individual self-interest may often lead to disaster for all involved. Because each individual may well have a strong interest in using more of the common resource than is their fair share, all suffer the consequences of depletion of that resource. Environmental pollution is a clear example where the common resource of clean air and water is abused by polluters who destroy this shared resource.

Trump is abusing the commons of trust in our political environment, and he is setting a clear example for other politicians to follow through his successful tactics. West Virginia Attorney General Patrick Morrisey and Kentucky Gov. Matt Bevin are adopting the post-truth tactics of condemning media as "fake news" whenever the media report stories unfavorable to them. As an example, Bevin personally attacked a journalist who reported on Bevin's purchase of a mansion for about a million dollars under market value from a hedge fund manager, likely a bribe in return for under-the-table political favors. Such trickle-down of post-truth politics points to its normalization within our political system, thus enabling corruption and undermining our democracy.

How do we stop this pollution of truth? The modern environmental movement has been dealing successfully with a tragedy of the commons: industrial pollution. The historical consensus is that the launch of the modern environmental movement came with the publication of Rachel Carson's *Silent Spring* in 1962. This and other similar publications brought about an awakening of the public to the danger posed by environmental pollution to individual and community health, and led to the coordinated movement of activists—Republican and Democrat—fighting for the environment.

As a result, environmental problems drew much wider public attention. Consider the 1969 fire on the Cuyahoga River in Cleveland. The river has had a long history of pollution, and in June 1969 oil-covered debris caught fire, causing $100,000 worth of damage to two railroad bridges. This event drew national attention and became a major story in *TIME*. Cleveland's mayor testified before Congress to urge greater attention to pollution by the federal government. Notably, the Cuyahoga River had experienced many other fires due to industrial pollution, such as one in 1952 that resulted in over $1.3 million in damage— 10 times that which incurred in 1969. This much bigger and more destructive fire, however, inspired little national attention—or efforts to change the situation—as compared with the conflagration of 1969.

The marked difference in the reaction to the two fires stemmed from the launch of the modern environmental movement, combining the coordinated actions of activists to seek out and highlight these problems with heightened public attention awareness of the danger of environmental pollution. We can do the same for the pollution of truth by launching a nonpartisan pro-truth movement. Such a movement would require a coordinated group of activists holding public figures accountable for deception as well as publicly highlighting the danger that post-truth politics poses to the health of our democracy.

Whereas the 1960s required the publication of books to raise awareness and launch a movement, our contemporary digital environment provides easier tools. One example is the Pro-Truth Pledge project at ProTruthPledge.org, which allows private citizens and public figures to take a pledge committing them to 12 behaviors that research suggests are most likely to lead to a truth-oriented society. This site both offers a coordination venue for those determined to roll back the tide of lies and protect our democracy, and raises awareness of the dangers of political deception. Hundreds of private citizens across the U.S. and dozens of public figures have already taken the pledge, including household names such as Peter Singer and Steven Pinker as well as over 20 Democratic and Republican politicians.

By launching a pro-truth movement uniting people across the political divide, we can avoid the normalization of post-truth politics. Doing so will help ensure that the kind of falsehoods uttered by Trump at the Phoenix rally get a response equivalent to the 1969 fire on the Cuyahoga river, rather than the 1952 one. Whether the pro-truth movement takes off depends on how many people choose to take the pledge at ProTruthPledge.org and join the effort to protect the health of our democracy from the pollution of truth.

References

Ariely, D., & Jones, S. (2012), *The Honest Truth About Dishonesty: How We Lie to Everyone--Especially Others*.

Braithwaite, V., & Levi, M. (Eds.). (2003). *Trust and governance*.

Hardin, G. (1968). The tragedy of the commons. *Science. 162*(3859), 1243-1248.

Hardin, R. (2002). *Trust and trustworthiness*.

Nyhan, B., & Reifler, J. (2010), "When Corrections Fail: The Persistence of Political Misperceptions." *Political Behavior, 32*(2), 303-330.

Nyhan, B., & Reifler, J. (2015). The Effect of Fact-Checking on Elites: A Field Experiment on US State Legislators. *American Journal of Political Science, 59*(3), 628-640.

Silveira, S. J. (2000). The American environmental movement: surviving through diversity. *BC Envtl. Aff. L. Rev., 28*, 497.

Vogler, J. (2000), *The Global Commons: Environmental and Technological Governance*, 2nd ed.

Conclusion

Congratulations! Since you've read this book, you now have realistic expectations and true beliefs, and can make the best decisions possible.

Just kidding! Learning about the research-based skills in this book is just the start. It might be a cliché, but it's also an accurate statement: truth-seeking is a journey, not a destination. More than that, truth-seeking is a skill, and research suggests that as any skill, it takes thousands of hours of deliberate practice to gain mastery. However, you can gain a pretty decent level in most skills in a much shorter time period, given appropriate instruction and an opportunity to engage in deliberate practice.

This book provides the manual for truth-seeking skills, and the world provides an unfortunate overabundance of opportunities for deliberate practice in this domain. Do not simply close the pages of this book and put it away: keep referring to its various chapters as you engage in such practice in the world around you. As you encounter various life situations that remind you of what you read in this book, return to the relevant chapter and reread it. Try out the strategies there, and see what works best for you. Adapt them to your life, preferences, and personality, following the approach described in the chapter on advice.

Practicing the skills of truth-seeking will help you develop more realistic expectations and accurate beliefs, which are necessary but not sufficient for making wise decisions that would help you achieve your goals. If you want to learn about these, check out the articles, videos, tip sheets, books, and apps at intentionalinsights.org and sign up to the Intentional Insights newsletter. To engage with the Intentional Insights community and ask questions about the methods described in our content, follow Intentional Insights on Facebook, Twitter, Pinterest, Delicious, YouTube, Instagram, Tumblr, StumbleUpon, Google+, SlideShare, and LinkedIn. If you wish to benefit from various forms of coaching, mentoring, and webinars, please become a member of Intentional Insights.

Also, I also invite you to join me in volunteering and/or donating today to support the work of this organization (I donate 10 percent of my income and volunteer dozens of hours a week as President of the organization). My doing so stems from my desire to help advance its mission of popularizing research-based strategies for truth-seeking, rational thinking, and wise decision-making for a broad audience. On a separate note, if you wish to support my own activism in creating content in this arena, I welcome you to become my patron on Patreon. This website enables you to support someone financially if you appreciate what they are doing, giving either a flat monthly donation or paying them per post they make: I make posts for each new article I publish, interview I do, speech I make, or any other similar public activism activity. My patrons provide me with the financial support needed to support myself financially while I pursue activist work such as doing interviews and publishing articles spreading ideas that help people pursue the truth, think rationally, and make wise decisions. It was such financial support that enabled me to put together this book, and if you enjoyed and benefited from it, I hope you will consider becoming my supporter on Patreon. Finally, if you wish me to present to your organization, company, or group about this and related topics, check out my speaking page here. I would also be glad to appear on your TV show, radio, podcast, videocast, or other media venue. In both cases, please email me.

Finally, I want readers to know that I took the Pro-Truth Pledge at ProTruthPledge.org, and believe everything in this book is accurate and factual, at least to the best of my knowledge at the time I either wrote it or accepted contributions by others to this volume. If you believe there is anything that is not accurate, please contact me at gleb@intentionalinsights.org, and let me know: I will be glad to update my beliefs, and issue any clarifications or revisions, per the Pro-Truth Pledge. You can look for such revisions or clarifications on my website, GlebTsipursky.com, which has a page dedicated to this book. For anyone who wants to get actively involved in the Pro-Truth movement, dedicated to fighting lies and promoting truth in public discourse, I welcome you to contact me by email as well. Please also email me any questions you might have about any aspects of the book, or with your feedback about the book; I also invite you to leave reviews on this link on Amazon.com and this link on Goodreads.com. Thank you, and I wish you well on your truth-seeking journey!

Appendix

Pro-Truth Pledge Text

I Pledge My Earnest Efforts To:

Share truth

- **Verify**: fact-check information to confirm it is true before accepting and sharing it
- **Balance**: share the whole truth, even if some aspects do not support my opinion
- **Cite**: share my sources so that others can verify my information
- **Clarify**: distinguish between my opinion and the facts

Honor truth

- **Acknowledge**: acknowledge when others share true information, even when we disagree otherwise
- **Reevaluate**: reevaluate if my information is challenged, retract it if I cannot verify it
- **Defend**: defend others when they come under attack for sharing true information, even when we disagree otherwise
- **Align**: align my opinions and my actions with true information

Encourage truth

- **Fix**: ask people to retract information that reliable sources have disproved even if they are my allies
- **Educate**: compassionately inform those around me to stop using unreliable sources even if these sources support my opinion
- **Defer**: recognize the opinions of experts as more likely to be accurate when the facts are disputed
- **Celebrate**: celebrate those who retract incorrect statements and update their beliefs toward the truth

Pro-Truth Pledge Frequently Asked Questions

Why do we need a pledge?

Brief Answer:
Unfortunately, we cannot trust politicians and other public figures to tell the truth. The pledge changes the incentive structure for public figures to promote truth-telling instead of lying. Through taking the pledge, and encouraging public figures to take it, you take the lead in fighting deception.

Full Answer:
While plenty of people have lied to get ahead in the past, this problem has gotten particularly bad lately. Recent political events in the United States, United Kingdom, and many other democratic countries have caused Oxford Dictionary to choose post-truth politics, "circumstances in which objective facts are less influential in shaping public opinion than appeals to emotion and personal belief," as its 2016 word of the year. Less and less people trust the media, in part due to the rise of alternative media, in part due to the growth of opinion-driven reporting, and in part due to criticism of the media by prominent politicians. The replication crisis in a number of scientific fields is eroding the credibility of scientists. The most popular sport in the world is mired in scandals based on deception. Leaders of organizations are lying more and more frequently, and usually do not get punished. It's not only a problem with public figures: fake news, more recently termed "viral deception," is sweeping social media, shared by ordinary citizens.

Sharing such misinformation is not necessarily intended to harm others or even deliberately deceive, as our minds are not intuitively set on seeking the truth. Research suggests our emotions and intuitions instead focus on protecting our worldview and personal identity rather than updating our beliefs based on the most accurate information. We are thus not naturally inclined to live by the maxim of "you will know the truth, and the truth will set you free." Being truthful thus requires the same kind of effort as any other sort of civilized, not-instinctive behavior.

Our society as a whole loses out by these lies, while individual liars often gain by their deception, a situation known as a "tragedy of the commons." A well-known tragedy of the commons is pollution: we all gain from clean air and water, but some individual polluters gain more, at least in the short term, by polluting the environment, harming all of us. Similarly, we all benefit from a society where we can trust each other to tell the truth, but some individuals gain more, in the short term, by abusing this trust and polluting the truth. Fortunately, the environmental movement of the 1970s has now resulted in a situation where many people started recycling and our society passed environmental legislation. In the same way, we can change individual behavior and public policy alike to be more oriented toward the truth through the Pro-Truth Movement, and the PTP is one aspect of this movement to help fight deception.

How does the pledge solve these problems?

Behavioral science research suggests that an important key to addressing such tragedies of the commons involve a combination of strategies. One is changing incentives, namely increasing rewards for behavior that is cooperative and helps society – in this case, telling the truth, and also increasing punishments for behavior that defects from the common good and harms society – lying. Another strategy involves reputation management, clearly showing who is being cooperative, and who is defecting. A third strategy centers around managing the choices available to participants, what is known as nudging. The PTP takes advantage of a fourth behavioral science strategy of precommitment – if you publicly commit to a certain course, you will be much more likely to follow it.

The PTP, created by a group of behavioral scientists, combines all of these strategies. By doing so, it provides a tool that motivates all who take it to share accurate information and avoid sharing misinformation.

Besides providing the motivation, the PTP spells out what it means to orient toward the truth. After all, it is very easy to say you share the truth, regardless of whether you do so. It is even easy to say you "verified" a source before sharing the information. However, if you verified it through checking a source known to be systematically unreliable, whether Occupy Democrats for liberals or Breitbart for conservatives, you have violated the standard of avoiding unreliable websites, and thus violated the pledge. As you will see below, if you retract your statement, you will not suffer any penalties from PTP advocates. The clear standard about truth-oriented behavior not only offers guidance to those who take the pledge, but also a basis for evaluating whether pledge-takers abide by their commitment. For more information, watch this Q&A video about the Pro-Truth Pledge.

What is considered misinformation?

Brief Answer:
Misinformation is anything that goes against reality. It can mean directly lying, lying by omission, or misrepresenting the truth to suit one's own purposes. Sometimes misinformation is blatant and sometimes it's harder to tell. For those tough calls we rely on credible fact-checking sites and the scientific consensus.

Full Answer:
Misinformation is anything that goes against the truth of reality. It can mean directly lying about the situation at hand, for instance when an athlete denies taking steroids that she was actually taking. It can mean lying by omission, as when a scholar publishes a study with a successful experiment, while hiding that he conducted 50 of the same experiments that failed, until by random chance one finally worked, a phenomenon known as publication bias. In some cases, misinformation is obvious, so that anyone can see it. In other cases, it is less so. For those cases, the PTP calls on pledge signers to rely on credible fact-checking websites and/or on the scientific consensus.

Rather than going through the process of vetting fact-checking websites, we have decided to outsource that work to Facebook, which is partnering with websites it has vetted and evaluated as credible. As of the initial unveiling, the websites include Snopes, Politifact, ABC News, and FactCheck.org, and more will be added over time. All these are members of a common coalition, the Poynter International Fact Checking Network, and have committed to a common set of principles. Any other websites that Facebook uses will be considered credible for PTP purposes. Someone who takes the pledge will be considered in violation of the pledge if they make a claim that is similar to those rated as "mostly false" or "completely false" by one of these websites (they use different language, but you get the idea). In a case where credible websites disagree, for instance one calls a claim "mostly false" and another calls it "mostly true," we will not consider the claim a violation of the PTP.

In some cases, fact-checking websites have not evaluated certain claims, but the claim will be opposed by scientific research. Since science is the best of all methods we as human beings have found to determine the reality about the world and predict the outcomes of our actions, someone will be evaluated as in violation of the pledge if they make a claim that goes against the scientific consensus. We are comfortable with the Wikipedia definition of scientific consensus as "the collective judgment, position, and opinion of the community of scientists in a particular field of study. Consensus implies general agreement, though not necessarily unanimity. Consensus is normally achieved through communication at conferences, the publication process, replication (reproducible results by others), and peer review. These lead to a situation in which those within the discipline can often recognize such a consensus where it exists, but communicating to outsiders that consensus has been reached can be difficult, because the 'normal' debates through which science progresses may seem to outsiders as contestation. On occasion, scientific institutes issue position statements intended to communicate a summary of the science from the 'inside' to the 'outside' of the scientific community." Thus, we can recognize scientific consensus by position statements by prestigious scientific organizations, such as this statement from 18 associations on climate change, or the result of meta-analysis studies (evaluations of a series of other prominent studies) that come to a clear determination, such as this study on the relationship of vaccines and autism. Since science gets ahead in part through individual scientists with expertise in a certain domain challenging the scientific consensus in that domain, those who are scientists do not have to abide by the scientific consensus in areas where they have expertise.

How are pledge-takers held accountable?

Brief Answer:
Pledge-takers are held accountable through crowd-sourcing the truth. For private citizens, the pledge relies on science-based strategies of personal commitment to the truth combined with community accountability. For public figures, we have volunteers who evaluate whether public figures violate the pledge by sharing misinformation. Violating the pledge does not mean a public figure is immediately punished for doing so, but it does mean is that someone from the PTP community will reach out in a private message. If the situation is not resolved, the matter is investigated more thoroughly by a vetted committee of PTP advocates. If they find that the public figure did share misinformation and refuses to take it back, the matter is widely publicized to all relevant media venues, resulting in sizable reputation damage to the public figure.

Full Answer:
The pledge is violated when you share misinformation. Violating the pledge does not mean you are going to be immediately punished for doing so, since the PTP is not intended to be primarily punitive. In putting facts first, we are not trying to play "gotcha" when someone makes an innocent mistake that causes a violation the pledge. After all, we aim to push ourselves and others who signed the pledge to be better than our natural inclinations – just like it is against the natural inclination of many of us to avoid a second piece of chocolate cake. Yet taking the second piece and thus violating our aspirations to eat well doesn't mean we drop our goal of having healthy eating habits, but simply try to figure out what went wrong and aim to do better in the future.

Similarly, each of us may well eventually fail to be oriented toward the truth, and make a statement that goes against a fact-checking website or the scientific consensus or the clearly visible truth of reality. We rely on a community of truth-oriented individuals to support each other and provide compassionate correction when we fail, helping advance open-minded thinking among all of us and thus improving our society, as research shows. A key piece of the pledge is that all pledge-takers will hold all others who took the pledge accountable for upholding the truth. If someone is unwilling to correct themselves when provided clear information about their mistake, it is the responsibility of each of us who took the pledge to hold that person accountable by publicizing that person's actions in appropriate channels, to penalize that person through harming that person's reputation. This applies especially to holding public figures who took the pledge accountable, as they have a bigger impact on public opinion and the common good of trust and truth in our society.

How does this accountability work in practice? While a public figure sharing misinformation by mistake suffers no penalty, one deliberately violating the pledge – as shown by a refusal to retract misinformation one shared – suffers substantial negative consequences. All of those who take the pledge have the opportunity to sign up for action alerts, and can also sign up to be a Pro-Truth advocate. Pro-Truth advocates can focus on a number of activities, including monitoring others who have taken the pledge, particularly public figures. If a Pro-Truth advocate finds that someone has violated the pledge, especially a public figure, the advocate would contact the person privately. As part of this process, the advocate would adopt "charity mode," meaning being more charitable toward the alleged violator than is one's intuition, and assuming an "innocent until reasonably shown guilty" perspective – perhaps the person misspoke, or you misheard something. Use curiosity and questioning to determine whether there is clear evidence that the pledge has been violated. If there is clear evidence, provide this to the alleged violator, and if the person retracts her/his words, the matter is resolved.

If the alleged violator does not retract her/his statement, the advocate may publicize the matter via the advocate's own channels, social media and otherwise. In doing so, the advocate must provide both: 1) Clear evidence of the violation, and 2) Clear evidence of a good-faith, reasonable effort to get the alleged violator of the pledge to address the violation. The advocate may also spread word to other PTP advocates with whom the advocate has contacts for them to publicize the information, as well as others whom the advocate considers salient to the deception at hand. If the individual is a private citizen, the matter ends there, as this sort of reputational blow provides a significant enough disincentive to cause the large majority private citizens who take the pledge to avoid lying.

If the alleged violator is a public figure, the advocate would escalate the matter to a PTP local, regional, or national mediating committee, depending on the status of the public figure. This committee includes a group of vetted volunteers who would evaluate the evidence provided by the advocate, contact the public figure for a chance for the person to offer an explanation, and make a ruling – either determining that there is a violation, that there is no violation, or that the evidence is insufficient to make a judgment. If there is a ruling of a violation, then this ruling is evaluated by a member of the PTP Central Coordinating Committee, to ensure fairness and accuracy, and provide an external perspective. In the case that the PTP Central Coordinating Committee member also determines that a violation has occurred, the committee then contacts the alleged violator, offering the person another chance to retract her/his words. By this time, the public figure had a number of opportunities to clarify the situation and correct it if a mistake has been made, rather than if the public figure aimed to make a deliberate deception to pollute the truth and hurt all of us. This process might sound a little convoluted, but it minimizes the possibility of the PTP being politicized or corrupted at a local level.

If the public figure still refuses to take her/his words back, the PTP mediating committee would issue a press advisory that the public figure is in contempt of the pledge to put reputational pressure on the thought leader, with clear evidence of the violation as well as the efforts it made to get the public figure to revise the violation. The PTP mediating committee would also contact relevant organizations with which the person who violated the pledge is affiliated, such as the radio station if it is a radio show host, or a university if it is a scientist. It would also issue a PTP Action Alert to those who indicated they want to receive such alerts – either at the local, regional, or national level, depending on the stature of the public figure – for them to email/Tweet and otherwise message the public figure encouraging her/him to revise the relevant statements, and writing letters-to-the-editor about the situation. Finally, the public figure will be listed on the PTP website as in contempt of the pledge. This provides considerable reputation pressure for a public figure to avoid being in contempt of the pledge – if the public figure envisions violating the pledge deliberately, s/he would be better off not signing it at all. To summarize, innocent violations of the pledge will not be penalized, only deliberate attempts to misrepresent the truth and thus undermine the public good of truth and trust.

Who will monitor the PTP mediating committees? Other pledge-takers, of course. The PTP mediating committees have strong incentives to ensure that their rulings are as fair and objective as is possible, because their whole reputation rests on such objectivity. The outcomes of their proceedings – if there is a ruling of a violation – will be provided as evidence for scrutiny by other pledge-takers, and the public at large. These outcomes will not be provided if the public figure retracts her/his words at any stage, to prevent reputation damage for the public figure, since the PTP is not meant to be punitive but corrective.

Violations of the pledge only apply to statements made in and about the public sphere. In other words, it does not apply to private interactions, such as when a wife tells her husband his new shirt makes him look really muscular, regardless of what she really thinks. It does not apply to semi-private contexts, such as when a fisherman tells tall tales about the size of the fish he caught. It also does not apply to religious or other values-based contexts, except in cases where the statement is a clear piece of misinformation about public policy. It also does not apply to cases that cannot be reasonably verified and/or have to do with personal beliefs and spiritual experiences, such as when a politician or a pastor says "I support this policy because of God's personal revelations to me," or an environmentalist says "I support protecting the environment because otherwise the spirit of Mother Earth would suffer" – it is not possible to verify whether God exists or made revelations to someone or whether the spirit of Mother Earth exists and experiences suffering if the environment is not protected. The pledge matters only in verifiable statements in the public sphere, such as when a private citizen shares a piece of viral deception online, or a journalist misquotes a source, or a pastor makes false claims about miracle healing and thus encourages parishioners to avoid going to doctors, or a scientist hides unfavorable experimental results relevant to public policy, or a politician spreads lies about her opponent.

While the pledge is only violated when you share misinformation, pledge-takers can choose to stick by the word of the pledge but go against its spirit through misleading if not explicitly false statements – what is known as "spin." In these cases, we encourage other pledge-takers to call out fellow pledge-takers who fail to live by the spirit of the pledge. In almost all cases, spinning the information will go against one of the truth-oriented behaviors outlined in the pledge. Bring this to the attention of the pledge-taker who fails to engage in this behavior, and encourage that pledge-taker to model the values of the pledge.

What are the rewards for taking the pledge?

Brief Answer:

All signers of the pledge benefit in building a more truth-driven public culture and cultivating socially beneficial habits of mind, word, and deed. Private citizens gain the privilege of being part of a nonpartisan community of people who support each other in abiding by the pledge in a compassionate, constructive manner. Public figures who take the pledge get the verifiable credibility of being constantly evaluated on how well they stick to the pledge by PTP advocates. An additional benefit for public figures who are competing with others, such as politicians, is that they can raise questions about why your opponent has not taken the PTP. We celebrate public figures who take the PTP in our newsletters and social media, offering them a reputational boost among an audience oriented toward the truth.

Full Answer:
First, let us consider the individual rewards for different groups of pledge-takers:

If you are an elected or appointed public official

- If you are an elected or appointed public official, you need to be perceived as trustworthy by citizens. The PTP provides you with that credibility, due to the presence of the monitoring mechanism. Citizens can easily look you up in the PTP database, and see if you are in contempt of the pledge or not. If you have signed the pledge a while ago and are not in contempt, they can be pretty confident that you have a high degree of honesty. You get an additional benefit if you are an elected official and your opponent for elected office has not taken the PTP, since you can raise questions about why your opponent does not wish to do so and what your opponent is choosing to lie about rather than be found to be in contempt of the PTP. Finally, you get benefits because when you sign up, we include your information in the PTP Updates we send to those pledge-takers who subscribed to these. Likewise, you can submit additional content to the PTP Updates that demonstrates why you care about the truth, ways that you oriented toward the truth when it would have been politically expedient to lie, as well as instances where taking the PTP caused you to act differently than you would have otherwise. If the content is a good fit for our mission, we will include it in the emails we send to the PTP Updates subscribers (contact us to get more clarity on what we're looking for in the PTP Updates content submissions). This provides you as a politician with positive recognition and reputation as being honest and credible to your constituents, and also offers you a base for furthering your political career since more people outside your locale find out about you and your pro-truth words and deeds.

If you are a media figure or thought leader (journalist, radio/podcast host, blogger, commentator/analyst, speaker/trainer, author, consultant, etc.)

- If you are a media figure or thought leader (journalist, radio/podcast host, blogger, commentator/analyst, speaker/trainer, author, consultant, etc.), you need to be perceived as trustworthy by the audience to which you communicate. The PTP provides you with that benefit due to the monitoring mechanism, and similarly to the politician described above, the longer you are signed up without being in contempt, the more credibility you get. Moreover, if your competitors do not sign the pledge, you will get a bigger audience, since their audiences will start flocking to you as a more trustworthy source of news/analysis/thought leadership. You can also get a broader audience engaged with you since you will get mentioned in the PTP Update when you first sign the pledge, and can get additional PTP-related content accepted into the PTP Update, as well as further your career by getting more recognition outside of your locale.

If you are a scientist

- If you are a scientist, you need to be trusted by your fellow scholars, science journalists, people in industries relevant to your research, and the broader public as a whole. They need to know that you perform your research honestly, in a way that can be replicated and avoids publication bias. For scientists in fields that have this option, we ask that pledge-signers by default engage in pre-registration of trials, and have a clear explanation of why they chose not to if they did not do so that would be found reasonable by fellow scholars in that field. Lacking such a clear explanation may – depending on the situation and the nature of findings – be cause for finding a scientist in violation of the pledge. In that case, if the scientist does not retract the experiment or published paper, the scientist may be found in contempt of the pledge. Likewise, if two attempts to replicate the findings fail – in ways evaluated by peer scholars in the same discipline as reasonably approximating the original experiment – the scientist would be asked to retract the experiment or published paper. Additionally, if credible data analysis methods such as the GRIM test and other ways to detect deception or insufficient rigor in studies find a significant likelihood of a deceptive outcome, we would ask the scholar for a retraction. Again, there would be no "gotcha" games, and the scientist would have plenty of opportunities to present a defense, from an "innocent until proven guilty" perspective. The PTP mediating committee would only issue a ruling of the scientist being in contempt if the scientist refuses to retract the paper, so it would be a last resort after other options failed. It would also make sure to consult with and get the input of peers in the scholar's discipline, to ensure that each scholar is evaluated based on the standards in that field. This special application of the pledge to scientists results from it being often really hard to determine if a scholar lied, since they are not fact checked and since they may have a very legitimate reason to go against the scientific consensus if they are breaking new ground. Because of these provisions of the pledge, those impacted by your research can have much more trust that your findings are credible, compared to someone who did not sign the pledge.

If you are an organizational leader

- If you are an organizational leader, you have a need to be trusted, both within and outside your organization, as leading with integrity. The monitoring and penalizing mechanisms of the PTP offer that benefit. Abiding by the PTP means being honest with employees about challenging topics such as potential job cuts, avoiding manipulation of financial statements and other forms of "cooking the books," avoiding misleading consumers and government regulators about your products, and so on. The PTP mediating committees welcome PTP advocates from inside organizations providing information demonstrating evidence of deceptions by organizational leaders and will readily use such documentation in its evaluations of pledge violations. It also welcomes external stakeholders of organizations providing information about PTP violations. Due to such monitoring, by internal and external stakeholders alike, organizational leaders who take the PTP have greater credibility than those who choose to avoid taking it.

If you are a private citizen

- If you are a private citizen, you need to trust that you are getting accurate information from officials, media figures and thought leaders, scientists, and organizational leaders. You also need to have a way of monitoring and penalizing those thought leaders who share false information. You also benefit from clear standards about what it means to have truth-oriented behavior, which the pledge outlines in detail. You gain the privilege of being part of a nonpartisan community of people who help support each other in abiding by the pledge in a compassionate, constructive manner. An additional benefit is having other people trust you more when you share information with them, since they know that you are being supported and monitored by fellow pledge-takers, thus ensuring a much higher likelihood of you avoiding sharing misinformation.

Finally, there are a number of benefits that accrue to all who take the pledge. All pledge-takers gain the benefits of cultivating socially beneficial – what many would call more moral and ethical – habits of mind, word, and deed. All gain the pride and self-satisfaction of standing up for your ethical and moral convictions. All gain the benefits in building a more truth-driven public culture, and fighting the pollution of truth in politics. All gain the benefit of being role models for others, whether ordinary citizens or public figures. All gain the benefit of joining a network of and collaborating with other truth-oriented people.

What is the impact of the Pro-Truth Pledge?

A candidate for Congress took the Pro-Truth Pledge. He later posted on his Facebook wall a screenshot of a tweet by Donald Trump criticizing minority and disabled children. After being called out on it, he went and searched Trump's feed. He could not find the original tweet, and while Trump may have deleted that tweet, the candidate edited his own Facebook post to say that "Due to a Truth Pledge I have taken I have to say I have not been able to verify this post." He indicated that he would be more careful with future postings.

A US Army veteran and member Special Operations community took the pledge. He then wrote a blog post about how it impacted him. He notes that "I've verbally or digitally passed on bad information numerous times, I am fairly sure, as a result of honest mistakes or lack of vigorous fact checking." He describes how after taking the pledge, he felt "an open commitment to a certain attitude" to "think hard when I want to play an article or statistic which I'm not completely sold on." Having taken the Pro-Truth Pledge, he found it "really does seem to change one's habits," helping push him both to correct his own mistakes with an "attitude of humility and skepticism, and of honesty and moral sincerity," and also to encourage "friends and peers to do so as well."

A Christian pastor and community leader took the Pro-Truth Pledge. He related how he "took the Pro-Truth Pledge because I expect our political leaders at every level of government to speak truth and not deliberately spread misinformation to the people they have been elected to serve. Having taken the pledge myself, I put forth the effort to continually gather information validating stories and headlines before sharing them on my social media outlets."

A former US intelligence officer, who retired from service after 4 decades, took the Pro-Truth Pledge. He later described how soon after taking the pledge, a piece of news "that played right to my particular political biases hit cable TV and then the Internet and of course my first inclination was to share it as quickly and widely as possible. But then I remembered the pledge I'd signed and put the brakes on. I decided to wait a bit to see how it played out (and boy-howdy am I glad I did.)… As it turned out the story was a complete dud, 'fake news' as they say. That experience has led me to be much more vigilant in assessing, and sharing, stories that appeal to my political sensibilities. I now make a much bigger effort to fact-check before I post or share."

Bill Cunningham is a prominent conservative talk show host who had Trump on his show, and is ranked 27 among "Most Important Radio Show Talk Hosts" in America by *Talkers Magazine*. We were invited to talk with Cunningham about Trump's allegations that Barack Obama wiretapped Trump Tower in the 2016 presidential election. Using strategies informed by the Pro-Truth Pledge, we had a civil conversation and this strong supporter of Trump acknowledged that Trump behaved inappropriately in tweeting his allegations without providing any evidence.

We did an interview in October 2016 with the well-known Christian conservative radio show host Scott Sloan, who had previously had a friendly conversation with Trump during the election campaign. Using the tenets of the Pro-Truth Pledge, we discussed whether Trump or Clinton would make the US more secure. While others experienced great difficulties convincing Sloan to acknowledge facts, we provided evidence specifically targeted to prove convincing to Republicans. Namely, we showed that prominent Republicans who served in the national security apparatus thought Trump would make us less safe than Clinton. As part of doing so, we showed that Trump's anti-Muslim rhetoric is not contributing to our security, due to the infinitesimally small chance of any given Muslim committing a terrorist attack. As a result, Sloan updated his beliefs and confirmed that from the perspective of safety, Trump is a worse choice than he previously thought.

The tenets of the Pro-Truth Pledge are sticky: people tend to remember them over time. For instance, after we did an interview in October 2016 on the radio show of the well-known Christian conservative radio show host Scott Sloan, we did another interview with him about a month afterward in November 2016. Sloan specifically recollected the October 2016 conversation where we talked about the low likelihood of any Muslim being a terrorist. He spontaneously stated that he remembered and re-affirmed that any individual Muslim is very, very unlikely to be a terrorist.

In January 2017, we had a radio interview with the well-known Christian conservative radio show host Scott Sloan, who had a friendly conversation with Trump during the election campaign. We talked with Sloan on why Republicans like himself should care about post-truth politics. After all, Trump won the presidency in part by using post-truth tactics, making it politically advantageous for Republicans to avoid calling out post-truth political engagement. We focused our conversation on key tenets from the Pro-Truth Pledge, and highlighted how post-truth politics would highly likely lead to corruption and authoritarianism. Since these issues are of major concern to Republicans as well as Democrats, Sloan agreed that Republicans should be concerned about post-truth politics and criticize lies, even by their own side. He subsequently showed greater willingness to acknowledge lies by Republicans, for instance on February 15, 2017 airing a segment about a Republican judge suggesting Trump should be impeached.

The 12 behaviors of the Pro-Truth Pledge can prevail even over very politically charged topics. The well-known Christian conservative radio show host Scott Sloan had a friendly conversation with Trump during the election campaign. We had a radio interview with Sloan two days after Trump fired FBI Director James Comey in May 2017, where we compared the evidence supporting Trump's explanation for the firing and the explanation of leading Democrats. We talked with Sloan about how behavioral science findings result in those with certain partisan beliefs to prefer the explanations offered by those who share their perspective. However, we then discussed with Sloan how many mainstream Republican leaders expressed concerns over Trump firing Comey and aligned more with the Democratic explanation. Thus, we encouraged Sloan to update toward that explanation. At the end of the conversation, Sloan did indeed change his mind more to perceive the Democratic narrative as more closely aligned with reality, and affirmed his previous commitment to acknowledging and criticizing lies from Republicans.

Why should I sign up for PTP Updates?

Public figures want to know that they will get recognition and positive reputation if they sign the PTP. The PTP Updates provide them with that benefit. We plan to send one every couple of weeks, with new public figures who signed the pledge, and also ones who signed it earlier to share about how they behaved differently due to having signed the PTP. The PTP would have a significantly bigger positive impact if the public figures knew that many people were signed up to the these updates. It would be especially impactful if you read through the updates and then Tweeted/emailed and otherwise messages public figures whose messages you appreciated in the PTP Update, especially ones in your locale. Still, despite this benefit, we decided not to make PTP Updates obligatory, to enable people who have a strong distaste for additional emails to participate in the PTP.

Why should I sign up for PTP Action Alerts?

We need to put pressure on public figures who are in contempt of the pledge, and PTP Action Alerts are a vital way of doing so. Once a PTP mediating committee makes a determination that a public figure not simply made an innocent violation of the pledge, but engaged in an intentional deception and is unwilling to back away, it would issue an Action Alert to those who indicated they want to receive such alerts – either at the local, regional, or national level, depending on the stature of the public figure – for them to email/Tweet and otherwise message the public figure encouraging her/him to revise the relevant statements, and writing letters-to-the-editor about the situation. To have meaningful reputational pressure, we need as many people signed up to receive PTP Action Alerts, and to take the steps necessary to mount this pressure. Still, despite this benefit, we decided not to make PTP Action Alerts obligatory, to enable people who have a strong distaste for additional emails to participate in the PTP.

Why should I give my address?

Having your address enables PTP advocates to know how many in their locale signed up to the PTP, and use this as a data point to advocate for public figures to sign the PTP. This is especially salient for local and regional elected officials, who always want to see the specific addresses of constituents to know who in their district signed the PTP. Another benefit of giving the address is that it enables PTP advocates who have the function of local organizers to reach out to you and help you participate in various PTP-oriented activities, getting you plugged into both Pro-Truth activism and Pro-Truth community activities. Finally, it enables us to send you PTP-related marketing materials that you can use to promote the pledge. Again, this is not obligatory but highly beneficial.

Why should I share that I took the pledge on my social media and to my email contacts?

Sharing that you took the pledge via your media channels enables others to have a greater confidence that they can trust you more and rely on you to keep your word. Moreover, it enables others who took the PTP help you abide by the pledge, and offer guidance and support when you might mistakenly go against the tenets of the pledge. Additionally, it can help motivate other people to take the pledge if they know that you took it.

Why should I sign up to be a Pro-Truth Pledge advocate?

Brief Answer:
PTP advocates are people who want to contribute to advancing the PTP and other truth-oriented activities. Being a PTP advocate involves any combination of the following six activities: organizing,

252

public promotion, lobbying, evaluating, behind-the-scenes work, and financial support. PTP advocates get support and training from the PTP core organizers as they lead by example.

Full Answer:

PTP advocates are people who want to contribute to advance the PTP and other truth-oriented activities. We estimate doing so might take a couple of hours a month at the lower level of activity. Regarding the PTP in particular, being a Pro-Truth advocate involves any combination of the following six activities: organizing, public promotion, lobbying, evaluating, behind-the-scenes work, and financial support. In all cases involving contributing their time, Pro-Truth advocates get various support and training from the PTP core organizers in their efforts, as well as various resources. For an example of the latter, here is a Google Drive folder with template email and Facebook drafts you can use to pitch the PTP; here is a Google Drive folder with marketing resources, such as flyers, business cards, sign-up sheets, and graphics; here is a Google Drive folder with materials for those who want to make public presentations on the PTP. For those who have **financial difficulties** impeding their ability to engage in the activities listed below, **take a look at the P.S. of this section for financial support options**.

- **If you do organizing**, you would help recruit and coordinate other people in engaging in PTP-oriented activities. Being an organizer for the Pro-Truth Pledge involves organizing other people to ensure that the outcomes of the Pro-Truth Pledge are met, namely that: 1) The PTP is promoted to the public, getting more and more people to sign it; 2) There is effective lobbying of public figures, especially politicians, to get them to sign it; 3) There is effective monitoring of public figures who signed the pledge, evaluation of any potential pledge violations, behind-the-scenes efforts to get public figures to revise problematic statements, and if not, then public pressure on them to revise problematic statements. See the three sections below on the specific steps you would be recruiting people to do, and especially the first step on public promotion on how to help yourself recruit other advocates who you would then organize. You should also be able to jump in and do any of the three activities described below, so that you know how they are done and can step in if a volunteer needs a brief break, as well as have the familiarity with the tasks necessary to be able to manage volunteers doing any of the three. You need to find other organizers to help you have life balance and be able to step away for brief periods as life stuff comes up. Finally, you need to be able to form a virtual or in-person community for volunteers to help them feel motivated and engaged and invested in the project. If you have leadership, follow-through, and planning skills, you may well make a good organizer. More details at this link.
- **If you do public promotion**, you engage in finding venues to tell private citizens about the PTP and encourage them to take it. This may involve solely focusing on people in your locale. For instance, you can gather signatures by attending appropriate events – rallies, meetings of service clubs and political clubs, churches and secular groups, events at schools, universities, and libraries – and gather signatures there. For spontaneous signature-gathering, libraries and universities are a good bet. You can also look for opportunities to speak at any of the venues listed above: PTP materials relevant to public speaking are in this Google Drive folder. A super-easy way to promote the pledge at these events and just in daily life is to purchase and wear PTP-themed merchandise, especially when you do PTP-themed activities, but also just out and about – it's a great conversation starter. Alternatively, you can focus on local-level social media, and go to various local Facebook groups and other relevant social media to promote the PTP there. You can write blogs in local venues or letters-to-the-editor in local newspapers about the pledge. If you do social media, you can also go broader than the local level, say in specific online discussion forums or social media venues that you believe would be interested in the PTP. You

can do a combination of all of the above, and any other things involved in getting the PTP out there. Then, as people get involved, you can either help organize them to promote the pledge, or connect them to another PTP advocate who does organizing. Here is a link to a documents folder that you can use with fliers, a sign-up form, and the option to make a binder for people to sign the PTP. Use these instructions and the materials in the folder linked above to create a PTP sign-up binder, which is very convenient to use when gathering signatures for the PTP in-person, and here is a link to a video with PTP-specific training on doing in-person signature gathering. If you have good communication skills, you would likely make a good promoter.

- **If you do lobbying**, you would work to get various public figures to sign the pledge. This may involve approaching the minister of your church or secular group leader, or local journalists and academics, or your boss in the company where you work, and convincing them to sign the pledge. This may involve traditional lobbying, such as going to the office of a politician to get her/him to sign the pledge. You can also get private citizens to sign the pledge and sign a separate statement calling for their local representatives to sign the pledge, putting pressure on the politicians. After you go to meet with a politician several times and the politician still refuses to sign the pledge, you can go to friendly media contacts – ideally ones you got to sign the pledge earlier – and tell the contact about the situation, as well as show them the signatures of ordinary citizens asking the politician to sign the pledge. This may result in a news story that would both spread word about the pledge and put some pressure on the politician to sign it, or be perceived as having something to hide. The benefits section of the PTP FAQ should serve you well in advocating for such public figures to sign the pledge. Information and templates on pitching politicians, journalists, and other public figures is in this Google Drive folder. If you have networking and advocacy skills, you probably would be a good lobbyist.

- **If you do evaluating**, you would keep track of public figures who took the pledge, and make sure they abide by it. You would read through their social media feeds and speeches, observe their actions, and browse their press releases. If you find something that smells fishy to you, you would investigate whether it violates the PTP. If you think it does, you would follow the process outlined above on holding people accountable. Those who have served for a while and successfully in monitoring may apply to mediating committees of vetted volunteers who make rulings in evaluate compliance with the PTP. Those who want to be PTP evaluators are welcome to check out the directions at this link, and follow the guidelines there for getting involved. If you have research and analysis skills, you would be a good evaluator.

- **If you do behind-the-scenes activities**, you would do things like programming, editing and writing, video and audio editing, administrative tasks such as inputting people who signed the pledge in person into the website, doing various research related to the pledge, and so on. The kind of behind-the volunteer activities available as part of this project are all described in this survey, which we invite you to fill out. The survey is for the nonprofit organization Intentional Insights, which runs the PTP project – indicate your focus on the PTP in the "What makes you excited about Intentional Insights?" section.

- **The last way to help out is financial support**. Plenty of people have insufficient time to help out on a consistent basis, and become checkbook advocates instead; likewise, many who contribute their time also contribute money. You can donate through this link to the account of Intentional Insights, the financial sponsor of the Pro-Truth Pledge. For the monthly donation option – which we especially appreciate, as it helps us make our financial plans going forward into the future – click the checkbox "monthly recurring donation." If you want to write a check, you can make it out to Intentional Insights, and mail it to 450 Wetmore road, Columbus, OH, 43214. Let us know by emailing info [at] protruthpledge [dot] org if you would like to make an ACH transfer or any other more complex form of financial gift, such as stocks or putting Intentional Insights into your will. These donations are tax-deductible against any income that you earn in the US, whether you are a US citizen or not. Regarding the amount, choose something that would make you happy and proud to support the fight against lies and the promotion of truth.

P.S. One of the many reasons we need donations is that we offer **financial reimbursements for PTP advocates** who have financial difficulties but have time available for doing PTP volunteering. For those with financial difficulties printing out the materials, purchasing a binder, travelling to an event, paying for parking, you can get up to $10 reimbursed for printing materials and purchasing a binder per month, and separately up to $20 for travelling to an event, such as gas, paying for parking, price of entry, and also up to $20 for event-themed costs, such as making a PTP sign for visibility at an event such as a march or political rally. If you can get a table at a promising community or political event, we can reimburse up to $100 for the table if you can commit to arranging for yourself or someone else to be present for at least three-fourths of the event (we trust you to pick relevant events). We will also reimburse up to $15 off the costs of PTP-themed merchandise, to ensure your visibility at events. To get reimbursements, first email finance [at] intentionalinsights [dot] org and describe your financial need: no need to provide documentation, just describe your situation in a paragraph, and get confirmation of approval. After that, just email finance [at] intentionalinsights [dot] org with the receipt for the purchase of the materials/binder, parking or travel by Lyft/Uber/Taxi/public transport or approximate gas money, or the approximate cost of paper and ink if you are printing at home, and any other expenses in similarity to these. Also explain what you used this money to pay for, so we can keep a clear track of reasons for expenditures, and a scan or clear photographs of all the signatures you gathered. Finally, please provide a PayPal account to which we can transfer the money (this is currently our only means of reimbursement – for setting up a PayPal account, which you can do with any credit or debit card, see here). We trust all PTP advocates to avoid abusing this system (after all, you signed the Pro-Truth Pledge yourself), and only use this as needed per your financial difficulties arranging for these needs otherwise.

What if I took the PTP pledge and want to renounce it?

If you are a private citizen, just email us and we will list you as having taken the pledge and later renouncing it. If you are a public figure, do the same, but keep in mind that any investigations will keep going. If we find a violation of the pledge, and you refuse to retract your statements, you will be listed as both in contempt of the pledge and also as having renounced it. This last clause is intended to make sure that public figures do not simply renounce the pledge when they have deliberately lied and want to renounce their taking of the pledge to avoid the negative reputation consequences of a ruling against them.

Who is organizing the PTP?

The PTP was created by a group heavy on social scientists and its implementation is organized by a non-partisan group of volunteers. It is part of a broader Rational Politics (RAP) project, which gathers thoughtful citizens of all political stripes devoted to fighting post-truth politics, meaning politics focused on emotions and personal beliefs and rejecting objective facts. We see these political methods as one of the worst problems for our global society in terms of how important, neglected, and solvable it is. In addressing this issue, we aim to use best practices in communicating and marketing both to get people to care about truth in politics and to provide them with the tools and resources to use evidence and reason in making wise political decisions that will benefit our society as a whole. To do so, we are launching the

Pro-Truth Movement to bring us from our post-truth present into a post-lies future. RAP is a subproject of Intentional Insights (InIn), a nonprofit organization dedicated to promoting rational thinking and wise decision-making in politics and other areas of life to bring about an altruistic and flourishing world. As a 501(c)(3) nonprofit, InIn does not engage in types of partisan political activity prohibited by the IRS, and the PTP is a form citizen advocacy for the non-partisan value of truth in politics and other areas relevant to our public sphere.

Select Annotated Bibliography

Ariely, Dan. *Predictably Irrational: The Hidden Forces That Shape Our Decisions.* New York: HarperCollins, 2009

Ariely, Dan. *The Upside of Irrationality: The Unexpected Benefits of Defying Logic at Work and Home.* New York: HarperCollins, 2010

Ariely, Dan. *The Honest Truth About Dishonesty: How We Lie to Everyone--Especially Ourselves.* New York: HarperCollins, 2012

- These three books seek to examine the systematic and predictable irrationalities inherent in human thinking. The author's aim is to make people aware of these irrationalities in the hope of helping individuals make more rational decisions, of helping policymakers make more pragmatic public policy and regulations, and helping organizations develop more effective methods of meeting their goals. The style of the book is to list various studies about how our brains go wrong, and then expand on the concepts behind them, while making some suggestions about how to improve our thinking and decision-making patterns.

Baumeister, Roy F. and John Tierney. *Willpower: Rediscovering The Greatest Human Strength.* New York: The Penguin Press, 2011

- This book on willpower and ego depletion is co-written by a prominent psychologist, Baumeister, and a New York Times science reporter, Tierney. Its style combines research, stories, and some advice. The book describes how self-control, which this book refers to as willpower, results in good life outcomes, and goes through how to improve willpower in a number of different contexts. Note that recent research

Goleman, Daniel. *The Brain and Emotional Intelligence: New Insights.* Northampton: More Than Sound, 2011

- This book summarizes the research on emotional intelligence. It examines the four fundamental domains of emotional intelligence: self-awareness, self-management, social awareness, and relationship management. In each of these domains, it explores how to gain better emotional intelligence to achieve our goals.

Goleman, Daniel. *Social Intelligence: The New Science of Human Relationships.* New York: Bantam Dell, 2006

- Social neuroscience is a recent subfield that has discovered that our brain's very design makes it sociable, inexorably drawn into an intimate brain to brain linkup whenever we engage with another person. That neural bridge lets us affect the brain and thus the body of everyone we engage with, just as they do to us. That link is a double-edged sword, as nourishing relationships have a beneficial impact on our mental and physical health, while toxic ones undermine our wellbeing. This book explores the recent findings in social neuroscience, and provides some ideas about how we can manage our mental and physical health in our social engagements, both ourselves and with those we interact.

Heath, Chip and Dan Heath. *Switch: How to Change Things When Change is Hard.* Broadway Books: New York, 2010

- The authors depict the primary obstacle in achieving positive change as a conflict that is built into our brains between the rational mind and the emotional mind. The book uses a story-driven narrative to describe how we can achieve transformative change at any level, from our personal health to society as a whole.

Kahneman, Daniel. *Thinking, Fast and Slow.* New York: Farrar, Straus and Giroux, 2011

- In this work the author, a recipient of the Nobel Prize in Economic Sciences for his seminal work in psychology that challenged the rational model of judgment and decision making, has brought together his many years of research and thinking in one book. The author aims to introduce into everyday conversations a better understanding of the nature of and the systematic errors in our judgment, choice, and behavior.

Restak, Richard. *The Naked Brain: How The Emerging Neurosociety is Changing How We Live, Work, and Love.* New York: Harmony Books, 2006

- The author argues that neuroscience is in the process of deeply impacting our society, and will become a powerful daily life element in the first half of the 21st century. This is because our expanded understanding of the brain is increasingly powerfully impacting our understanding of how people think and behave.

Thaler, Richard H. and Cass R. Sunstein. *Nudge: Improving Decisions About Health, Wealth, and Happiness.* New Haven: Yale University Press, 2008

- The book draws on research in psychology and behavioral economics to defend the concept of libertarian paternalism, namely "nudging" people into being happy and successful through public policy. Sunstein and Thaler state that "the libertarian aspect of our strategies lies in the straightforward insistence that, in general, people should be free to do what they like-and to opt out of undesirable arrangements if they want to do so" (pg. 5). The paternalistic portion of the term "lies in the claim that it is legitimate for choice architects to try to influence people's behavior in order to make their lives longer, healthier, and better" (pg. 5).

Watts, Duncan J. *Everything is Obvious: Once You Know the Answer.* New York: Crown Business, 2011

- The author questions people's reliance on common sense assumptions to understand how other individuals and groups will make decisions and behave. People's common sense assumptions of the behavior of others are based on their own common sense understanding of the world, which differs to a smaller or larger extent, from the way other people think about and thus behave in the world; moreover, people generally do not take important environmental factors into consideration when thinking about and predicting the behavior of others. The author suggests instead the need to question our common sense beliefs, to reflect on how other people might have a different common sense than we do, and to rely more on social science to explain how other people will think and behave.

Biographies of Contributors

Jeff Dubin: Jeff Dubin is a Clinical Social Worker, an aspiring rationalist, and the volunteer Vice President of the Humanist Community of Central Ohio. He is happy and proud to help Intentional Insights raise the sanity waterline. dubin.8@osu.edu

Joel Lehman: Joel is an academic artificial intelligence researcher, currently working for Uber AI labs. His PhD research culminated in a popular science book he co-wrote, entitled "The Myth of the Objective: Why Greatness Cannot Be Planned." lehman.154@gmail.com

Hunter Glenn: Hunter Glenn is a writer who wants to use writing to communicate the ideas to people that will let them make of their lives and their world what they want. In his spare time he enjoys making music and talking to interesting people. hunterglenn92@yahoo.com

Diogo Gonçalves: Diogo Gonçalves is a behavioral scientist interested in developing behavioral policies that deliver social and economic value. He lives in Lisbon, Portugal, where he is responsible for several initiatives related with the promotion and development of behavioral policy, namely the "There are Free Lunches" Lectures, and the Nudge Portugal think thank. diogo.goncalves@yahoo.com

Max Harms: Max Harms is an artificial intelligence researcher, software engineer, community leader, and author. He's been engaged for years in developing the art of better thinking, first in Ohio where he ran a rationality dojo, and now in Northern California. raelifin@gmail.com

Peter Livingstone: Peter Livingstone is an evidence-based investor, business process improvement expert, and mining industry consultant. He is a leader in several non-profits focused on helping people improve their lives through wise decision making and healthy lifestyles. peternlivingstone@gmail.com

Gleb Tsipursky: Dr. Gleb Tsipursky is a tenure-track professor at Ohio State University and President of the nonprofit Intentional Insights. He is a best-selling author, and his forthcoming book is The Alternative to Alternative Facts: Fighting Post-Truth Politics with Behavioral Science. gleb@intentionalinsights.org

Agnes Vishnevkin: Agnes has a passion for helping people improve their lives through tools based on the latest behavioral science. With over a decade of experience in the nonprofit sector, Agnes oversees the operations of Intentional Insights, which she and Gleb Tsipursky launched in 2014. agnes@intentionalinsights.org

Amy K. Watson: I coach purpose-driven leaders dealing with difficult relationships to find hope, strength, and direction. But my clients would tell you that my real specialty is uncovering their hidden genius and using that to make their lives easier. Amy@CareerLeadershipAlignment.com

Alex Weissenfels: Alex has developed and compiled paradigms to help people learn different problem-solving skills and succeed at understanding others' motivations and perspectives. At Intentional Insights, Alex leads the informal coaching project for people learning how to deal with struggles and achieve their goals. He is excited to demonstrate and spread effective approaches for empowering people. Alex has a optical engineering degree and works at a medical software company. exceph@gmail.com

81041030R00156